A History of Burma

A HISTORY OF BURMA

by Maung Htin Aung

Columbia University Press

New York and London

1967

Maung Htin Aung was the Rector of the University of
Rangoon, 1946–1958. He is the author of *Burmese Drama*
(Oxford University Press, 1937), *Burmese Folk-Tales* (Ox-
ford, 1948), *Burmese Law Tales* (Oxford, 1962), *Folk
Elements in Burmese Buddhism* (Oxford, 1962), *The
Stricken Peacock: Anglo-Burmese Relations 1752–1948*
(Martinus Nijhoff, 1965), *Burmese Monk's Tales* (Columbia
University Press, 1966), and *Epistles Written on Eve of
Anglo-Burmese War* (Nijhoff, 1967).

*To the memory of my great-great-grandfather,
Maha Minhla Mindin Raza, and of my
eldest brother, U Tin Tut*

Preface

There is a Burmese folktale that tells of a magic mirror in which a person sees only what he wishes to see. History is such a mirror; and a historian, however much he attempts to be objective and detached, often finds that he cannot completely overcome his human frailties of prejudice and preference. The reader therefore may find that this history of Burma gives too flattering a picture of the Burmese people. Nonetheless, it seems obvious that a nation which has preserved its identity, its social institutions, and its religion for nearly two thousand years, although hemmed in on all sides by other larger ones with different cultures and traditions, surely must possess some enduring qualities of character. In order that the reader may become acquainted with views of Burmese history different from mine, I have given in Appendix III of this book detailed references to the works of two eminent writers on southeast Asian history. The reader is invited to read in that appendix the opening paragraphs, in which I explain the nature, scope, and limitations of my book.

The writing of this book was planned in 1959, when after I had retired from the service of the University of Rangoon it appeared that I was to lead a life of leisure. Professor U E Maung, his wife (my sister) Daw Mya Mu, and the late U Po Lat, Director of Archaeology, were to have collaborated with me. I received an appointment in the Burmese Diplomatic Service, however, and accordingly left Rangoon. Had it been possible for them to be joint-authors of this book with me, the chapters on the ancient kingdoms of Prome and Pagan would have been fuller because of their great knowledge of the Burmese inscriptions.

The book was begun in the academic year 1964–1965 in the School of International Affairs at Columbia University, while I was a visiting professor there, continued in 1965–1966 at Wake Forest College, and completed in the summer of 1966 at the State University of New York at Buffalo, Brockport, and Oswego. I take this opportunity to thank my various friends and colleagues at these institutions for their many courtesies.

MAUNG HTIN AUNG

Winston-Salem, North Carolina
June 1967

Contents

x   *Contents*

A History of Burma

1 Burma in Southeast Asia

Burma lies on the western edge of that huge peninsula that used to be known as Indo-China and is now called mainland southeast Asia. Surrounded on three sides by mountains and on the fourth by sea, Burma forms a distinct geographical unit. By both southeast Asian and European standards it is a large country—about the same size as Thailand or France, but by American standards it is small, being no larger than the state of Texas and having a population of only 24 million. Shaped like a diamond, but with a "tail" attached, its greatest width is 600 miles and its length 800 miles plus the 500 representing the "tail." As in other southeast Asian countries, the mountains and rivers in Burma run from north to south. The Irrawaddy river divides the country in two and its valley constitutes the real heartland. The Chindwin river in the west and the Salween in the east run parallel to the Irrawaddy, but after flowing southward for some three hundred miles the Chindwin turns southeast and joins the Irrawaddy. The Salween river, after flowing through Yunnan, bisects the eastern part of Burma and at a certain point forms the political boundary between Burma and Thailand.

The climate of Burma is classed as tropical monsoon. It has three definite and regular seasons, the hot dry season from March to May, the rainy season from May to October, and the cool dry season from November to February. This climate is determined by the monsoon winds, which blow from land to sea for half of the year and then change their direction and blow from sea to land. All over the country rainfall is heavy except in the central region, known as the dry zone, where the annual rainfall is less than 30 inches. Dense forests cover the mountain slopes, and as in other southeast Asian countries wet rice cultivation is practiced in the valleys and dry rice cultivation on the hills. This cultivation of rice has been the basis of both the culture and the economy of Burma.

The mountain barriers have kept Burma separate from her neighbors, but it was from beyond the northern mountains that successive migratory waves of Tibeto-Burmese tribes came into the country. Five thousand years ago there were stone-age people living in the valley of the Irrawaddy whose primitive culture was unique enough to earn the name Anyarthian from anthropologists, but whether they died out or merged with the newcomers of historical times cannot be known. In addition, it is possible that Negritto tribes were the first to settle in Burma as they were in neighboring countries. However, when the first migration of Mongolians took place, centuries before the beginning of the Christian Era, Burma was almost unaffected because she was merely on the fringe of the area hit by the Mongols. They were the Proto and Deutro Malays, and their original home was probably the region which is now southern China. West of that region lived people speaking languages belonging to the group called Austro-Asiatic by anthropologists and students of linguistics. These Austro-Asiatic people moved southward, but unlike the Malays who had gone by sea they followed the great Mekong river. Of these people, the Khmers formed the eastern wing of the movement and came to occupy what is now Laos and Cambodia. The Mons formed the west wing and settled in the region that is now Thailand. The third migration of Mongolians affected Burma rather than the other parts of the Indo-Chinese peninsula; these were the Tibeto-Burmese from the southeastern slopes of the Tibetan mountains. Whereas the reason for the migrations of the Malays and the Mon-khmers could be only conjectured, there is evidence that the Tibeto-Burmese migrations were for political reasons. The two kingdoms of Tibet and China were locked in bitter rivalry, and the Tibeto-Burmese were hemmed in between them. They had reached the same level of culture as the Tibetans and the Chinese of the time, but they considered their independence and social institutions to be more valuable than their material culture, and accordingly they fled from their homeland. After trekking across icy mountains and through dense forests, some of them entered Burma from the northwest and others skirted the northern mountains to enter from the northeast. The last migration took place in the thirteenth century, when another Mongolian group, the Tai-Shans, overran Burma and the regions occupied by the Mons.

Situated on the western edge of the peninsula, Burma has a common frontier with China, India, and, since 1947, with Pakistan also. Indian cultural influences had the greatest effect on Burma, reaching her by both land and sea before they passed on to the rest of southeast Asia. In early history the sea was considered more dangerous than land, and trade between India and Indo-China and China was carried on through Burma. Even after the sea route had come into general use, for a long time ships did not venture out into the sea but preferred to hug the coast; they were blown toward the Burmese coast by the southwest monsoon and were sped back to India and Ceylon by the northeast monsoon. Thus Burma was the gateway to Indo-China and China. Even when advances in the science of navigation enabled ships to bypass her, Burma remained important as the back door to China. Through this back door passed an embassy from a Roman caesar to the emperor of China, and through it also came the Tatar armies like wolves attacking a fold. This passageway was the bone of contention between France and England in the nineteenth century and finally led to the fall of the Burmese kingdom to the English; in 1941 the Japanese armies came marching in to close this door.

Because of her special geographical position Burma often played the role of leader among the kingdoms of southeast Asia. Burma introduced Buddhism to her neighbors and later became the champion of this faith in southeast Asia. She took upon herself the enormous task of shielding southeast Asia from foreign intrusion. She successfully dammed the flow of the Tai-Shans into southeast Asia in the eleventh century, and when the dam broke in the thirteenth century, southeast Asia was overrun by them. She fell, fighting desperately to stop the Tatar armies in the thirteenth century, but she was able to repulse the Chinese armies in the eighteenth. She kept the Portuguese out of mainland southeast Asia and attempted to keep out the British, with disastrous consequences to herself. She lost her independence at the same time her neighbors lost theirs, and she led them in the struggle to become free of colonial rule. Thus the history of Burma is one aspect of the history of southeast Asia as a whole.

II Early Kingdoms: The Mons and the Pyus

Burmese chronicles and Theravada Buddhist traditions claimed that two Mon merchants from Lower Burma obtained from the Buddha some hair relics, and on their return they enshrined them in a small temple, which later became the kernel over which the great Shwedagon pagoda was built. There is no inherent impossibility in the legend, first because the particular spur on which the pagoda now stands was high above water level long before the Irrawaddy formed its delta a thousand years ago, and second because there must have been at least some coastal trade between the opposite shores of the Bay of Bengal. The *Jatakas* clearly mentioned Indian merchants sailing to Suvarnabhumi, "the land of gold" across the ocean. Although it is possible that the *Jatakas* were collected only after Buddha's passing away, they had been compiled at least by the time of Asoka, the emperor who united India into a single political unit for the first time in her history and who made Buddhism the official religion of his kingdom. He sent to distant lands a number of religious missions, one of which reached Suvarnabhumi, converting its people to Buddhism. The capital city of Suvarnabhumi was Thaton in Lower Burma.

Burmese and Mon traditions asserted that the monks leading the mission established a monastery at Kelasa mountain on the outskirts of the city. In any case, a delegation of Mon monks headed

by the Abbot of Kelasa monastery was present at the consecration
ceremonies of the great stupa built by Duttagamani, the hero-king
of Ceylon, in the second century B.C. Some Thai scholars insist that
Suvarnabhumi was the region which is now Thailand and that its
capital was at Nakorn Pathom, on the evidence that very ancient
Buddhist remains have been excavated at that place. But Nakorn
Pathom is inland, far away from the sea, and Burmese and Sinhalese
chronicles clearly indicated that the capital was a port. However,
Suvarnabhumi did not mean Lower Burma alone but the entire
region occupied at that time by the Mons. The lower valley of the
Menam was their heartland, but Thaton was their window to the
sea and the great world of Buddhist India. The Mons, being nearest
to India, thus fell under Indian commercial and cultural influences,
and their civilization was shaped to a great extent by Indian custom
and thought. They later passed on that culture to the races near
them, namely, the Khmers and the Tibeto-Burmese, and later the
Tai-Shans. But the great failing of the Mons was that they were never
politically ambitious and accordingly never attempted to found
for themselves an empire of their own, unlike the Khmers, the
Burmese, and the Tais. They never exploited the initial advantage
that history had given them.

According to Burmese chronicles, the first Burmese kingdom
was at Tagaung in northern Burma, and it was founded by an Indian prince who had lost his kingdom in India. In the absence of
archaeological evidence European scholars have summarily rejected
the existence of this particular Burmese kingdom. But again there
is no inherent impossibility in the legend. Indian merchant ad-
venturers who dared to sail the seas would have dared first to go
overland, and there must have been some commercial contact
across the northwestern mountains between India and Burma even
in those remote times. The chronicles never claimed that the Burmese were Aryans or that they came from India, a point missed by
European critics of the chronicles. All that they claimed was that
the earliest dynasty of kings in Burma was Indian in origin. How-

ever, by the term Burmese, Pyu was actually meant, for the vanguard of the Tibeto-Burmese tribes in the Irrawaddy valley was
the Pyus. The journey of the Pyus down the Irrawaddy valley must
have taken at least a century or two, and surely they must have
dotted the country from north to south with settlements that later
became kingdoms. Tagaung could have been one of those. As early
as 128 B.C. there was an overland route across the north of Burma
along which goods from China passed through India to points
farther west. The emperor of China even endeavored to control
this trade. An embassy from the Roman empire passed along this
route to China in A.D. 97 and again in A.D. 120. The very fact that
embassies could travel in safety across northern Burma clearly
showed that the country by that time was politically developed.
Besides Tagaung, two kingdoms founded by the Pyus in Upper
Burma were Halingyi and Peikthanomyo. Archaeological evidence
has been discovered in both places.

The city of Halingyi was definitely on the overland route, but
unfortunately little is known regarding the history of the place.
However, a legend exists that, in spite of its folk-tale elements,
clearly embodies some authentic facts regarding the kingdom. The
king had a younger brother, the crown prince, whose smile always
resulted in a shower of gold falling on the city. One day an embassy
from China arrived, and the king, desiring to give a present of gold
to the visiting dignitaries, ordered his brother to smile. But as he had
just discovered that the queen was plotting to assassinate the king,
his brother could not smile but only weep. As the king shouted in
anger there was an earthquake, and the city together with the king,
the queen, the crown prince, and the Chinese envoys went up in
flames. Halingyi was obviously the same city in Central Burma that
third-century Chinese historical texts referred to as Lin-Yang. The
Burmese pronounce Halingyi as H'lingyi and perhaps the Pyus pro-
nounced it in the same way. If that was so, to Chinese ears it would
have sounded very much like Lin-Yang. Peikthanomyo, which
means Vishnu City, right in the center of Burma, was recently

excavated by the government's archaeology department and a full report is in preparation. It has been announced, however, that carbon tests of the objects found there indicate the site is about 2,000 years old, which makes it one of the oldest cities of southeast Asia.

Pyu political power was centered at Prome, which was then at the apex of the mouth of the Irrawaddy river, as its delta had not yet been formed. It was only a few miles away from the sea, and ships could come up the deep mouth of the river. Thus Prome established an alternate and easier trade route to China. By sea it was halfway to Thaton and other Mon ports beyond, where cargoes could be discharged and carried over the portage routes across the narrow isthmus to ships waiting on the other side on the Gulf of Siam. These portage routes saved the ships from making a long, tedious, difficult, and dangerous journey round the Malay peninsula. Thus in A.D. 131 an embassy from the Roman empire to China used the portage route across Tenasserim, and in A.D. 166 a trade delegation from the Roman empire to China used the same route. Prome is the anglicized version of the Burmese word "pyay," which means "the capital," for later generations of Burmese showed a great regard and respect for this ancient city of the Pyus. To the Pyus themselves it was known as Sri Ksetra, "The Fortunate Field."

Across the chain of mountains to the west, known as the Arakan Yomas, there were other kingdoms also. The Burmese chronicles stated that some Burmese tribes migrated into that region along the mountain passes from the Irrawaddy valley. This region of Arakan is nearer to India but is separated from it by marsh and mangrove forests, which prevented or at least did not facilitate migrations from India. Arakanese speech is merely Burmese with an archaic pronunciation, and when written down it does not show any difference from Burmese. Although the earliest inscriptions found in Arakan and earliest Arakanese silver coins date only from the fourth century, the kingdoms must have been founded much earlier. These Mon, Pyu, and Arakanese kingdoms reached their full development as a result of the great Indian commercial expansion in southeast Asia in the first century A.D. On the other hand it was possible for that great expansion to take place so rapidly and almost over-night only because these kingdoms were already in existence as trading centers.

Various reasons for this increase of Indian commerce have been suggested by scholars, but the most logical is the one put forward by Professor G. Coedes. Following the foundation of the Maurya (Asoka) and Kushan empires in India and the rise of the Seleucid and Roman empires in the west, a great expansion of trade between the two regions occurred. As the balance of trade was so much in favor of India there was a great drain of gold from the Roman empire, and Emperor Vespasian (A.D. 69–79) was constrained to prohibit the export of gold from his dominions; India was then forced to turn to southeast Asia for a new source of gold. This gold crisis coincided with the great advance in navigation as a consequence of the "discovery" of the monsoon winds by "outsiders." (Of course, the nature and course of the monsoon had been known long before to the people actually living in the costal regions of the Bay of Bengal.) Since the beginning of history Burma must have pro-duced a great amount of gold. As stated above, Lower Burma and the heartland of the Mons in the Menam valley were the original Suvarnabhumi. The ancient chronicle of Ceylon and the Burmese and Mon chronicles never ceased to refer to the region as Suvarna-bhumi, and if, as some scholars suggest, the Malay peninsula was Suvarnabhumi, it became so only later when the supply of gold from Lower Burma had become exhausted. The third-century Chinese historical texts noted that the Pyus used knives and halberds made of pure gold. According to another Chinese historical text, Fan Shih Man, King of Funan on the Lower Mekong, conquered many kingdoms on the Malay peninsula and then died as he was preparing to invade Chin-lin, meaning "gold frontier," which was a populous kingdom toward the west situated over a big bay. Ob-viously Chin-lin was the Mon kingdom of Thaton.

Although the Pyus arrived on the seacoast much later than the

Mons, they were more vigorous and more united and thereby were able to make the Mon kingdoms their vassal states. Burmese chronicles asserted that Pyu dominion extended over the whole Malay peninsula; at least they controlled all the portage kingdoms. According to the Chinese *Old Tang History* the Pyus claimed sovereignty over eighteen kingdoms, mostly to the south of Burma, even including Palembang and Java. European scholars consider this to have been an empty vaunt, but surely if the Chinese compiler of the history had considered the claim ridiculous he would not have mentioned it. The Burmese chronicles told of Pyu kings sailing to Ceylon, the Malay peninsula, and the islands beyond. Because of the strategic position of their capital, Prome, they were able to extract at least nominal tribute from ships sailing to and from neighboring kingdoms. However, the Pyus never founded a closely knit empire. Even Burma itself did not become a single unified kingdom, because it was dotted with city states that sometimes gave allegiance to the most powerful among them and at other times challenged its authority. Sri Ksetra was by far the most powerful, and for many centuries it demanded and received tribute from other Pyu city kingdoms.

The Pyus were essentially agricultural. Their main crop was rice, but they also grew millet and sugar cane. They were obviously delighted with the fertility of the soil and the climate in their new settlement; they named their great city "The Fortunate Field." Like other Pyu cities Sri Ksetra was surrounded by inner and outer moats and a massive wall of glazed bricks. The embankments of the moats were also of glazed bricks. It was the largest city ever built in Burma, and it occupied an area much larger than that of the eleventh-century Pagan and nineteenth-century Mandalay. Unlike later cities, Sri Ksetra was in the form of a circle, which doubtless gave rise to the legend that the king of the gods had held the naga dragon's tail as it moved in a circle, thus marking the perimeter. There were twelve gates. Only the southern half of the city was taken up by the palace, monasteries, and houses; the entire northern half consisted of rice fields. Together with the moats and walls, this arrangement ensured that the city could withstand a long siege by enemies. The king's palace and the monasteries were of brick. The halls and rooms were painted bright colors and decorated in gold and silver, and the floors were covered with embroidered rugs. The houses were of timber and were roofed with tiles of lead and tin. Inside their city the Pyus led a life of elegance. When the king went forth in the city, he was borne on a golden litter, but when he wished to travel outside the city he rode on an elephant. The men wore on their hats gold ornaments, jewels, and kingfisher feathers. The women wore in their hair gold and silver ornaments and strings of pearls. Their skirts were blue, their scarfs were of gauze silk, and they carried fans.

According to the eighth-century Chinese historical text *Man-shu*, the Pyus esteemed modesty and decency; their disposition was peaceful; they were men of few words. They were courteous and charming and greeted each other by grasping the arm with the hand and bowing. Their laws were humane; chains, fetters, and prisons were unknown. Criminals on their first offense were given three strokes with a whip; for repeated offenses, five strokes, but criminals found guilty of murder were executed. There was also a great white image of the Buddha one hundred feet in height, before which litigants in civil suits knelt and made their oaths. In time of national calamity and danger the king himself lit incense before the image and took an oath to rule his people with justice. In front of the palace there were two bells, one of silver and the other of gold, to be sounded in time of war. The Pyus were fond of music and dancing. The musicians and the dancers wore golden hair ornaments and jewel-studded golden bracelets and anklets. They had a variety of musical instruments including the phoenix-headed harp with fourteen strings, the crocodile-headed zither with nine strings, the dragon-headed lute with three tuning pegs and frets, and many kinds of drums.

The Pyus were devout Buddhists. The Chinese texts noted that the Pyus, both men and women, wore silk-cotton cloth instead of true silk because the manufacture of silk involved the taking of life. There were many monasteries, and both boys and girls on reaching the age of seven shaved off their hair and became novices in monasteries and convents; when they reached the age of twenty, which was the minimum age to take the higher ordination, most of them would not consider themselves worthy and would leave the monasteries or convents. In addition to the great image, there were pagodas at the four cardinal points of the city. Three of those four pagodas are still in use as places of worship. The best preserved is the Bawbawgyi pagoda. It is one hundred and fifty feet high with a hollow shaft in the center, crowned with a flattened cone. These pagodas are cylindrical and of plastered brick. In addition to these pagodas there were also small vaulted chapels, which are probably later in date than the stupas, but still definitely Pyu. Built of brick and with the true pointed arch, they were the prototypes of the temples to be built later during the period of Pagan's greatness.

The colossal Buddha image of white stone did not survive the fall of the city and it may well be that it was brought from Arakan, the land of colossal images, but of course the Arakanese images were in bronze or gold. The Pyus were not fond of making images in the round of considerable size, and they seemed to have preferred to make large stone sculptures in relief, as many stone slabs with fine sculptures in relief have been found in excavated Pyu sites. In addition to being expert stone carvers, they were also skillful metal workers, and Pyu craftsmen were definitely superior to the craftsmen of Pagan. They made small and exquisite images in the round in green glass, jade, amethyst, rock-crystal, gold, silver, bronze, and lead; and some had detachable haloes. In addition, they made beautiful miniatures of the finest craftsmanship. The ruins of Sri Ksetra have yielded a treasure house of fine miniatures—rings, trays, cups, bowls, bells, cane balls, lion heads, flowers, lotuses, boats, butterflies, ducks, deer, tortoises. If they were just ornaments, they must have delighted both the carver and the wearer; if they were offerings, they must have delighted both the craftsman and the worshiper.

With such skilled gold- and silversmiths, the Pyus were probably the first people in southeast Asia to use silver and gold coins as currency. Although the Chinese texts mentioned both gold and silver coinage, only silver coins have survived. They ranged from the size of a Burmese Kyat (or an Indian rupee) to that of a quarter Kyat. They have been found not only in the entire Irrawaddy valley but also in the remoter regions including the Shan plateau and the Salween valley. Probably the silver coins of Arakan issued by its Candra dynasty in the fourth century A.D. were modeled on them. The Pyu coins were of such beautiful artistic design that they were often perforated, strung, and worn round the neck. The designs on one side were more or less uniform, namely that of a throne within a circle of moons. Some coins, however, had a different design, the rising sun, also surrounded by a circle of moons. Both the throne and the rising sun represented the power of the king at Sri Ksetra, and very probably he was already making the claim that Burmese kings belonged to the sun race, from which the Buddha himself had sprung. The designs on the other side of the coins were different and varied, but they all included objects associated with good fortune, peace, and prosperity, such as the conch shell, the eel, the sun, the moon, the stars, and the swastika. They were symbols not only of good fortune itself, but of the "fortunate field" that was Sri Ksetra. A coinage was necessary because of the extensive trade of the Pyu kingdom. Its products were wheel-made pots, glazed jars, and white silk-cotton cloth. The chief item of import from the remoter areas of Burma was beeswax, which after being mixed with incense was made into candles, not only for lighting homes but for offering to the images and pagodas.

Because the country was dotted with city kingdoms, the Pyus of Sri Ksetra often had to fight and subdue the others. However, because of the Pyus' religion and characteristic peaceful disposition, disputes were often settled before resorting to use of armies, either by single combat between two representatives or by an agreement that the army that was able to complete the construction of a stupa or an alms hall in the shortest time should be the victor. When the enemy was a queen, the opposing king settled the dispute by marrying her. Thus, according to the chronicles, Peikthanomyo, ruled by a queen, attacked Sri Ksetra until an alliance was effected by the king's marriage to the Peikthano queen. This account seems to be confirmed by the discovery of a miniature cylindrical stupa, made of silver gilt, with four seated Buddhas carved around it. The inscription in mixed Pali and Pyu mentioned the names of the Fortunate Ruler Varma (in this case, a contraction of "Vikrama") and Fortunate Ruler Devi. European scholars have thought that they were the names of a king and a queen who donated the statue. Actually, the stupa was a treaty of friendship between the contending king and queen.

Another discovery, a beautiful stone image, bore an inscription in mixed Sanskrit and Pyu. It tells of two cities, one ruled by a king with the dynastic title of Vikrama and the other by a king with the title of Varman. The second king was referred to as the younger brother; between the two kings, the inscription reads, there was much love and friendship due to the influence of a common teacher, a Buddhist monk. The concluding verse expresses the hope that love and friendship between the two kings and the two cities will continue for many generations of kings to come, until the end of the world. European scholars were misled by the term "younger brother" and were puzzled by the two brothers' having different dynastic names. In Burmese diplomatic parlance, a king who paid tribute to another king was described as "younger brother," so as to differentiate him from a king of equal rank, who would be referred to as "friend." Again, this stone image is really a treaty of friendship, marking the end of a war between two rival cities and the restoration of peace through the intercession of a Buddhist monk.

There can be no doubt that the religion of the Pyus was Buddhism of the Theravada school. Chinese texts emphasized this fact over and over again, and if there existed any indications of the prevalence of Hinduism the Chinese texts would certainly have described the kingdom as consisting of "Little Brahmins" as they did of a kingdom to the north of Burma. The Siva cult of Hinduism scarcely had any influence on Burma, but the cult of Vishnu seemed to have penetrated Lower Burma to some extent. But even this cult entered the country in a semi-Buddhistic form. In India, the Vishnu cult had made some compromise with Buddhism by making Buddha an Avatar of Vishnu, just as Rama was. The Buddhists returned the compliment by recognizing Rama as an earlier incarnation of the Buddha and accepting Vishnu as the guardian god of Buddhism. The kernel of the epic of the *Ramayana* was after all merely a *Jataka* (*Dasaratha Jataka*), and ancient Ceylonese chronicles begin their story with an account of the charge given to the king of the gods by the dying Buddha to look after the establishment of the religion in Ceylon, a charge the busy god passed on to Vishnu. The legend that Vishnu was one of the builders of Sri Ksetra, along with the very existence of Peikthanomyo, "Vishnu City," testified to the regard the Pyus extended to Vishnu. But he was never worshiped as Buddha was worshiped for he was considered to be far inferior. Even the great Kyansittha of Pagan in the eleventh century did not dare to claim that he was a Future Buddha, but did claim that he was the reincarnation of Vishnu.

That the king of Sri Ksetra married the Peikthano queen and persuaded her to abandon her city could mean that the Vishnu cult was suppressed. The recent excavations at Peikthanomyo brought to light no religious building except the semi-religious one where the queen's great drum was kept, and this would perhaps show that the city was the only one where Buddhism did not prevail. Some stone sculptures of Vishnu have been found at the site of Sri Ksetra, but they by themselves do not prove that the cult was ever strong with the Pyus. Unlike with the Mons, Hindu ideas were not generally accepted by the Pyus. Of course the source of Pyu culture was Indian, as it resulted from trade contacts with India. But, since Asoka's time, the relationship between Lower Burma and Ceylon was indeed very close, and the fact that Ceylon was the center of the Theravada school of Buddhism prevented Hinduism from penetrating too deeply into Burma. The Hindu cult of the divine king was never accepted in Burma, although the ritual of coronation was followed and the death of a king was euphemistically described as his going to the abode of the gods. However, even more flattering language was used to describe the death of a Buddhist monk— he had *returned* to the abode of the gods.

Like the Hindus the Pyus burned their dead but, unlike the Hindus, they preserved the ashes in urns. For ordinary people the urns were earthenware, for the rich they were of copper, but for royalty they were of massive stone. The urns were buried at random or placed on long brick platforms, which were later covered with earth and buried. Urns containing the ashes of donors of pagodas were put in the vaults of those pagodas. Hundreds of these urns have been discovered not only near the site of Sri Ksetra but also at other Pyu sites and even at Tagaung. This custom of urn burial was neither Hindu nor Buddhist and the Burmese did not continue it. There was, however, one Hindu cult that was tolerated in the Pyu kingdom: astrology. Buddhism frowned upon astrological practices and predictions, as could be seen from the *Vinaya* rule prohibiting Buddhist monks from indulging in astrological learning and pursuits. Nonetheless, because astrology remained so popular with ordinary people, both Theravada and Mahayana Buddhism had to permit it. In all countries of southeast Asia, the calendar was of Indian Hindu origin. The days of the week came to bear the Hindu names of the planets, and the adjustments between native lunar years and the solar years were worked out by Hindu astrologers. The Pyu king, like his contemporaries in other southeast Asian countries appointed Brahmins from India as his royal astrologers to enhance his prestige and authority and to assist him in the coronation and seasonal purification ceremonies. These Brahmins spread the cult of astrology beyond the palace circle. The Chinese texts noted the fact that in the Pyu kingdom there were many astrologers.

The Pyus did not accept the Hindu Code of Manu either. In other countries of southeast Asia the idea of the divine king and the general principles of the code were accepted, and in some ways one was a corollary to the other. The only source of law known to the Burmese was custom, and the idea of a divinely revealed law was unknown to them. The aim of Burmese justice was to attempt to reach a compromise if possible before the actual trial started. This seems to have originated with the Pyus, for the Chinese texts noted that litigants were encouraged to burn incense in front of the great image, to consider their own faults, and then come to some understanding if possible. To give prestige to their customary laws, the Burmese did use the name of "Manu the law-giver," but that was done only in the thirteenth century after Pagan had fallen. Mon chronicles hinted at the existence of Indian Hindu colonies in Lower Burma, but they were only temporary trading settlements, and in any case they surely came into existence only after Sri Ksetra had lost her glory and her power. The Burmese had always been surprised at the caste distinctions prevailing among the Hindus; their word for Indians is Kula, meaning "caste people," and it may well be that they inherited the word from the Pyus. The debt that the Pyus owed to the Indians for their culture was great, but it was owed to the Indian Buddhists and not so much to Indian Hindus. In addition, contact with the Buddhist Sinhalese was continuous throughout their history.

Traces of Mahayana Buddhism were found in the ruins of Sri Ksetra, namely statuettes of the Future Buddhas, especially Avalokitesvara. Hundreds of terra-cotta votive tablets have been found, bearing Sanskrit words and Pyu signatures, as well as two Sanskrit documents. On the other hand, two gold plates, a stupa stone, and a book of twenty numbered gold leaves, all containing long extracts from the three divisions of the Pali scriptures, testify to the popularity of the Theravada form. They also show that the Abhidhamma scriptures were studied at Sri Ksetra, and it must be remembered that the Abhidhamma is known only to the Theravada School. The school of Buddhism that generally prevailed in southeast Asia was the Mahayana, and that was because the period of Indian commercial expansion coincided with the period of the decline of Theravada Buddhism and the development of Mahayana Buddhism in India. In A.D. 80 the Pyus abandoned the Buddhist Era in favor of the new Sakra Era, which had come into being in India two years before. This era later won general acceptance not only in India but all over southeast Asia. It was supposed to mark the ascension in A.D. 78 of a famous Kushan king, but it also marked the occasion of the holding of a Great Synod of Buddhist monks in which the Mahayana school came out triumphant over the Theravada school. The introduction of this era into the Pyu kingdom could have marked the temporary victory of Mahayana over Theravada, but until the fall of the kingdom Theravada Buddhism prevailed among the Pyus. The hundred monasteries and the novitiates mentioned in the Chinese texts were obviously Theravada. To this victory of the Theravada school, the great Buddhist commentator Buddhagosa contributed greatly. This eminent monk, who lived in the fifth century A.D., crossed over to Ceylon, studied the scriptures there, and wrote a series of commentaries.[1] It was even claimed for centuries that he was a Mon and that he died in Suvarnabhumi. This claim has been questioned by modern scholars, but the very fact that such a claim could have been made testifies to the strength of Theravada Buddhism in Lower Burma.

The actual dates of the rise and fall of the kingdom of Sri Ksetra are a subject of controversy among European scholars. Many of them found it difficult to believe that any Tibeto-Burmese tribe could ever have a kingdom of its own earlier than the eighth century A.D. Even when some burial urns were excavated and the following inscriptions in Pyu language were found on them, "Suriya Vikrama died in the year 50   Hari Vikrama died in the year 57   Siha Vikrama died in the year 80," they refused to accept the dates as they were written. The era was obviously the Sakra Era, which the Burmese later called the Pyu Era, but they insisted that it was the

[1] See below, p. 23.

Burmese Era established only in A.D. 638 and interpreted the dates on the urns as 688, 695, and 718. The argument that Burmese history could not have begun before A.D. 800 had long ago been refuted by general acceptance of the account of Asoka's mission that reached Burma even in the third century B.C., and by archaeological evidence. The Sanskrit and Pali scripts found in the inscriptions on the Buddha images mentioned above and the urns could not be later than the fourth century A.D. and could possibly be earlier than the second. Another ground for controversy is the total difference between the names of kings given in the chronicles and those found on the images and the urns. It must be remembered that Burmese chronicles tended to use the personal names of kings rather than their official titles. According to the chronicles the founder of Sri Ksetra was Duttabaung, which in Pyu language only meant "the great king." But he was obviously the founder of the Vikrama dynasty, as Mon chronicles referred to him as Duttabaung Rama. In addition, the name "Vikrama" was retained by the Burmese at Pagan as a title of nobility.

The chronicles stated that Sri Ksetra fell in A.D. 94, and that has also given rise to controversy for the Pyu kingdom continued to exist for several more centuries. The *Man-shu* stated that the Pyu capital fell in about 800, but it was referring to a later Pyu capital. It seems likely that the chronicles were speaking of Duttabaung's dynasty only, and therefore it was the dynasty that fell and not the kingdom itself. It was replaced probably by its rival, the Varman dynasty. "Varman" as a dynastic title was widely used all over southeast Asia, meaning "protégé of Siva." To the new Pyu king, however, it must have been just a title and no more. According to an eleventh-century inscription that was put up by King Kyansittha at a famous pagoda just a few miles away from the site of Sri Ksetra, the date of the fall of Sri Ksetra was given as A.D. 656.

Although the term "fall" was used, it may well be that the city was gradually abandoned, as was the case with Peikthanomyo. The chronicle account of its abandonment by the queen and people of

Peikthanomyo was confirmed by recent excavations. Although building after building was unearthed, not a single skeleton or weapon was found. The chronicles mentioned that the empty city was destroyed by King Anawrahta of Pagan in the eleventh century because he feared that unscrupulous rebels might occupy it and use it as a fortress. The same chronicles, when describing the fall of the dynasty in A.D. 94, explained that the three main racial groups, which together had established the dynasty, broke away from each other, and the king and his Pyus migrated back to the upper valley of the Irrawaddy. It is conceivable that some decades before A.D. 656 the ruling dynasty with its followers might have migrated northward in search of a new capital. There were many reasons that could have prompted this. The Irrawaddy had rapidly formed its delta and Sri Ksetra was now far away from the sea. After centuries of experience in sailing the same seas and with the help of developments in the art of navigation, sailors were now bypassing Sri Ksetra, going straight to the Mon ports near the portage routes. Small Indian trading settlements were appearing in the delta region, and the Mons were pushing farther and farther west into the same delta region. Thus the sea route became closed to the Pyus, and it became imperative that they concentrate on controlling the overland route to India.

The Chinese pilgrim Hsuan-tsang in about A.D. 648 and I-tsing in about A.D. 675 mentioned Sri Ksetra in their accounts of Buddhist kingdoms in southeast Asia. There are many possible explanations of why they should still mention Sri Ksetra after it had ceased to be the capital; for example, they could have been speaking of the kingdom rather than the capital, or the city could have remained for several more years under a governor. The Tang dynasty histories and the *Man-shu* gave detailed accounts of the Pyu kingdom at the beginning of the ninth century, but by that time the Pyu capital was no longer Sri Ksetra but another city in Upper Burma. Much of their information, however, was obviously based on earlier accounts and they were thus describing the old capital of Sri Ksetra, of which the new was merely a replica. The Tang histories especially mentioned the arrival at the court of the Chinese emperor of an embassy from the Pyu capital in A.D. 801 and noted the presence in it of the king's younger brother, "the lord of Sri"; it is possible that he was the lord or governor of the forsaken capital, for there was no other Burmese town which had Sri as part of its name. The actual site of this new capital is a matter of conjecture, except that it was on the overland route to India. Some European writers think that it was at Halingyi. Burmese scholars, however, believe that Halingyi was much earlier than Sri Ksetra because the stone work found at its site does not have the style and finish of Sri Ksetra stone work, which testifies that the Pyus at Halingyi were still unskilled. They think that the new capital was at Rajagaha, which is mentioned in the chronicles as an early capital. It was much nearer to the Indian frontier. The Chinese texts mentioned that the Pyu capital was the city of Sariputra, the chief disciple of the Buddha. It seems obvious that the Chinese historians mixed up the Rajagaha of India with the new Pyu capital; after all, the Pali name Rajagaha means only "the king's abode."

The history of the Pyus after their withdrawal from Sri Ksetra is not definitely known. Toward the close of the eighth century the Tai kingdom of Nan-Chou followed an expansionist policy and, taking advantage of the waning of Pyu power, it obtained control of the trade route to India. The Tais raided the Mon kingdoms of Lower Burma and then went farther east and besieged even Hanoi. Although according to *Man-shu* the king of Nan-Chou styled himself "lord of the Pyus," it is not likely that the Tais actually held Upper Burma; at least they never held Lower Burma. In fact, although they were able to sack one or two Mon cities, their raids were generally repulsed by the Mons. They gave the death blow to the already dying Pyu power, however, by sacking the new capital and taking away some three thousand of its inhabitants as captives. But it was during this period of defeat and disaster that the Burmese came to the forefront of history. According to the chronicles, even in the second century a new merger of Tibeto-Burmese tribes was taking place. Leaving the Kanyans and the Thets in possession of Arakan and the lower Irrawaddy valley, respectively, the king of the first Sri Ksetra dynasty established a new settlement in Upper Burma. A fresh merger of the tribes must have taken place in the seventh century after Sri Ksetra had been abandoned. Out of this merger, the Burmese appeared.[2]

So the Mons were left supreme in Lower Burma. There was definitely some conflict between the Indian settlers and the advancing Mons. According to Mon chronicles two princes from Thaton, Thamala and Wimala, founded Pegu on an island that had recently emerged from the sea as part of the Irrawaddy delta in A.D. 825. The island had been discovered already by an Indian merchant ship, but the Mons were able to hold it despite Indian claims for its possession. Then the elder brother sent the younger to be educated in southern India, but when the latter returned the king ignored him. The younger brother then rose in rebellion, slew the king, and took the throne. The son of the fallen king was saved by his mother and given to an old couple in a remote village to be brought up as their son. He grew up into a handsome young man of courage and vigor. Soon after he attained the age of sixteen an Indian merchant ship arrived, bringing a challenge that the king should fight with an Indian warrior, "seven feet tall," with Pegu as the stake. The king, finding that he was unable to accept the challenge himself, called for a volunteer to champion his cause, and the young villager came forward. In the ensuing single combat the young man emerged victorious, and when his identity was made known he was declared to be the crown prince. In spite of such conflicts, the Mons seemed to have followed a policy of compromise. They gave Pegu the official name of Ussa, after Orissa in eastern India, and they freely intermarried with the Indians so as to absorb their small community, with the result that the Mons came to be known also as Talaings,

[2] This problem of the coming of the Burmese is discussed in detail in the next chapter.

or "people from the Talangana coast of south India." When Hinduism and Buddhism later became rivals for supremacy in southeast Asia, however, the conflict between Indian and Mon changed into conflict between Hindu and Buddhist.

Mon power and prestige depended much on their relationship with Buddhist Ceylon. Coedes and other modern scholars of early southeast Asian history, while giving due emphasis to the part played by India in the diffusion of culture in the region, have neglected to consider an equally important part played by Ceylon. Although Buddhism first came to southeast Asia from southern India, after Asoka's death and the emergence of the Mahayana school in India Ceylon became the center of the Theravada tradition, and it was Ceylon that continued the tradition of missionary zeal. The ocean currents and the monsoon winds favored direct intercourse between Ceylon and Lower Burma and between Ceylon and Malaya. In the early centuries of the Christian era, when under the enlightened Guptas Hinduism and Buddhism could exist side by side, the Bay of Bengal became a Buddhist lake across which pilgrims and monks traveled between Ceylon and southeast Asia. The names of two Malay kingdoms, Lankasuka and the great Sri Vijaya, testified to this, for Lankasuka meant "happiness of Ceylon" and Vijaya was the hero-king who first founded the kingdom of Ceylon. As the Chinese pilgrim Hsuan-tsang duly noted, Lower Burma was known also as Kama Lanka or "delight of Ceylon." The gradual resurgence of orthodox Hinduism and its growing intolerance of Buddhism, both in the Ganges valley and in south India, were checked for a time by the appearance of the erudite and brilliant monk-scholar Buddhagosa in the fifth century, whose detailed commentaries on Theravadian scriptures shook the religious world of Ceylon, India, and southeast Asia. Although the Mon claim that this great scholar was a Mon himself was doubted even by medieval Burmese scholars and is rejected by modern European scholars, it is definite that at least some of his pupils, using their teacher's name of Buddhagosa, went and preached to the Mons.

Even during those Buddhist centuries, Lower Burma and the valley of the Menam were merely Theravadian islands floating precariously in the sea of Mahayanist and Hindu ideas and traditions. The Malay peninsula was always dominated by Mahayanists and Hindus, and the portage kingdoms were inhabited not only by Mons and Buddhists but by Indians and Hindus. Less democratic than the Pyus, the Mons adopted both the Hindu idea of the divine king and the Hindu law code of Manu. Accordingly, Brahmin astrologers were more numerous at the court of a Mon king than at the court of a Pyu king. But the Siva cult, which became so popular in the Khmer and Javanese empires, could make no great headway among the Mons because of their long tradition of Buddhism. Some European scholars have tried to prove that the patron saint of the Mons, Gavampati, was really a Hindu deity. There is no doubt that there was a Sivite god by the name of Gavampati or "lord of cattle," but the Gavampati that the Mons worshiped was one of the arahats who were mentioned again and again in the Theravadian scriptures. After all, Gavampati could be just a personal name, in the same way as Gotama is still a personal name in India, and mere similarity of names by itself cannot prove anything. Otherwise, one could even argue that the Hindu hermit Kaundiya, the mythical founder of the first Funan dynasty, was a Buddhist arahat of that name. The same scholars were also intrigued by the Mons' describing Gavampati as "son of Buddha," because historically the prince who later became the Buddha had only one son, Rahula. But in Mon and Burmese writings and translations of the Buddhist scriptures, all Buddhist monks were described as "sons of Buddha," and the Buddha was always quoted as addressing his monks as "Beloved Sons," "Beloved Son Ananda," "Beloved Son Sariputtra." The Mons believed that, even during the lifetime of the Buddha, Gavampati visited Thaton and that he did not enter Nirvana until he had helped in the building of Sri Ksetra and felt assured that Buddhism would "shine in Lower Burma for five thousand years."

The Mons never went up the Irrawaddy valley nor did they

ever penetrate Arakan. They concentrated their attention on the delta region. Pegu was the farthest north they went and it was built only after Pyu power had been broken in Upper Burma. Dagon (modern Rangoon), Twante, and Syriam at the mouth of the Irrawaddy were Mon settlements before the Pyus came and before the formation of the delta. When Pyu power waned, these settlements must have declared their independence along with Thaton, and thus Sri Ksetra was often raided by Mons from the south and the east. When the Pyus had withdrawn themselves, the Mons went farther west and founded the port of Kosama (modern Bassein), right on the other side of the delta. The seventh, eighth, and ninth centuries constituted the period of Mon power and glory in southeast Asia.

About the same time as the Pyus were abandoning Lower Burma, on the other side of mainland southeast Asia the great Funan empire of the Malays was declining and disintegrating. The fall of the Funan empire in the east and the fall of the Pyu empire in the west made it possible for the Mon-Khmer races living in the center to divide the entire region among themselves. The Khmers, starting with Chenla, proceeded to found their empire. Their cousins, the Mons, were not able to establish an empire but they did evolve a loose federation of Mon states. The Mons in the lower valley of Menam founded the kingdom of Dvaravati, with its capital at Lavapura (modern Lopburi). It reached the zenith of its power in the seventh century, and from it in the eighth century a new kingdom was colonized in the north by the name of Haripunjaya (modern Lamphun). According to Mon and Siamese chronicles, it was founded by a devout Buddhist queen of Lavapura. The kingdom of Thaton acquired the northern portage kingdoms and the Irrawaddy delta. These three kingdoms, united by a common language, a common racial origin, and a common religion, formed the Buddhist confederacy of Ramanna. Ramanna was another name of the Mons, and originally these three regions were known as Ramanna Desa or "Land of the Mons," but later on Lower Burma alone retained that name. Again, originally, the "three Mon lands" consisted of

Dvaravati, Haripunjaya, and Thaton, but later came to consist only of Bassein, Pegu, and Martaban. Martaban was an ancient port, and its importance increased when Thaton ceased to be a port as the Sittang silted up its delta; Thaton was sacked in the eleventh century by the Burmese.

Without question the Mons were the most cultured of all the races of southeast Asia. Through Thaton, their window to the cultured world of India, they absorbed Indian culture and then transmitted it all over southeast Asia. Both the Pyus and the Khmers were in many ways pupils of the Mons. The oldest Mon inscription, found near Lopburi, goes back only to the eighth century, but the Mons must have learned to write long before that date. Their influence on all races of southeast Asia can be seen from the fact that many words of Mon origin are to be found in most of the languages of the region. The Thaton Mons were great stone carvers, working on laterite and red sandstone. They made stone images of the Buddha and their patron saint, Gavampati. They were also skilled in bronze. Unlike the Pyus they made images in the round, but they sculpted in relief as well. Their statues of the Buddha were neither colossal as in Arakan nor minute as in the Pyu kingdom, but life-sized. The postures had not yet been conventionalized, and the work was therefore more free and lifelike (at Moulmein there is an ancient Mon statue of the Buddha sitting on a bench with feet dangling freely without touching the ground). In spite of their high achievements in culture and their great influence over other racial groups, the Mons failed to seize their chance of founding a great Mon empire and of dividing the entire region of mainland southeast Asia between themselves and the Khmers. They were a vigorous nation from the point of view of military might, as could be seen from the way they forced the Pyus to withdraw from the delta region and from their ability to withstand the Nan-Chao raids. Their failure to consolidate themselves into a single empire invited attack from without and dissension from within the confederacy itself.

The final fall of the Pyus, the Nan-Chao raids, and the fall of the Tang dynasty in China, all within the second half of the ninth century, disturbed the pattern of trade and the balance of political power in southeast Asia. The unstable conditions in Upper Burma stopped all overland trade between Burma, India, and China and also affected the overland trade through the passes in the mountains of Arakan and river trade down the Irrawaddy. Sittang was rapidly forming its delta and Thaton's harbor was becoming shallower. The Nan-Chao raids gradually ceased, but many members of the raiding armies remained behind all over southeast Asia as freebooters and mercenary soldiers. Above all the Cholas of south India conquered Ceylon, and with their powerful navy they played the role of champions of the resurgent Hinduism.

The fall of Ceylon to the Hindus was disastrous to the cause of Theravada Buddhism in southeast Asia. Although Buddhism in its early days needed no protection from the secular arm, since Asoka's time it had been able to expand and survive only through the patronage of local kings, and such patronage became more and more difficult to obtain as the monarchs were gradually drawn back into the influence of Hinduism through their selfish but understandable desire to be looked upon as divine kings. To retain that patronage Buddhism had to find a compromise with Hinduism, and Mahayana Buddhism was able to survive in India only because in many ways it modified the original doctrines of the Buddha and accepted certain Hindu ideas.

In southeast Asia also, matters were coming to a head and Theravada Buddhism was faced with a crisis. According to Mon chronicles, a king of Pegu was completely won over to the side of Hinduism and started to persecute Buddhists until his selfless and courageous queen won him back to the fold. The inscription on a stone statue of a standing Buddha found near the modern town of Pa-an seems to show that at Martaban, also, a queen had to struggle against the rising tide of Hinduism. The Cholas, in their quest to expand their commerce and at the same time to attract Buddhists to Hinduism, patrolled the seas and even attacked the

Mahayanist Buddhist maritime empire of Sri Vijaya, south of the Malay peninsula. The Khmers, who were Saivite Hindus with a touch of Mahayanist ideas, were becoming more ambitious and aggressive with their native armies strengthened by sprinklings of Nan-Chao mercenaries. Assailed on all sides, dissension now appeared among the Mons. Dvaravati and Haripunjaya went to war against each other.

To add to the disunion and confusion among Theravada Buddhists, the king of the Theravada kingdom of Ligor (Tambralinga) to the south of the Mon portage kingdoms now invaded Dvaravati from the sea. He had no real quarrel with the Mon kingdom but wanted to take advantage of two situations independently of each other; the Mons were at war, and his overlord, the king of Sri Vijaya, was preoccupied with a war against Java. Malay by birth, he perhaps dreamed of establishing another Malay empire in mainland southeast Asia. Officially the religion of his kingdom was Theravada, but it was mixed with strong Mahayanist and Hindu elements. He conquered Dvaravati in no time and turned his attention to Haripunjaya, where he was repulsed. His queen was a Khmer princess, and his son, succeeding to the two kingdoms of Ligor and Dvaravati on his death, claimed the throne of the Khmer empire. A moderately devout Theravada Buddhist, he led the Buddhist Mons of Dvaravati to attack the Khmer empire and was helped by pro-Buddhist Khmers themselves. After ten years of fighting he became king of the Khmer kingdom (Cambodia) in 1011, with the title of Suryavarman I. Once he had won the Khmer empire, however, he shed the cloak of Buddhism. Although to the end of his reign he extended religious tolerance to both forms of Buddhism, he gave his patronage to the Siva cult, with its emphasis on the divinity of the king. In Mon Dvaravati itself, which was now merely a part of the Khmer empire, this meant the defeat of Theravada Buddhism. To add to the plight of Buddhists, a cholera epidemic broke out in Haripunjaya and, in fear both of the epidemic and the prospect of falling under Khmer Hindu rule, thousands fled to the neighboring

kingdom of Thaton. In Thaton itself, the Mons feared Khmer conquest and, hoping that they could save themselves, made some compromise with Hinduism. This must have been the period of the two
great Mon sculptures in relief showing the four-armed Vishnu
sleeping placidly on Ananta naga dragon, with the holy trinity of
Hindu gods, Brahma, Siva, and Vishnu himself, ascending from his
navel to the sky, and of the four-armed fighting Siva mounted on
the bull Nandi and with his goddess Parvati resting on him, crushing the demon in the guise of a buffalo. In 1050 Suryavarman died
and was succeeded by his son Udayadityavarman, who was a devout
Hindu. Thus the end of Theravada Buddhism in southeast Asia
seemed to be imminent, and the situation gave the opportunity to
the Burmese from the north of Burma to emerge as the new champions of the stricken faith.

III The Kingdom of Pagan and the First Burmese Empire

The exact date when the Burmese took over leadership of the allied tribes from the Pyus can be only conjectured. The chronicles suggested that after the Pyus withdrew from Sri Ksetra there was a new merger of tribes and gradually the Burmese appeared. Their emergence was so gradual that the Chinese continued to speak of the Burmese as Pyus until 1271, when they suddenly realized that the people in the Irrawaddy valley were "Mien" (from the Burmese word *Mrama*), and by that time the Pagan empire was nearly at its end. The Burmese had founded a small settlement or kingdom of their own while supporting and merging with the Pyus, as the Kanyans and Thets had done before. Theravada Buddhism in Upper Burma, after being cut off from its source in Ceylon, gradually weakened, and from India along the overland route had come Mahayanist doctrines. Native animism also had a resurgence. The Burmese in the year A.D. 638 adopted a new era based on astrology.

After the Pyu capital had fallen to Nan-Chao raids and three thousand of its inhabitants were taken away in captivity, the leadership of all the allied tribes passed on to the Burmese. European writers assume that the entire Pyu population disappeared from history with the fall of their capital. Surely the Pyus must have numbered much more than three thousand, however, and the three thousand who were taken away included only the royal family, chief administrative officials, and other prominent persons. In spite of the king of Nan-Chao's claim that he was the conqueror of the Pyus, his excursions into Burma were more in the nature of raids and sacking of cities rather than actual conquests. The Burmese kingdom survived probably because it had no fortified city and the Nan-Chao armies did not think it worth their while to raid it. Moreover, the climate was too hot for Nan-Chao troops to stay for any length of time except during six or seven weeks of the cool season. However, the Burmese must have lived in the shadow of Nan-Chao power and many of them with a lust for adventure and booty fought in the Nan-Chao armies both as conscripts and volunteers. The discipline in the Nan-Chao army, especially for conscripts, was rigid and merciless, and the Burmese together with the Pyus, Thets, and other allied tribes gained valuable training and experience in the new methods of warfare the Nan-Chao commanders were using. When the Nan-Chao armies melted away and their raids ceased, the Burmese felt themselves strong enough to build a fortified city of their own. Thus Pagan came into being at a fork of the Irrawaddy river just below its junction with its great tributary, the Chindwin.

The new kingdom was as yet far from stable and the chronicles told of struggles for the throne and changes of dynasties until the advent of Anawrahta in A.D. 1044. His father had been forced to become a monk and give up the throne to a usurper when Anawrahta was still a child. Anawrahta was probably brought up as a royal cadet in the army, and when he came of age he challenged the usurper to single combat and killed him. He offered his throne to his old father, who declined however. Anawrahta strengthened the army by selecting and appointing four great paladins as commanders, and Burmese, Mon, and Thai chronicles described the king and his four warriors as leading the armies, wearing armor of gold, and riding on demon horses. The exploits of these heroes became the subject of legends and folk-tales all over southeast Asia. From the accounts of battles given in the chronicles, it seems that

Anawrahta introduced to southeast Asia new military tactics. He was the first to use elephants on a large scale and, like tanks in modern warfare, they led the infantry in battle while the cavalry raided far behind the enemy lines. He was a very strict disciplinarian and the slightest disobedience of his orders brought the penalty of death. Using this newly strengthened army he brought stability and unity to his kingdom.

He was dissatisfied with the prevailing religion of his people, which was a mixture of Mahayana Buddhism with native animistic beliefs. He resented the enormous authority and prestige of the Ari monks, whom he considered depraved. At this juncture a Mon monk, Shin Arahan by name, arrived at Pagan. He was one of those few who disapproved of the acceptance of Hindu ideas at Thaton and, preferring exile to being a party to what he considered the corruption of Buddhism, he had come all the way to the Burmese capital. It was a bold and desperate move on his part, for he was alone and without a single follower and he was entering, as it were, the camp of enemy barbarians. His ascetic and saintly personality stood in contrast to the heavy-eating and arrogant Ari monks, and within a short period of time he was able to convert Anawrahta to Theravada Buddhism. Anawrahta, who must have been already planning to conquer the Mons and extend his frontiers to the sea-coast, was now seized with genuine religious zeal and assumed the role of a champion of his new faith.

Accordingly he sent out feelers to the Mons. Pegu was ready to submit. She was on the extreme edge of the Mon lands and was exposed to attack by Indians from the sea and by the Burmese from the north. Anawrahta then politely requested that the king of Thaton, Manuha, give him the copy of the Theravada Buddhist scriptures that he possessed. The king of Thaton, however, sent back an insulting reply, calling the Burmese barbarians. Both the Burmese and the Mon chronicles emphasized that Anawrahta's message was courteous and Manuha's reply was rude. The request for the scriptures could be explained in two ways. It might have been a genuine request because the Burmese did not have a copy, Ceylon was under the Cholas, and to make another copy would have been not only laborious but nearly impossible in the absence of trained scribes and learned scholars among the Burmese. On the other hand, it might have been just a demand for submission couched in diplomatic language.

Anawrahta's armies now came down to the south and besieged Thaton. After a siege lasting three months and ending with a great battle in which the four paladins won undying fame, Thaton submitted and was sacked. The copy of the scriptures, King Manuha himself with golden shackles on his legs, and members of his court were put on elephants and taken back to Pagan, as exhibits in a great victory parade. Monks, scholars, scribes, and artisans were also taken as captives for resettlement at Pagan. In the words of the Mon chronicles, "The great capital of Thaton was in ruin and silence reigned supreme. In contrast, Pagan, which really deserved its official name, *Tramplers on Enemies,* shone in glory and in triumph, as if it had become the abode of gods." Anawrahta's conquest of Thaton shook the Mon world, and Haripunjaya, which had become closely allied with Thaton since the time of the cholera epidemic, also submitted. Although the Burmese chronicles did not mention it specifically, Anawrahta must have demanded and received tribute from the kingdom of Dvaravati, which prompted its overlord, Udayadityavarman, to invade Tenasserim. But the Khmer empire was in the throes of mutinies and rebellions and Anawrahta did not consider the invasion important enough to warrant his going down to Lower Burma; he instead sent his four paladins, who easily repulsed the invaders.

The Burmese chronicles mentioned briefly this Khmer invasion and its subsequent defeat and noted Anawrahta's conquest of Chengmai. They also referred to the kingdom of Cambodia as the southeastern limit of the Pagan empire and listed various kingdoms in the Menam valley among the states that revolted against Burmese rule when Kublai Khan's Tatar armies seized Pagan in 1287. The

Thai chronicles definitely asserted that Anawrahta conquered the entire Menam valley and received tribute from the Khmer king; one stated that Anawrahta's armies invaded the Khmer kingdom itself and sacked the city of Angkor, and another went so far as to say that Anawrahta even visited Java to receive his tribute.

As this tradition of Anawrahta's conquest is so strong in Siam, as the Thai chronicles were so persistent, and as there was no reason at all why Thai chroniclers should flatter the Burmese, W. A. R. Wood, in his *History of Siam*, accepted it as true, pointing out that the final triumph of Theravada Buddhism in the Menam Valley and the first acceptance of Theravadian ideas by the Khmer populace dated from Anawrahta's time. The folk-tales in the entire region of Indo-China contain many accounts of Anawrahta often visiting the region riding on his magic lance. The legend of The Emerald Buddha, which is enshrined in the royal palace at Bangkok, narrates that the Emerald Buddha was a gift from the king of Ceylon to Anawrahta, but the ship carrying it to Bassein was driven off course to the Isthmus of Kra where it was taken to the Menam valley; Anawrahta, in great anger, flew over on his magic lance but relented when he saw the devotion of the people to the emerald image. The Buddhist initiation ceremonies still performed in Thailand, Laos, and Cambodia are modeled on the Burmese one, and in many parts of northern Siam the Burmese water festival of the new year is still celebrated. It seems that throughout the Menam region the Burmese Era and the Burmese calendar came to be in general use as the result of Anawrahta's conquest. Even before 1050 A.D. the city of Pagan was mentioned in a Cham inscription, and at the present day the best kind of brick in Thailand is called Pagan brick.

Anawrahta's political aims were to wield the geographic region of Burma into a single kingdom and then surround it with kingdoms paying tribute to him. He was thus the founder of the first united Burmese kingdom and also the first Burmese empire. In the former Mon kingdoms of Lower Burma he replaced the kings with governors, except at Pegu, whose king he allowed to remain as a tribute-giving king in appreciation of services rendered in the conquest of Thaton; after that king's death, Anawrahta did appoint a governor. Anawrahta invaded Arakan, but taking into account the geographical barrier of the Arakan mountains he allowed the Arakanese king to remain semi-independent. He made an alliance with the Buddhist kingdom of Pateikkaya, northwest of Arakan on the Indian border. On the request of the king of Ceylon, then locked in a desperate struggle for supremacy with the Cholas, he sent money and other valuable gifts to help re-equip the Sinhalese armies. When after achieving victory the king of Ceylon requested Anawrahta's help in restoring Theravada Buddhism to Ceylon, the Burmese king sent a mission of monks who ordained or re-ordained the entire clergy of the island.

Now that the danger of attack by the Khmers no longer existed, Anawrahta turned his attention toward Nan-Chao. Assuming the role of avenger of the Pyus, he led a campaign against the Tai kingdom and met with very little resistance. Ostensibly, he went to request the gift of the sacred relic, the Tooth of the Buddha, which was in Nan-Chao's possession. As in the case of the request for the scriptures from Thaton, this request was really a demand for tribute, and Anawrahta was pleased when the Nan-Chao king submitted by showering him with gifts, including a replica of the Tooth. The chronicles hinted that Anawrahta tried to substitute Theravada Buddhism for Mahayana Buddhism then prevailing in Nan-Chao but was not successful. Anawrahta was more than satisfied, however, for his main object in invading Nan-Chao was to prevent interference with his campaign to subdue the Tai-Shans on the eastern part of his kingdom. So on his return from Nan-Chao he toured the Shan states, receiving allegiance from the Shan chieftains, who were given the rank of minor kings or "kings of the sunset." However, in case they should be ever tempted to rebel against Burmese authority, he built a line of strong forts on the edge of the Shan plateau. His subjugation of Nan-Chao and the

Shans of Burma saved mainland southeast Asia from further raids and invasions by those warrior tribes for the next two hundred years.

In making Buddhism the official and national religion of his people, Anawrahta was acting under advice from Shin Arahan, whom he appointed as the primate of his empire. A strict disciplinarian, he was intolerant of and punished ruthlessly any departure from orthodoxy. He handled the opposition from the Aris with skill, executing the leaders but conscripting the rank and file for his armies, and, according to traditional accounts, with their well-fed and vigorous bodies the unfrocked Aris fought well in the elephantry. Nonetheless, he had to come to some compromise with spirit worshipers. In spite of his stern measures, he was successful in making Buddhism the national religion of the people only because the majority accepted it. Under Shin Arahan's directions, the monks went to the villages, established monasteries, and taught the people not only religion but also reading and writing. Anawrahta aroused mass enthusiasm by breaking open the relic chambers of pagodas at Sri Ksetra and bringing the relics in triumphal processions. He staged similar processions when bringing the copy of the scriptures from Thaton and when receiving the replica of the sacred Tooth from Ceylon.

Wherever he went on his victorious campaigns, he left, instead of victory pillars, hundreds of terra-cotta votive tablets with a short Buddhist prayer in Pali or Sanskrit and his signature in Sanskrit. He was the first of the great temple builders, and he made Pagan the center of Theravadian learning by inviting scholars from the Mon lands, Ceylon, and especially India, where a dying Buddhism was being given the *coup de grâce* by Muslim conquerors. He encouraged artisans, architects, carvers, and artists to settle in Pagan. Some scholars have written that the Buddhism at Thaton was far from pure and the chronicles were wrong in suggesting that Theravada Buddhism came to Pagan from Thaton. But the chronicles were referring to the coming of Shin Arahan to Pagan and the obtaining of the copy of the scriptures from Thaton. If the religion at Thaton was pure, there would have been no occasion for Shin Arahan to go to Pagan and persuade Anawrahta to champion the stricken faith. The Mon chronicles hinted that Manuha was reprehensible for making a compromise with Hinduism; they stated, "Manuha was defeated because he did what he should not have done."

The greatest achievement of Anawrahta was his consolidation of various tribes into a single nation. He was careful that his own people, the Burmese, should not flaunt themselves before other tribes, and he continued to show regard for the Pyus, who had recently fallen from greatness. For some time he retained the name of Pyu for all the allied tribes, although they were being molded into a nation under the leadership of the Burmese. Thus the Chinese for a long while were not aware of the change of leadership in Burma; the Arakanese chronicles recorded that Anawrahta came and conquered Arakan with his Pyu army, and in the inscription set up at Buddha-Gaya in India by an embassy sent by Anawrahta's successor, Kyansittha, the latter was described as "King of the Pyus."

Once Thaton had fallen, Anawrahta showed regard for the Mons and encouraged his own tribes to sit at their feet and learn their culture. Although he allowed his troops to sack Thaton, he saw to it that the defenders were not wantonly slaughtered, and Manuha and his family were treated with consideration and courtesy; even his shackles had to be specially made of gold. Anawrahta was ruthless and stern not to any particular racial group but to all his subjects, for he felt that harsh measures were needed in building up a new nation. He never accepted the cult of the god-king, and he was impatient even with gods that his people worshiped; men came to say that he beat up gods with the flat of his lance. He achieved his aims, but only at the price of his own popularity. His subjects admired and feared him, but did not love him. His execution of two young heroes for a trifling breach of discipline after the conclusion of his Nan-Chao campaign angered the people, and to appease them he declared that the two dead heroes were now gods who could be worshiped. His forcing of Kyansittha to become a fugitive increased his unpopularity, although this action at least was justified, for the great paladin, like Lancelot of the Round Table, was in love with one of the queens.

The chronicles hinted that Anawrahta's enemies ambushed and killed him, and then disposed of his body in such a way that it was never found; their account of his death was that a god whom he had whipped appeared in the guise of a wild buffalo and gored him to death, and demons then took away the body. However, even his mysterious death could not shake the kingdom he had so firmly built, and his young son, Sawlu, succeeded to the throne. The inscriptions affectionately referred to him as the "Boy King." Because he was inexperienced his ministers advised that the great Kyansittha should be called back from exile. Kyansittha served his young master well, but it was discovered that he was continuing his old romance and so he was again exiled. Remembering his past services, however, Sawlu softened the blow by appointing Kyansittha "lord" of Htihlaing, the village in the remote west, which was the place of his exile.

The young king now chose as his boon companion the son of his former wet nurse. Anawrahta had engaged, probably for political reasons, a Mon lady of noble birth to be his son's wet nurse, and for the same reasons Sawlu had appointed her son as governor of Pegu. Neither the name nor the personal title of the governor has survived, for the chronicles referred to him as Raman-Kan or the "Blind Mon," because he was blind in one eye. It was obviously an insulting term, which came into use only after he had broken with the king. During his frequent visits to the court he must have noticed the inexperience of the young king, and perhaps he even suggested to his master that independence should be restored to the Mons. In spite of the good treatment received at the hands of the Burmese, the Mons felt not only the loss of their independence but also the loss of their control of trade over the portage routes.

The chronicles described the final breach between the governor and the king in a dramatic way. The two were playing at dice and the governor won; as he romped about in joy at his victory, the king taunted him, "If you are so clever, why do you not rebel against me?" The governor went back to Pegu and, taking the king at his word, raised the flag of rebellion. He must have fought in Anawrahta's armies and was familiar with Burmese military tactics. He sailed up the Irrawaddy river with his army and took a strategic position on an island some miles below Pagan. Sawlu recalled Kyansittha from exile and together they marched down the river, reaching at nightfall the island where the governor was encamped. Sawlu was impatient and against Kyansittha's remonstrance he took advantage of the moonlight and attacked. But the governor was expecting such a surprise attack and had prepared his positions well. The result was a general rout of the Burmese army and the king was taken prisoner.

Kyansittha rode back in haste to the city, where the ministers elected him king, thinking that Sawlu was dead. Kyansittha refused the throne, saying that he would go back in search of the king. Learning from spies that the king was a prisoner, he entered the enemy camp in the darkness of the night and attempted to carry off the captive king. But the latter was uncertain about Kyansittha's intentions and so, deciding that it was safer to trust his erstwhile boon companion, gave the alarm. Kyansittha in disappointment and disgust threw the king down and escaped by swimming across the river. He went straight back to the capital and, rallying the remnants of the army around him, he retired to Mount Popa to re-form and to re-equip. It was the first defeat for the Burmese since Anawrahta had ascended the throne. The governor executed the captive king and marched on to Pagan. It was Kyansittha's personality that prevented the surrender of the kingdom to the Mons. The ministers shut the gates of the city and the Mon army started its siege. When all was ready, Kyansittha staged a counterattack and forced the Mon army to retreat. The governor lost his nerve and fled down the river in his house boat, but Kyansittha sent a trusted horseman after him. The horseman caught up with the boat and at a bend in the river he killed the governor with an arrow. With the death of their leader, the Mon rebels surrendered.

The Mons braced themselves to receive their punishment from the victorious Burmese, but the expected blow never fell, for Kyansittha very wisely followed a policy of conciliation. The rebels were pardoned, and Mons were allowed to serve in the army and in the administration as before. At the capital, Mon craftsmen and Mon scholars were encouraged and honored as before. The Mons remembered Kyansittha's battles on their behalf against the Khmers in the past, and remembered also his romance with the Mon queen. She was the daughter of the king of Pegu, and after Kyansittha's victory over the Khmers she was sent in Kyansittha's care to Pagan to be Anawrahta's bride; during the long journey they had fallen in love. His popularity with the Mons grew when he raised the lady to be his queen.

Kyansittha's mysterious birth with a touch of scandal had made him an intriguing figure. His mother was a princess of an Indian kingdom who was sent by her father to be Anawrahta's bride in the early years of his reign. The Burmese envoy who escorted her to Pagan fell in love with her and on arrival at the Burmese capital, to hide his guilt and also to win her for himself, he reported to Anawrahta that he was doubtful whether the lady was really a king's daughter. Believing him, Anawrahta refused to make her a queen. But the chronicles were silent as to whether Anawrahta made her his concubine or whether she became the wife of the envoy. But Kyansittha never claimed to be Anawrahta's son and he always referred to Anawrahta and Sawlu as his masters. During his exile, Kyansittha took as his wife the niece of an Ari monk who himself was a fugitive from Anawrahta's wrath. After Kyansittha had become king, she appeared at the palace with a little son born to her soon after Kyansittha had left in response to Sawlu's summons.

All this made Kyansittha a romantic hero in the eyes of the Mons. During his long service in the army he probably had learned to speak Mon, and in his inscriptions and proclamations he now used the Mon language. His predecessors had used Pali or Sanskrit as the official language, because scholars were still endeavoring to evolve a Burmese alphabet and the Pyu language was rapidly ceasing to be spoken; also perhaps they were reluctant to use Mon because it might amount to an admission of inferiority. Kyansittha in contrast was sure that the Burmese were now secure in their position of leadership and could afford to make gestures of goodwill toward the Mons.

Perhaps his decision to ease the burden of religious persecution was also part of his policy of conciliation toward the Mons. Worship of the Hindu god Vishnu was no doubt introduced into Lower Burma by Indians but gradually it was accepted all over Lower Burma, and especially by the Mons. As stated before, he was brought into the fold of Buddhism by making him a guardian god of Buddhism. Kyansittha, with the advice of Shin Arahan, who was still the primate, made the connection between Vishnu and Burmese Buddhism even closer. He declared that in his previous life he had been Vishnu himself. European scholars have misinterpreted his action as proof of his going over to Hinduism or as an acceptance of the cult of the divine king. On the contrary, his idea was to show that Vishnu was greatly inferior to the Buddha and was no greater than the king himself. In some ways, his action could be compared to the action of the Medieval Christian Church in including the Gotama Buddha in the calendar of its saints.

Kyansittha also declared that he, together with the naga king and Gavampati, built the city of Sri Ksetra. It was a neat piece of propaganda because the Mons were reminded that they had shared with the Tibeto-Burmese tribes the glory and the greatness of Sri Ksetra, and it was suggested that they should also share the glory and greatness of Pagan. It may be noted that he used the same tactics to make the relationship between the animistic gods of the Burmese themselves and Buddhism closer when he declared that the chief among those gods, the "Lord of the Great Mountain," was a fellow worshiper of his in a previous existence. Like himself, he was an ardent servant of Buddhism. He also claimed that a naga dragon had hidden him when Anawrahta's soldiers were searching for him. He made himself the heir of Anawrahta's supposed supernatural powers by claiming that when Anawrahta, furious at discovering his romantic intrigue with the Mon queen, threw the magic lance at him, the lance merely cut the ropes that bound him, and he had picked up the lance and escaped.

He adroitly exploited the enthusiasm of the people for him. His theme was peace and prosperity in his kingdom. Pageants and processions were staged on every possible occasion, and even collection of taxes was made in a gay and festive atmosphere. It was a time of plenty for the kingdom and he could say with sincerity in one of his inscriptions:

From the faces of those who had been weeping, of those who were parted from their beloved ones, of those who were sickened at heart, the king will wipe away the tears and wash away the nasal mucus, and with full loving-kindness and with the purest compassion, he shall pour upon them benefit after benefit. To all his people, he shall give with his right hand rice and cakes, and with his left hand ornaments and raiments. Like happy children resting in their mother's bosom, they shall be happy under the protection of their king.

He was by all accounts a just and merciful king. Although in his inscriptions he claimed that through his father he belonged to the sun race and through his mother he was a descendant of the bale-fruit stock, he allowed his parentage to remain a subject of mystery. The bale-fruit stock was a clear reference to his mother's being a princess of Vesali, but the reference to the sun race was not precise, and he left the question open as to whether he was claiming descent from the Pyu kings or from Anawrahta. He always acted as if he were a mere caretaker of his master's throne and he would not name his own son as the crown prince. Instead he married his daughter to Sawlu's son, who because of a physical defect could never succeed to the throne. When a son was born, he placed the new-born child on the throne and anointed him king, saying, "My lord, my grandson, this is thy throne and I am thy servant, a mere caretaker."

In spite of his conciliatory policy toward the Mons and his easing of religious tension, it would be wrong to consider Kyansittha as reversing all policies followed by Anawrahta, for he continued the work of consolidating the kingdom and establishing Theravada Buddhism. He was a strong king and saw to it that discipline and good order remained unimpaired throughout the country. His great achievement was that throughout his long reign there were no rebellions. He kept the Khmers, the Shans, and Nan-Chao well checked and he sent an embassy to the Sung emperor of China, which the latter welcomed with full honors accorded to an embassy of a sovereign king. He continued Anawrahta's policy of friendship with Ceylon and encouraged pilgrims and merchants to travel freely between the two countries. He sent a mission with a treasure-loaded ship to repair the great temple at Buddha's place of Enlightenment at Gaya in Bengal, which dated back to Asoka's time but had fallen into neglect and decay after the Muslim conquest of India. He continued his kingdom's friendly relations with the Buddhist-Indian Pateikkaya, so that its crown prince became a frequent visitor to Pagan. However, when the latter fell in love with his daughter and requested marriage, Kyansittha refused because he feared that a deluge of Indian immigrants would result from the marriage. He completed the construction of Anawrahta's Shwezigon pagoda, which enshrined the replica of the tooth relic presented by the king of Ceylon. He built a number of temples whose style of architecture, although showing both Pyu and Mon influences, was in a direct line of development from the vaulted temples at Sri Ksetra.

He was not by any means such a blind admirer of the Mons so as to forget his own origins and the origins of his people. He styled himself not as the king of the Mons but as the king of the myriad Pyus. As his predecessor had done, he encouraged scholars to reduce the Burmese language to writing, and by the end of his reign Burmese was able to take its honored place by the side of Pali, Pyu, and Mon languages in an inscription. His official title in Pali meant "Fortunate Buddhist King, Sun of the Three Worlds," which summed up his aims and achievements. His people insisted on calling him with affection Kyansittha, the "Soldier Lord," or Htilaing Min, "Lord of Htilaing," because they remembered him as a dashing young commander or a lover who chose exile for the love of his mistress. He was indeed a great king, but it is unfair to Anawrahta to say that Kyansittha was greater than Anawrahta, for one was complementary to the other.

In 1112 the great king lay dying. He was seventy-two years old and had reigned for a full twenty-eight years. He had named and trained his grandson as successor, and the only person who could upset the arrangement was his own son, upon whom he had conferred the title of Rajakumar or "Royal Prince" and appointed to be the viceroy of the Seven Hill Districts between the Arakan mountains and the Irrawaddy river. The region was far away from the capital but it was not meant as an exile, for there were only two or three regions whose governors were given the rank of viceroy. The prince now hurried back to the capital and assured the king of his utmost loyalty and gratitude by setting up a golden image of the Buddha, endowing it with all the lands he had inherited from his royal mother, and saying to the king, "My lord, remembering the many great favors which you have showered upon me, I have done this deed of merit, and may my lord be pleased to take a share." The king, even in the extremity of his sickness and on the point of death, smiled upon his son and said, "Well done." After the king died, so that there should be no doubt in the minds of the king's subjects as to his intentions, the royal prince set up a stone on which was inscribed a full description of his last meeting with his father in four languages, Pali, Pyu, Mon, and Burmese.

The new king, Sithu the First, also had a long reign, toward the end of which he came to be known as Alaungsithu or Sithu, the Future Buddha. He had been trained in the army and was an expert horseman and archer. His tutors were Shin Arahan himself and a distant cousin, the former Prince of Seinnyat, who had joined the Order in his youth and was now a learned and senior monk. Under such teachers he learned to be fluent in both Pali and Mon. According to the chronicles, he standardized all weights and measures; such standardization was now necessary because of the growth of trade and because the medley of different tribes had become a nation. He imposed the Burmese customary law all over his kingdom, and because the Mons were not familiar with it he issued an official collection of his judgments to be followed as precedents by all courts of justice. Alaungsithu was a great traveler and went on long sea voyages, visiting Bengal, Ceylon, and Malaya. The chronicles stated that he was well received by the king of Ceylon, who gave him his daughter in marriage, and he left there an Indian as his envoy, but the Ceylon chronicle made no mention of the visit.

His frequent journeys to Malaya were really to the portage routes, and they were made to ensure that the Burmese control over them remained unimpaired. He feared Khmer aggression, for that empire under Suryavarman II was again following a policy of aggrandizement. He probably encouraged the Mon state in the lower Menam valley to attack the Khmer empire. His frequent absences from the capital were a strain on his ministers, who had to run the government in his name, but his reign was singularly free of rebellions except in a corner of Arakan, where there was a sub-king ruling over the Thets, and in Tenasserim, where there was a Mon governor. He led a punitive mission to Tenasserim himself because of the importance of the portage routes, but he sent one of his commanders to deal with the Thets. In Arakan itself, the sub-king was deposed by a usurper but as the latter continued to send tribute Alaungsithu did not interfere, treating it as a domestic matter. However, on the plea of the son of the deposed king, who had come all the way to Pagan, he led an expedition to Arakan and restored the throne to the supplicant.

A reign of peace and prosperity was enjoyed again, and Alaung-sithu built temple after temple and became so religious that people felt convinced that he was a Future Buddha. This should not be taken to mean either that the king had gone over to Mahayana Buddhism or that the Burmese had accepted the cult of the divine king, for in Theravada Buddhism also men do pray to become a Buddha, and not all Burmese kings were believed to be a Future Buddha. That Alaungsithu deserved his reputation of being a pious king could be seen from the inscription in faultless Pali verse that he set up at his most beautiful temple, the Shwegugyi pagoda. In it he gave a learned résumé of the main events in the life of the Buddha and of his teachings, and then went on to declare his ambition:

For this great deed of merit in building the pagoda, I may seek any boon; however, I have chosen to seek a boon that will profit not only myself, but all beings. I do not desire to be born as a Brahma or a great god or a Titan, nor do I want even to be reborn as a king in all his splendor. I do not pray even to be an arahat. I wish to be a Buddha, as I want to build a causeway across the whirlpool of rebirths, so that I shall be able to pull the drowning humanity to safety and lead them to the City of Eternal Peace.

Both the reigns had been long but, unlike his grandfather's, Alaungsithu's reign was to end in struggle and conflict. After many long years of friendship and regard, Burma and Ceylon quarreled over the rigid control exercised by the Burmese over the portage routes. Alaungsithu had always been suspicious of possible Khmer designs on the Isthmian region, and he was angered by the opening of diplomatic and commercial relations between the Khmer empire and Ceylon. He especially disapproved of Ceylon's action in favoring a power that had traditionally been anti-Buddhist. Fuel was added to this fire of suspicion by false reports received from his envoy in Ceylon. The deterioration in political relations was followed by deterioration in trade and cultural relations. Although Ceylon had elephants in her own forests, there was a great demand for Burmese elephants specially trained either for domestic or military use. Alaungsithu felt that the trade in elephants was causing a drain on the Burmese supply and he imposed a royal monopoly on the export of elephants and raised the prices. When the commercial agents of Ceylon protested, they were made to water the plants in the palace gardens with pestles tied to their feet as shackles, a a form of punishment usually meted out to Burmese officials for neglect of duty. When a trade mission arrived from Ceylon with a petition asking for restoration of free trade in elephants, he arrested the members of the mission and imprisoned them in the isthmian region. The result was wholesale smuggling of elephants by Sinhalese ships. To shop this illicit trade the Burmese king arrested a Sinhalese teacher and a Sinhalese scholar, long resident at Pagan, and forced them to sign an agreement undertaking to stop all Sinhalese ships from coming to Burma, and then sent them back on an ill-equipped ship. Finally, a Sinhalese diplomatic mission taking a Sinhalese princess to the Khmer king was intercepted and seized on its journey through a portage route.

This breach of diplomatic immunity angered the Sinhalese king, who was none other than the great military leader Parakramabahu I, especially because he himself had respected the diplomatic immunity even of the "slanderous" Indian who was the Burmese envoy. Of course the Sinhalese account of the dispute is the one recounted here, but the Burmese version cannot be known because their chronicles did not mention this episode except for a passing remark that the Indian appointed as the Burmese king's representative in Ceylon was disloyal. The Sinhalese chronicle went on to describe the great armada that Parakramabahu sent on a punitive expedition. Because of a storm, however, only six ships were able to reach Lower Burma. They raided Bassein and another port that cannot be identified and finally attacked the city of "Ukkama" where they killed the "ruler." There was no city of that name in Burma, and so it must have been either Muttama (modern Martaban) or Ukkalapa (modern Rangoon). The ruler killed was obviously the local governor. The Sinhalese chronicle made it appear that it was a great war followed by a glorious victory. But the inscription set up by Parakramabahu in 1165, to witness a grant of land to the leader of the expedition as a reward, clearly showed that it was a mere raid. The inscription mentioned the sacking of Bassein but made no mention of either the conquest of Ukkama or the death of its ruler. Moreover the inscription made it clear that the reward was not for any great military achievement but for contribution toward the successful negotiation of a treaty of friendship between the two countries. The inscription also did not mention the official leader of the expedition, who, according to the chronicle, was merely the king's treasurer.

The fact that the expedition was not led by any one of the regular commanders of the Sinhalese army also showed that from the very beginning the expedition was meant only as a punitive raid. The raid did achieve its purpose, for friendly relations were soon restored through the intervention of monks, both Burmese and Sinhalese. Perhaps both sides came to realize that the trouble was really started by the mischief-making Indian representative of the Burmese king, whose falsehood and disloyalty the chronicles of both countries noted. Another reason was the easing of the political situation, as the possible aggressive designs of the Khmer king were now checked by his death, followed by attacks on Cambodia itself by the Chams from the other side of the Indo-Chinese peninsula.

For the weary king Alaungsithu, now infirm and old, further trouble was in store. The king of Pateikkaya sent his daughter to be his bride and Alaungsithu became very fond of her. His elder son resented her arrival from the beginning, and there developed a coolness between father and son. One day the prince came to see the king and found him sitting on the couch with the young Indian princess. Expecting her to get up and stand aside, he knelt before the king, but the princess remained on the couch. Shouting, "Am I inferior to this Indian wench?" he stormed out of the palace. Another unfortunate incident soon followed. The king gave a golden robe, which only a royal prince could wear, to a junior official, and when the latter came to the palace on a ceremonial occasion wearing the robe he was manhandled by the prince and the robe was torn off. The king heard of the incident and fearing that his son was planning rebellion exiled him immediately to a town in the north. Soon after, the king fell ill and lost consciousness and the younger son, thinking that his father was on the point of death, removed him to the Shwegugyi temple. The king recovered consciousness, however, and summoned his son to come and explain his action in moving him to the temple without his permission. The prince came, and when he saw that the king was shaking with anger he seized hold of the bedclothes and smothered him to death.

This younger son then ascended the throne, and his elder brother gathered an army, planning to march down the river and surround the city. The younger prince now asked the primate to intervene and, swearing a great oath, promised to surrender the throne to the rightful heir. During Alaungsithu's reign, the great Shin Arahan had died, as had the other royal tutor, the former prince, who had been appointed in his place. A monk well known for his piety and austerity, Shin Panthagu, was now primate. Shin Panthagu perhaps did not wield the same influence over the court as Shin Arahan had. Austere to the point of extreme, he wore robes made of shrouds abandoned at the cemetery and so was an incongruous figure at the court; furthermore, he was unfamiliar with the wiles and intrigues of the palace. So when the younger prince Narathu so readily swore and promised, he believed him implicitly and persuaded the elder prince, Minshinsaw, to come down to Pagan without waiting for his army to assemble. Minshinsaw was received warmly by his younger brother, who after kneeling and greeting him humbly led him to the throne, where he was anointed king. Then the younger brother gave a great feast and set a special dish before his brother. The dish was poisoned, and even as Minshinsaw ate the food he died. When the primate, on hearing the news, came rushing in and protested, Narathu replied with a leer, "My lord, my lord, have I not kept my promise? Did I not place my brother on the throne?" The primate left the palace in anger and soon sailed away to Ceylon. The people were seething with rage, but as three great kings in succession had made the monarchy so strong, there was no rebellion.

The king, burdened by his sense of guilt, shut himself in his palace. To console himself, he raised the young Pateikkaya princess to be his queen, but she despised him as a murderer and for his unclean habits. She refused his advances and in a fit of anger he killed her with his own hands. But the people did nothing, except to glare at the palace in sullen anger and to view the dark temple the king built as an expression of the terrors of his soul. Revenge came from outside. The king of Pateikkaya, mourning his daughter, sent to Pagan a mission consisting of captains of his guards, disguised as Brahmin astrologers. On arrival at Pagan they were received by Narathu. Pretending to offer their felicitation and holding conches in their hands, they approached the king. Suddenly drawing their swords, which had been well hidden under their robes, they hacked him to pieces. Then, as the Burmese guards rushed toward them, they committed suicide. Narathu became known in history as the Kalagya Min, meaning the "king who was felled by the Indians."

Narathu was succeeded by his elder son, Naratheinkha, who promptly appointed his younger brother Narapati as the commander of his armies. This itself was a significant change, and probably it was Narathu who first gave up command of the army, for Anawrahta, and even Sawlu, Kyansittha, and Alaungsithu had all been soldier kings. The dynasty truly had become arrogant, and Narathu's conduct had lowered the prestige of the monarchy. The chronicles hinted that there was an attempt to regain lost popularity; a young woman, belonging to the bale-fruit stock, in other words a descendant of Kyansittha's mother, was brought to the capital to be the king's bride. The chronicles stated that the king rejected her because her ears were too long, but the crown prince married her after lopping her ears to the right length. As Kyansittha's mother was an Indian princess, perhaps she had handed down to her descendants the custom of wearing heavy solid gold earrings. The marriage definitely made Narapati more popular and, realizing his mistake, the king sent his brother to the frontier and seized the princess. Narapati rushed back to the capital, sending in advance his trusted servant, who stealthily entered the palace and assassinated the king. Narapati ascended the throne as Sithu II. He obviously chose this title as a reminder to the people of the glories of Alaungsithu and also as a promise that he would repeat those glories. His task was not easy.

The recent domestic troubles of the dynasty encouraged the Kadus in the Tagaung region and the Mons of Tenasserim to break out in rebellion again and again. Even from Pegu, bands of Mon rebels once came up the river. But the Mons were leaderless and their only hope was that the great-grandson of Manuha, who was living in Pagan, would join the rebellion. But this young man could not come to a decision whether to join or not and, probably fearing arrest and playing for time, he fled to the Popa region carrying with him the ceremonial boat, which was his heirloom. Narapatisithu followed him there, and, to appease him and also to keep the Mons leaderless, he gave his daughter in marriage to him, making him his loyal supporter. Like Alaungsithu, Narapatisithu was a great voyager and visited the portage cities many times. Noting that assassinations of kings had been too easy, and to discourage such attempts on him, he instituted a praetorian guard whose sole duty was to guard the palace and the king. He retained command of the army although he seemed not to have led any expedition against rebels. At least in the later part of his reign the country was free from rebellions.

During his reign Burmese culture reached its highest level and, although his immediate successor was able to maintain that level, there followed a period of decline and decay. During Alaungsithu's reign four or five inscriptions in Burmese were set up, but the style clearly showed that scholars were still unsure in the use of the language. In Narapatisithu's reign, however, Pali, Sanskrit, and Mon languages were discarded and Burmese replaced them as the language of inscriptions. As the reign advanced the style became more and more refined and beautiful, and for the first time in those inscriptions the writers boldly used the name "Mranma" or "Burmese," for their leadership was now unquestioned. Pagan scholars were by this time so proficient in the study of the scriptures that they were producing commentaries and grammatical works of their own. These commentaries were accepted in Theravadian countries as part of the scriptures, ranking only below the great commentaries of Buddhagosa himself. It was a tremendous achievement on the part of the young nation. Shin Panthagu stayed on in Ceylon and was therefore not in Burma when Narapatisithu ascended the throne, although he did come back soon afterward. In any case his office had lapsed with the death of the king who appointed him. Narapatisithu appointed another learned monk as primate. This primate led a mission to Ceylon, taking with him a copy of the great Pali grammatical work that Pagan scholars had produced for formal presentation to the clergy of Ceylon, and the mission was a complete success. Narapatisithu was another great temple builder, and in some of his magnificent temples he enshrined relics obtained from Ceylon. Under his patronage Theravada Buddhism continued to spread beyond the boundaries of the Burmese empire and penetrated even Cambodia.

Yet, as the chronicles clearly hinted, there was some conflict between the Buddhist clergy and the Burmese king. During the absence of the primate in Ceylon, the clergy was supervised by lay officers in the name of the primate. It is not known whether the two offices of Ecclesiastical Censor and Commissioner of Ecclesiastical lands originated during this reign, but in view of the need for discipline among the ranks of the clergy, whose numbers were increasing day by day, and because of the loss of revenue over lands endowed for the use of temples and monasteries, similar offices must have evolved by then. The primate died soon after his return, and the king wanted to appoint a certain great Mon monk-scholar to succeed him. Because this monk had a physical defect, however, he was considered unsuitable, and so a Burmese monk was appointed as primate.

For the first time in Pagan's history, racial conflicts began to appear. When the former primate went to Ceylon leading the religious mission, he took with him a Mon novice by the name of Chapata. This Chapata became a fully ordained monk while in Ceylon and stayed behind when his teacher returned to Pagan. After his teacher's death he returned with three other monks, one of whom was the son of Jayavarman VII of Cambodia, who had embraced Theravada Buddhism and driven out the Chams. But Chapata was critical of the Burmese clergy. "When my master was primate," he declared publicly, "the affairs of the clergy were managed by him. But these Burmese monks have allowed Burmese lay officials to control their affairs, and with such depraved monks I cannot hold the fortnightly confessionals." The result was a schism in the ranks of the clergy. The king would not take sides, and gave his patronage to both the sects.

There was another incident after this. While the king was riding along a mountain road, he saw a ruby sparkling in an old river bed below him. He hastened toward the place and after picking up the priceless jewel he decided that he would build a great temple on the spot. So he summoned the people from the nearby villages and forced them to fill up the river bed. Hearing of the villagers' plight, Shin Panthagu arrived on the scene and said, "Great king, your deed is not meritorious; in fact, it is a deed of demerit, for you are ill-treating the people." The king replied, "I cannot agree with you, my lord." "Wicked king," scolded Shin Panthagu; "from this day henceforth, I will not accept any alms from such a tyrant." "My lord," sneered the king, "I own this kingdom and the property of my people is my property. Therefore, my lord, how can you refrain from accepting almsfood from me, unless you leave the kingdom?" The monk in great anger decided to go back to Ceylon, but there were protests from all over the kingdom, and the king was constrained to beg forgiveness from the monk in a great public ceremony.

Perhaps the king was unduly fearful of unpopularity. He probably restrained his lay ecclesistical officials in their work, and a certain laxity appeared among the Burmese clergy, which could be seen from the fact that Chapata required all monks in his sect to take ordination again. This must not be viewed as an attempt to impose Sinhalese Buddhism on the Burmese. A general re-ordination was resorted to only when certain laxities appeared among the ranks of the Order. As stated above, Anawrahta sent a mission of Burmese monks, on the request of the king of Ceylon, to re-ordain the Sinhalese monks because during the country's struggle with the Cholas certain corrupt practices had entered the Order. In the same way, during the time of troubles beginning with Alaungsithu's assassination, some of the monks became lax in their morals. Although Narapatisithu approved of Chapata's breaking away from the main sect, he failed to make a clear-cut decision and flinched from suppressing the lax practices. The result was the rise of yet another sect, the forest-dwellers, whose reversion to the practice of magic and alchemy the king would not suppress.

Narapatisithu continued the work of his predecessor Alaungsithu in the establishment of a common system of law, the Burmese customary law, for the whole kingdom. Accordingly he begged the learned Mon monk with the physical defect to compose a work on Burmese law to supplement the book of judgments compiled by Alaungsithu. The monk, granting his request, wrote a book of law, which came to bear his name of Dhammavilasa. The work was written in Pali but was soon translated into both Burmese and Mon. By the time Narapatisithu died in 1210 he had fully restored the power, the prestige, and the popularity of his dynasty, and the succession of his son to the throne was smooth; there was no rebellion in any part of the country.

The new king, although he had an official title, was affectionately called by his people Nadoungmya, meaning "Many Earrings," which emphasized his connection with the line of Kyansittha's mother. He was a worthy successor of his father and continued the latter's policies, but he gave up the command of the army and none of his successors to the throne ever took it up again. This perhaps was a sign that the dynasty had lost its vigor. He was the last of the temple builders and his endowments consisted of lands, not near Pagan but in the remote west, which clearly showed that the royal treasury was getting empty. He was a devout Buddhist and a scholar but, flinching like his father from taking strong measures against the forest-dwellers, he avoided conflict with the clergy. He continued to honor the Mon monk-jurist Dhammavilasa. The work of government was getting heavier and more complicated as the kingdom developed, and he appointed a privy council consisting of five ministers, which in later reigns gradually developed into the High Court of Hluttaw, the supreme administrative and judicial organ of government. There was only one rebellion during his reign, among the restless tribes to the north of Tagaung, which was suppressed by the commander-in-chief. The king died in 1234 and was succeeded by his son Kyaswa.

The economic basis of Pagan's power was both agriculture and trade. The agricultural implements of the Burmese were simple, the hoe, the axe, the pick-axe, and the wooden harrow, and their draft animals were the elephant, the bullock, the buffalo, and the horse, used both as plough animals and as beasts of burden. They were skillful horsemen and their conquests right up to the Indian border were made on horseback. Even today the Manipuri word for horse means "Burmese animal." They were able to practice both dry rice cultivation on hill slopes and wet rice cultivation on the plains. They built, in the Kyaukse district especially, efficient and highly organized systems of irrigation canals, the maintenance of which was the king's duty. Burmese society, with its emphasis on the liberty and dignity of the individual, was always very difficult to discipline and Anawrahta's people first learned discipline in digging and maintaining the irrigation systems, then in his armies, and finally, when peace came, in the restraint of the national faith, Buddhism. In addition to canals, "tanks" (ponds) were dug, which not only stored water but supplied additional food in the form of fish, waterfowl, and duck. Rice was the main crop and there were two harvests a year. Although they used mulberry wood to make bows, they wanted to avoid taking life as much as possible and were not interested in the rearing of silk worms, which had also been the case with their predecessors, the Pyus.

That reluctance to take life unnecessarily, however, did not prevent them from fighting for their kingdom or from eating meat. There were butchers and hunters, but during the period of Pagan's greatness the people were not overly fond of meat. They enjoyed fish, and it was made into paste for eating in the summer months when the ponds and streams were dry. They drank a great amount of milk and were specially fond of butter and other milk products. In those places where the land was less fertile, the palmyra palm, the mango, the tamarind, and many other fruit trees were grown. The palmyra palm was specially useful; its leaves were woven into baskets and containers, thatch for roofing, broad-brimmed field hats, and monk's fans; and its juice was drunk, made into jaggery, and brewed into wine. They chewed betel leaf with betel nut and lime, and the king and the great officials were attended by a special servant, the betel-box carrier. Tea was drunk and its leaves pickled and eaten with fried garlic and roasted sesame seed. According to folklore, it was Alaungsithu who discovered the tea plant and the gods themselves always welcomed a dish of pickled tea as an offering.

However rich the agriculture was, the kings and the people of Pagan could not have built their great temples on an economy based merely on agriculture. The great wealth of the kingdom must have accrued as a result of both internal and external trade. The chronicles boldly stated that the people of Pagan were double-tongued and with polite and persuasive words they sold their merchandise and became wealthy. A comparison of land values and agricultural prices with the heavy cost in wages of building a temple will clearly illustrate that Pagan must have had a source of income in addition to that from agriculture. The price of a pai of fertile land (equivalent to 1.25 acres) was 20 Kyats near Pagan, but only 1 to 10 Kyats away from the capital; a basket of paddy fetched .50 Kyat; 10 viss of cow's milk, 1 Kyat; a viss of honey, 1.25 Kyat; a thousand betel nuts, .75. Wages paid by Narapatisithu for architects, masons, carpenters, carvers, painters, gold- and silversmiths, and laborers for building a temple amounted to 44,027 Kyats; wages for building an "Indian-type" big monastery by a private donor amounted to 30,600 Kyats. These wages were in addition to free food and clothing issued to workmen during the period of employment. This was a requirement of Burmese customary law, as testified both by the law book of Dhammavilasa and the inscriptions.

The increase in the volume of trade could also be seen in the appearance of bankers, referred to in the inscriptions as "rich men." But surprisingly, the Pyu practice of issuing gold and silver coinage was not retained, and a system of barter was re-introduced. There was much use of copper, silver, gold, and precious stones as mediums of exchange. The relative value of precious metals was as follows: 1 Kyat of gold was worth 10 Kyats of silver, 1 Kyat of silver was worth .50 Kyat of copper, 1.50 Kyats of silver was worth 1 Kyat of mercury. Kyat was not a unit of value, but a unit of weight, being $\frac{1}{100}$ part of a viss. (A viss was approximately 3.6 pounds, avoirdupois.) Silver was the most common medium of exchange, and although there were many kinds of silver, differentiated according to the degree of purity, a Kyat, unless specified, always meant a Kyat of silver. It was also usual to resort to actual barter, for example, goods were exchanged for paddy or cattle. Sometimes wages were paid in kind, for example, one horse to image makers (number not specified), and one horse paid to a mason carpenter. However, that was probably a special arrangement, for in the same list another group of image makers were paid 10 Kyats of silver; a cartman for bringing timber, 10 Kyats of silver; painters, 20 Kyats of silver; another group of painters, 54 baskets of paddy; and a group of masons, 140 baskets of paddy.

The surplus wealth of the kingdom was used to build countless temples at Pagan, some five thousand of which still stand at the present day, many still in daily use as places of worship. Thousands more were destroyed in the great fire that ravaged the city in 1225, in the sacking of the city by Kublai Khan's troops in 1287, and in the burning of the city by Shan usurpers in 1299. Hundreds of monasteries were also built but did not survive the disasters because they were usually of wood. The temples were of two main types, the solid stupa, and the hollow, vaulted, artificial "cave." The first of the great temples, Anawrahta's Shwezigon, was a pyramidal structure, bell-shaped toward the top, ending in a copper spire, and crowned by a copper and gold hti (umbrella). The whole structure was covered with gold leaf and the hti was studded with precious stones. Most of the temples built by later kings were of the "cave" type and the earlier ones consisted of one story only; later ones added an upper story or two stories, which were used as libraries. As with the other type, there was a gilded spire at the top, again crowned with a hti.

Inside the building at the center, bearing the weight of the spire, was a massive block of masonry. On each of the four sides of the central block there was a large image of the Buddha; the images were placed back to back. Four separate corridors led to this central chamber. The walls of the cave temple were entirely covered with paintings in vivid colors of floral designs, gods, goddesses, and scenes from the life of the Buddha and from the *Jatakas*. Sometimes there were pictures of the Buddha. One inscription noted that 14,619 Buddhas were painted on the walls of a temple. There was a relic chamber underneath the structure itself in the case of the solid pagoda, and in the central block in the vaulted temples. The chamber of course was permanently closed before the temple was completed. In the relic chamber were enshrined bodily relics of the Buddha and small images of gold, silver, ivory, crystal, or precious stones. Both the stupa and the cave temple stood on low platforms. The solid base and the tapering spire together gave the temple the appearance of soaring into the sky. Thus each single temple expressed the character of the Pagan people; their feet were firmly planted on the mundane world but their spirit soared toward the skies.

The monastery usually consisted of a number of buildings surrounded by a wall. Besides the main building, in which the monks resided and assembled, there were the abbot's quarters, an ordination hall, a preaching hall, and a rest house for laymen to come and stay on sabbath days and for travelers. In addition, at one corner there stood a stupa or a cave temple with a library attached. Some monasteries were decorated with wood carvings or with wall paintings as in the temples. Brick monasteries were not common and they were called "Indian-type." The style of architecture gradually evolved and developed throughout the period until Nadoungmya's reign, but it would be wrong to divide it into separate Mon and Burmese periods. The vaulted temple was a direct descendant of the vaulted temples at Sri Ksetra and the art of gilding the pagodas and painting frescos on the walls came from the Mons. Both the architecture of the Pyus and the art of the Mons flowed from the same source, namely, India. The Burmese of Pagan never had any doubt that their culture was the joint effort of all the racial groups, and far from claiming the credit for themselves they went on calling their brick monasteries "Indian-type." The Mons, being conquered people, were more conscious of the difference in racial origin but, far from claiming credit for themselves, they noted in an inscription that a pagoda was built by "Mon workmen, Burmese workmen."

The temples at Pagan were not built by forced labor. They were deeds of merit pure and simple, and once a temple was dedicated it became the property of the public. The donor always saw to it that the workmen were well paid and well looked after, because the success of the undertaking depended so much upon them. The temples could have been built only by a society where individual liberty and individual equality prevailed. In the inscriptions the terms "king," "ruler," "lord," and "headman" were almost interchangeable, and the fact that all those offices were originally elective was always remembered. Even when Anawrahta had established a strong dynasty, the ministers as elders were able to elect Kyansittha to the throne. There did not exist a hereditary nobility, for the nobles, the senior administrative officials of the king, held their offices only up to the end of each reign although, of course, they could be re-appointed by the new king. Some historians have tended to regard the office of "Myothugyi" or headman of a cluster of villages as hereditary; actually it only appeared to be so because, other things being equal, a preference would naturally be given to the son to succeed his father.

The nearest approach to feudalism among the Burmese of Pagan was in the practice of the king in giving lands to families whose members would be liable to give personal service to the king, under well-defined conditions and in well-defined capacities. For example, some families would be liable to serve in the palace guards, some to serve as royal messengers, and others to serve as purveyors of royal food. Again, outwardly it would appear that all these duties were hereditary. In actual practice, however, the son of a royal gardener would not *ipso facto* become a royal gardener him-self. But the chances were that he would succeed his father, because he would have been trained and experienced in the work since child-hood. But at the time he attained the legal age of maturity, he would be free to seek employment outside the king's service.

During the period of Pagan the Burmese had a peculiar institu-tion of slavery. Slaves were of two main categories, hereditary and non-hereditary. With hereditary slaves, their offsprings became slaves also. Non-hereditary slaves were undischarged debtors, or prisoners captured in battle. However, both hereditary and non-hereditary slaves could buy their freedom or they could run away to another village. The price of freedom was the price of the slave on the open market, which was not high at all, five viss of mere copper. A runaway slave was considered guilty merely of a civil offense of the nature of a breach of contract or a nonpayment of debt, and not of any crime. Inscriptions mention a number of litigations over slaves, and all were cases of misappropriation of slaves; in other words, the slaves had run away from one master to another and the actions were against the new master and not against the slaves themselves. The slaves possessed rights against their masters for adequate food and clothing, and for medical care and good treatment. They were in reality indentured laborers. There were also temple slaves, whose duties were clearly defined; some were for general labor, some were scribes, some were craftsmen, whose duty was to keep the pagoda in good repair, some were musicians, and so on. Land was endowed to cover the cost of their food, clothing, medical care, and wages. There was no stigma attached either to ordinary slaves or to pagoda slaves, and it was quite common for a king to give his sons to a pagoda as slaves and then redeem them by paying the cost of redemption to the temple. Perhaps some craftsmen and artisans preferred to be pagoda slaves, as permanent employment for life was assured.

Women took full part in the activities of society. Inscriptions mention women "headmen" of villages, women officials, women high officials, women scribes, women secretaries at the king's court, women bankers, women artisans, women musicians, women scholars, and nuns. Many donors of temples were women, and women were usually the litigants in disputes over wrongful possession of slaves.

The temples and the monasteries were the center of social life and attracted throngs of laborers, merchants, farmers, artisans, hill peoples, great lords and ladies, and foreigners. The artists watched these gay crowds and, sharing their joy, they painted their likenesses on the walls. From those frescos we can know that the people of Pagan dressed simply. Both men and women wore a skirt-like dress, made of cotton or silk-cotton. Men did not usually wear any jacket but had scarves over their shoulders. Women wore tight-fitting jackets and also had scarves over their shoulders. Like the Chins of later times, both men and women often wore long robes. Lords and ladies wore jackets of vivid designs. Women wore golden bracelets, chains, pendants, and earrings. Sabbath days were not only religious but joyous occasions. Before the kingdom became too large and the affairs of government too complicated, the king himself would come forth to receive not only adulation but also taxes from his people. There was much music and dancing. Singers, musicians, and dancers were both men and women. Some were attached to the temple itself. The fondness of the Pagan people for music was well illustrated by a prayer contained in an inscription set up by a minister: "For this deed of merit, may I attain Buddhahood, but before attaining Buddhahood, may I always enjoy the bliss of being awakened in the mornings by the music of the drum and the horn." The inscriptions mention no form of dramatic entertainment, but even without dramatic shows the life of the people was definitely pleasant and gay. Buddhism has never been a religion of pessimism, and this is well illustrated by the fact that the Burmese in this greatest period of their history were inspired by the ideals of their religion, and amidst their victories and triumphs their outlook on life was one of serenity. This spirit of serenity achieved by the people of Pagan was noted and reproduced by the nameless sculptor who chiseled the stone figures of King Kyansittha and the Primate Shin Arahan, which are still to be seen in the Ananda temple at Pagan. For more than eight hundred years, these two makers of the Burmese nation have knelt serene and confident, gazing up at the colossal figure of a standing Buddha, with hand raised in a gesture of infinite compassion.

IV The Decline of Pagan and the Mongol Intrusion

The ascension of Kyaswar to the throne left vacant by the death of his father Nadoungmya in 1234 marked the beginning of a period of decline for the kingdom of Pagan. This decline was not due to foreign attack or internal rebellion, but rather it was merely a natural process of exhaustion and decay in a great empire. The dynasty itself was able to produce only weaklings, who tried to hide their inadequacy by a show of arrogance.

Although Kyaswar was a very learned scholar in the Buddhist scriptures and was a just king, his reign was marked by failure, despite its favorable beginning. He took back lands that his predecessors had given for the use of certain temples and monasteries, for reasons which neither the inscriptions nor the chronicles recorded. Some scholars think the reason was economic, for the royal treasury was feeling a loss of revenue as a direct consequence of the use of the best fields for the upkeep of religious institutions. There is no doubt that even in Nadoungmya's time the royal treasury was becoming empty. But land values and the prices of agricultural produce were never high and the economic stress must have been caused primarily by a decline in trade. Therefore, the reason for the king's seizure of monastic lands must have been his disapproval of the magico-religious sect of forest-dwelling monks, who were now living in great monasteries and buying lands, because they had become popular with the people. The sect founded by Chapata and others criticized the forest-dwelling monks, who no longer dwelled in the forest, broke the vow of poverty, and were gradually becoming too fond of toddy wine. The king also proclaimed a code dealing with crimes all over the country, with a view to suppressing robbery and theft, which were becoming too prevalent in the kingdom.

However, his measures to suppress the laxity of conduct among certain sections of the clergy and to wipe out banditry were not successful. Public opinion against any seizure of monastic land forced him to return the land. He started building a temple but never completed it because there was no one skillful enough to supervise the construction, and he could not pay the laborers adequately. He would not stoop to completing the temple with forced labor and said proudly, "In my life, I have done nothing except deeds of virtue." Frustrated, he left the administration of his kingdom to his deputies and his ministers, and he spent his time composing religious writings and giving his patronage only to orthodox sects. The forest-dwellers neither needed his patronage nor feared his authority. Thus toward the end of his reign, meat and liquor were openly and freely offered to those monks by their devotees. The meat and liquor were consumed by the monks and their worshipers during great victory feasts and were referred to as "victory meat and drink." The drink was not merely the sweet or unfermented toddy wine, which Mahayanist monks drank, but definitely fermented liquor. The feasts, although outwardly in celebration of the completion of some deed of merit, were obviously ritualistic.

For the people to have lost their serenity and turned again to magic and alchemy there must have developed certain circumstances creating an atmosphere of stress and insecurity. Was this malaise in society merely a natural reaction to a great period of national achievement, or was it part of the general malaise that had fallen upon the whole of southeast Asia like a dark curtain of locusts on the gold of ripened corn? In island southeast Asia, the long, late summer of Sri Vijaya's greatness was rapidly drawing to a close, and the Javanese kingdom of Kediri was in swift decline. On the other side of mainland southeast Asia the great Khmer empire was at the beginning of its final decline. The trade between southeast Asia and India was almost at a standstill because of India's own pre-occupation with her Muslim conquerors, and the trade between southeast Asia and China had been extinguished by the Sung dynasty's economic troubles and its need to concentrate all attention on the Tatars.

Kyaswar's son, Uzana, became king in 1250. He seemed to care only about chasing elephants and drinking liquor, and he left the task of administration to his chief minister, Yazathingyan. When Uzana was killed in an elephant hunt, his eldest son prepared to ascend the throne but there was a personal feud between him and Yazathingyan. Yazathingyan won the other ministers to his side and they elected the younger son, Narathihapati, to the throne. Narathihapati was the son of a concubine who was the daughter of a village turner and therefore he had no real claim to the throne. The experienced and wily chief minister believed that he would continue to be the power behind the throne, but he soon found that the young king was quick-tempered, arrogant, and ruthless. Narathihapati at once took over the administration and promptly exiled the old minister. This was the signal for Tenasserim and Arakan to rebel, and Yazathingyan was recalled and given command of the expeditions against the Arakanese and the Mons. In a short time he was able to suppress the rebellions but died on his return journey to the capital.

Yazathingyan had done his work well and there were no more rebellions, but his death removed from the scene the only person who could have controlled the ruthless king. Unlike his father, Narathihapati was interested in religion, and during his reign there were exchanges of pilgrims, monks, and religious missions between Burma and Ceylon. But he failed to suppress the forest-dwellers. He built a great pagoda but as his treasury was empty he resorted to forced labor until his people, sinking under the burden of his rule, whispered, "When the pagoda is finished, the king shall die." All this devotion to religion was merely to enhance his prestige as a great Buddhist ruler, and he was not at all learned in the scriptures. He spent most of his time at play with his queens.

In the palace circles he was secretly despised and his rule resented. The fact that he was merely a turner's grandson, with no real right to the throne, was remembered and the people gave him the nickname "King Dog's Dung." But he was ruthless. When he discovered that one of his favorite queens had plotted to assassinate him by poisoning his food, he promptly burned her in an iron cage as if she were a wild animal.

But his nemesis was slowly coming. Seeing that both Burma and Cambodia were on the decline, and encouraged by the defeat of the Sungs by the Tatars, the Tai Shans were on the warpath again. There were fresh migrations, and the Shan mercenaries who were serving in both the Burmese and Khmer armies were showing signs of restlessness. In 1215 a group of migrating Tais founded the small kingdom of Mogaung in north Burma but, not daring to venture farther south, they went toward the west into Assam and founded their Ahom kingdom in 1229. Another group, moving down the Salween river skirting the eastern frontier of the Burmese kingdom, founded the kingdom of Muong Nai in 1223 and then went farther south to the middle Mekong valley. The Shan mercenaries now wanted kingdoms of their own, but as the power of the Pagan king was still strong, the first blow was struck in the Khmer empire. A Tai mercenary in the service of the Khmer king and married to a Khmer princess mutinied, and after driving out the Khmer military commander he founded the Tai kingdom of Sukhotai in 1253.

Kublai Khan, the Tatar commander, who had now conquered northern China, decided to contain the Sungs in the south with an encircling movement by occupying Yunnan and then going on to Hanoi. So in 1253 the Tatar armies occupied Nan-Chao and in 1257,

Hanoi. The Tais had lost their main kingdom of Nan-Chao, but as a consolation prize the entire Indo-Chinese peninsula was open to them, except that the bulwark of the Burmese kingdom stood in their path. Many of them either joined or were forced into the Tatar armies, which gave them an opportunity to learn the new military tactics and methods of the Tatars. Kublai Khan in the meantime had re-formed his armies and in 1260 started his final campaign against the Sungs. His brother, the supreme leader of the Mongols, Khan Mangul, died during the campaign and Kublai Khan became not only the supreme leader of the Mongols but also the emperor of all China. As the heir of the Sungs he was determined that all the kingdoms of southeast Asia that had recognized the Sungs as their ultimate suzerain should also recognize him in that capacity. Being a Tatar commander and a conqueror, however, he wanted to make their tributary status clear and definite; he therefore forced their kings by might of his arms to come to him in person and swear allegiance. In 1257, after he had finally destroyed all resistance by the Sungs, he sent out instructions to his viceroys to demand tribute and allegiance from southeast Asian kings.

The instructions to the Burmese king reached the Tatar viceroy of Yunnan in 1271. The kingdom of Pagan, at least since Anawrahta's time, had never paid tribute to China, and the Burmese missions to the Chinese capital had been received with honors due to a fully sovereign state. In fact, Anawrahta had even obtained tribute from China's vassal state, Nan-Chao. Perhaps the viceroy of Yunnan would have given time and consideration to the matter had not the Tai chiefs, who were poised on the northern Burmese border, suggested that he should humble the Burmese king. He therefore sent an embassy to Pagan demanding payment of tribute. Narathihapati, with the full support of his country, refused to give audience to an embassy bringing such a preposterous demand. Two years later an imperial envoy arrived, bringing a letter from Kublai Khan himself. According to the chronicles, the envoy, as the direct representative of the emperor, behaved as if he were the emperor himself and refused to remove his shoes during the audience with the king. The king at once arrested the envoy and his retinue and later ordered their execution. The ministers remonstrated, pointing out that the life and liberty of envoys were inviolate, but the king took the view that this immunity could be lost by gross misconduct on their part. Undoubtedly, the envoy must have been difficult, as were all Tatar imperial envoys; in Java an imperial envoy demanding similar tribute was manhandled, and in Cambodia another imperial envoy and the members of his mission were arrested and later executed. The Chinese records were silent about the execution of the envoys by the Burmese king but noted that they never returned to China. It is easy to criticize Narathihapati's action as foolish and arrogant, and equally easy to be wise after the event and say that he should have bowed to the storm. It must be remembered however that the king had his difficulties. His dynasty had been losing prestige, and to accede to the Tatar demand would have been considered tantamount to surrender of the kingdom's independence and would have encouraged rebellion all over the kingdom. Moreover, he must have felt that it was his duty to hold the Tatars and the Tai-Shans from overrunning the Buddhist kingdoms of mainland southeast Asia.

Kublai Khan was busy consolidating his conquered territories and for the time being took no further action against the Burmese. But the Tais were giving the Burmese trouble, and when their little state of Kaungai on the edge of Yunnan submitted to China the Burmese believed that it was now necessary to punish the little state. The Burmese obviously thought that if those buffer states on the frontier submitted one by one the Burmese kingdom would become exposed to the Tatar armies. Therefore in 1277 the Burmese armies invaded Kaungai, which was now technically within the Mongol frontier. Kublai Khan naturally ordered that the Burmese invaders be swiftly repulsed, and the viceroy of Tali sent out a force of 12,000 veteran Mongol cavalrymen. The Burmese had 60,000 infantry with a sprinkling of cavalry and 2,000 war elephants. The Burmese, as had been usual throughout the period of Pagan's greatness, relied on the elephantry, by its shock tactics, to overcome the enemy. The Burmese were skillful bowmen, but they perhaps did not realize that the standard of archery was far higher among the Tatars than elsewhere in southeast Asia. As the Burmese had expected, in the initial stage of the battle the Mongols reeled under the attack by the elephantry, but the ground of the battle had been well chosen by the Mongol commander. As the Burmese elephants advanced headlong, the Mongol horsemen retreated into the nearby woods. Then they dismounted and from behind the trees they discharged a barrage of arrows aimed, not at the foot soldiers following the elephants nor at the soldiers mounted on the elephants, but at the elephants themselves. Maddened by the pain, the elephants turned and fled, trampling the infantry. Then the Tatar soldiers swiftly remounted their horses, cut down the Burmese soldiers before they could recover from the confusion, and the Burmese army broke.

A second Tatar army under the viceroy of Yunnan followed in the wake of the routed Burmese army and destroyed some forts within the frontiers of the Burmese kingdom, but the Tatars, finding the heat of the Upper Irrawaddy valley unbearable, went back to Yunnan. Neither the king nor the people thought of surrender, and in 1278 a new army under a new commander was sent to the frontier fort of Ngazaunggyan. Another army was sent to the next frontier fortress of Kaungzin. The Tatars, however, were not ready and five more years passed, during which time the Burmese king sent his three sons to Lower Burma to discourage the Mons from breaking out in rebellion and to deny Lower Burma to the Tatars should Pagan fall to them. Although the Tatars were quiet, their followers, the Tais, were not, and skirmishes between the raiding Tais and the Burmese soldiers were frequent. In self-defense the Burmese soldiers pursued the raiders into Mongol territory. In Tenasserim the Mons rose in rebellion. In 1283 a huge Tatar army swelled by Tai soldiers of fortune entered Burmese territory and overwhelmed the Burmese. Ngazaunggyan fell, and one week later Kaungzin also fell with its garrison of 10,000 soldiers, who were mercilessly put to the sword by the victors. The two Burmese commanders rallied their broken forces and accomplished a good retreat, hoping to make a stand at Pagan. But Narathihapati now lost his nerve and fled in haste down the Irrawaddy, for which cowardly act he came to be known in the chronicles as "Tayokpyaymin," "the king who ran away from the Chinese." The senior commander was killed in rear-guard action and his death, together with the news of the king's flight from Pagan, turned the retreating Burmese army into a rabble of frightened men. The road to Pagan now lay open.

The Tatars, however, were reluctant to follow the defeated Burmese army to Pagan for the climate of the Irrawaddy valley was too hot and moist for them, and their own losses, although far fewer than the Burmese casualties, were heavy. In addition, they were now quite far away from their bases in Yunnan, and to march farther south would unnecessarily expose their flanks to Burmese guerrilla attacks. Accordingly, they again sent an embassy to Pagan, calling upon the king to surrender, and of course the king was not to be found. In the meantime the Burmese commanders, although abandoned by their king, re-grouped their forces at Tagaung, the only frontier fort remaining to them. But the garrison was ill-armed and dispirited, and in 1284, when the Tatars, not having received any communication from the king, again mounted a savage attack, Tagaung quickly fell. The advent of the monsoon, however, prevented the Tatars from advancing to Pagan. Considering Burmese resistance to be finally broken, the Tatars declared Upper Burma a new province of China, naming it "Chiang-Mien" or "Burmese province" with Tagaung as the provincial capital.

Narathihapati, on learning about the Tatar mission that failed to find him at Pagan, now sent his primate, Shin Ditharparmoukka, to Kublai Khan. The chronicles did not mention this mission from the Burmese king and the primate's own inscriptions did not give the exact message that he carried to the Tatars. The monk, on his own responsibility, pleaded for Tatar withdrawal, pointing out that Burma was such a small kingdom compared to the vast possessions of Kublai Khan. The monk was well received and returned to Lower Burma. Probably Narathihapati had asked for time so that he could journey back to Pagan and prepare the kingdom for formal submission to the Tatars. In any case, the Tatars remained at Tagaung for three years without advancing farther, and the king in 1287 left Bassein and sailed up the Irrawaddy river. On his arrival at Prome, a full regiment of soldiers, on the orders of his second son, the local governor, surrounded the royal boat and forced the king to take poison. To refuse would have meant death by the sword, and with a prayer on his lips that in all of his future existences "may no man-child be ever born to him again," the king swallowed the poison and died. The governor then sailed down to Bassein and, rushing into the chamber where his elder brother lay sick, he hacked him to pieces. After accomplishing this treacherous deed he sailed to Dallah, whose governor was his younger brother. The news of his murders had preceded him and one of the Mon guards shouted insults as his boat approached the harbor. In great anger he bent his crossbow to shoot down the Mon guard, but his hand slipped and he was killed by his own arrow. The king's sole surviving son, the governor of Dallah, whose name was Kyawswar, now took charge of the whole of Lower Burma (except Tenasserim) and the Mons remained loyal to him.

Ten years had passed since the first terrific battle between the Tatars and the Burmese, and Kublai Khan felt that its back door to the outside world must be pried open, especially as the front door via the sea was still closed. So he sent his own grandson to take command of the Tatar army at Tagaung. Soon after Narathihapati's death the Tatars pushed into the Irrawaddy valley without meeting any official resistance, but the losses were heavy because of guerrilla action on the part of Burmese patriots. He reached Pagan in a few weeks' time and, wishing to punish the Burmese for their resistance, sacked the city. Those inhabitants of Pagan who had not fled the city—monks, men, women, and children—lost their lives in the looting and burning. The temples and the monasteries were stripped of their gold and silver fittings and decorations. It was the idea of the Tatars to make Central Burma another province of China, but mainly because of the weather and partially because of the possibility of fresh guerrilla attacks they swiftly departed from Pagan, with their horses loaded with the treasures of the fallen city. From Tagaung the Tatars declared Central Burma to be the second Burmese province of China with the name of Chung-Mien. But they left no garrison at Pagan and made no attempt to administer Central Burma.

All this information is from Chinese sources only because Burmese chronicles did not give details of the fall of Pagan. An inscription set up in 1293 by three Shan brothers claimed that they had defeated the Chinese army. Therefore it could well be that the Tatar army was forced to withdraw from Central Burma by guerrilla action. The fall of Pagan in 1287 was the signal for Arakan, Pegu, and the various Mon states of the Menam valley to rise in rebellion and declare their independence. But the Mon rebels were still loyal enough to the fallen dynasty of Pagan to allow Kyawswar, governor of all Lower Burma, to return to Pagan. For two years the Burmese did not know what action to take with regard to the monarchy, but in 1289 the fiery queen Saw, widow of Narathihapati, and some ministers who survived the blood-bath of the Tatars elected Kyawswar as the new king. His position however was most insecure. His rivals were the three Shan brothers, who considered him only as a petty king, not fully sovereign, like themselves.

The Shan brothers' power had begun early. During Narathihapati's time a younger brother of a Shan chieftain on the Shan plateau, owing allegiance to the Burmese king, had taken shelter in the Kyaukse district as a political refugee. He married a daughter of a Burmese banker and settled down in the small town of Myinsaing. Three sons and one daughter were later born to him. A former mercenary himself, he took his three sons to Narathihapati and offered their services to him. They were half Burmese, and like all Shans on the Shan plateau they were Buddhists. Above all, they were skillful fighters. The king therefore was pleased to take them into his army. After a few years of service they were given minor titles of nobility and appointed joint commanders of the garrison at Myinsaing. The king also arranged the marriage of their sister and his son Thihathu, who later became the governor of Prome. During the troublesome times they must have fought well against both the Tatars and their Shan followers, because they considered themselves Burmese.

After Narathihapati had fled they strengthened their fortress at Myinsaing and gradually took over the entire district of Kyaukse, which was the granary of Pagan even when Pagan was at the height of her glory. But now the lands around Pagan were uncultivated and barren because of the war. Perhaps as they claimed in their inscription in 1293 they did force the Tatar army to withdraw from Pagan. They possessed a small but well-disciplined army of fighting men who were veterans of many a skirmish with the Tatars, whereas Kyawswar had no one around him. In these circumstances Kyawswar had no choice but to seek their support by recognizing them as lords of Kyaukse district. Accordingly he appointed the eldest brother as viceroy of Myinsaing, the second brother as viceroy of Mekkara, and the third brother as viceroy of Pinle. Actually the territories they were named to govern were very small, but the great king of Pagan himself now ruled over only a few square miles; it was the title of viceroy that attracted them.

The real power rested with the Shan brothers and there naturally were conflicts between them and the king. Finally the king felt that his position was untenable and in January 1297 he sent his son, the crown prince, to the Tatars at Tagaung, offering submission and asking for recognition. This action on the king's part was resented not only by the Shan brothers but also by the dowager queen Saw, who considered it a betrayal of national interests. The Shans were ambitious and realized that Tatar support of the king would reduce their own power, but notwithstanding this selfish motive they were genuine patriots who could not forgive the Tatars for their countless acts of cruelty and vandalism and could not forget that they themselves took a leading part in driving the Tatars out of Pagan. The reply from the Mongols came in the following March, and the promptness of the reply and its conciliatory tone convinced the three brothers that the Tatars were eager to avoid further trouble with the Burmese. In his reply the Mongol emperor recognized Kyawswar as king of Burma, conferred some Chinese titles on the brothers, and abolished the Chung-Mien province. The dowager queen and the Shan brothers now plotted to overthrow the king.

In the following December the brothers invited the king to Myinsaing, their stronghold, to take part in the dedication ceremony of a monastery built by them. The king probably thought that it was an overture of submission and conciliation on the part of the brothers, now that he had the Mongols behind him. He was encouraged in this opinion by the dowager queen, and he foolishly went to Myinsaing and led the dedication ceremony. But as soon as the ceremony was over he was arrested, dethroned, and forced to become a monk in the very monastery he had dedicated. At Pagan the dowager queen and the ministers put Saw Hnit, a younger son of Kyawswar, on the vacant throne. The three Shan brothers became bolder and when an embassy from the Mons of Lower Burma to Kublai Khan came up the Irrawaddy, with a safe-conduct guaranteed by the Tatars, they not only barred the way but threw the members of the mission into prison. The news of the dethronement of Kyawswar reached the Tatars the following June. According to Chinese sources, the news was carried there by another younger son of Kyawswar, who managed to escape arrest by the brothers, but according to the Burmese chronicles Saw Hnit himself sent a request to the Tatars to come and restore Kyawswar to the throne. Saw Hnit might have been playing a double game, or, on the other hand, the brothers could have deliberately put the blame on Saw Hnit so as to belittle him and make him unpopular with his own people. In any case, as the Tatars prepared to invade Central Burma again the brothers put Kyawswar to death, invaded Upper

Burma, which was now a Chinese province, and occupied two important towns. The Tatars, in June 1300, received the news of Kyawswar's death and declared a Burmese prince who was with them, by the name of Kumara Kassapa, as the new king of Burma.

In January 1301 a Tatar army entered Central Burma. Unlike previous campaigns this one was conducted without much enthusiasm and the invading army soon suffered heavy losses from guerrilla attacks by both Burmese and Shans. However, the Tatars did manage to reach Myinsaing and lay siege to it. The brothers had well fortified their town, however, and were fully prepared to withstand a long siege. As the Tatar army continued to sustain losses through guerrilla action and the unfavorable climate, their commander began looking for an excuse to withdraw; when he was offered a bribe by the brothers, he readily accepted it as tribute. As the brothers celebrated their great victory, the broken Tatar army slowly made its way back to Tagaung. On arriving there the commander and his chief-of-staff were promptly executed by order of Kublai Khan. Kumara Kassapa, who had easily installed himself as the king of Pagan when the Tatar army was besieging Myinsaing, went back to Tagaung with the retreating Tatar army. The Tatars saved face by recognizing Saw Hnit as the rightful king of Burma. However, no one was interested in Saw Hnit any longer. The three brothers did not even take the trouble to arrest and dethrone him. In 1303 the Tatars abolished the province of Chiang-Mien and withdrew entirely from Upper Burma.

Of the three brothers, the youngest, Thihathu, was the most ambitious, the most able, and the most ruthless. By 1295, although they were ruling as a triumvirate, he already had visions of glory and assumed the title of "Lord of the White Elephant," and one year later, the title of the "Great Lord." At that time Kyawswar was still king, and perhaps the assumption of these royal titles by Thihathu was one of the reasons he sought Tatar help. After the Tatars had gone in 1309 he crowned himself king. Obviously he considered Saw Hnit to be of no importance. He wanted now to rule all Upper Burma by himself, and when one of his brothers died he poisoned the other. He realized that to become the real king of Upper Burma he should have a capital on the Irrawaddy. The obvious place was at the junction of the Irrawaddy and Myitnge rivers, but it is likely that the dowager queen from Pagan saw to it that a less suitable site should go to Thihathu, because she still had her dreams and plots of making Pagan the great capital again. So she perhaps arranged to have unfavorable omens occur on the site, and the king thus decided to build the capital at a less strategic position. So the new city of Pinya and a glittering golden palace were built.

Thihathu was determined that he should be accepted as the successor to the great kings of Pagan. In 1297 after he and his brothers had dethroned Kyawswar, he even raised Kyawswar's queen, already with child, to be his consort in order to heighten his prestige. He now sent a message of good will and regard to the dowager at Pagan and invited her to come to Pinya and install him in the new palace. The old queen was quite insulting in her reply but he again sent a humble message. The old queen finally came and in a great show of regal splendor she installed Thihathu in his new palace. By this action she, in effect, declared him to be the rightful king of Burma and announced to the people that the great Dynasty of Pagan would reign no more. It was the year 1312 A.D. The Mongols were gone, but almost the whole of Indo-China was now ruled by Tai-Shan kings. As a good Burmese patriot, he had tried to wrest Lower Burma from both the Mons and the Tais, but he had become resigned to the fact that Lower Burma, Arakan, and the Menam valley were beyond recovery for him. He had grown older, less fiery, less ambitious, and so he settled on a policy of peace. At the dedication ceremony of a temple that he built at Pinya there were present his new allies, the king of Arakan, and the Tai kings of the Menam valley, namely those of Chiengmai, Sukhotai, and Linzin. Following the tradition of the Pagan rulers, in addition to building the temple he appointed a monk from the orthodox sect as his primate.

Thihathu was fortunate in that he was accepted by the Burmese, in spite of his racial origin, as the legitimate successor of the Pagan kings. Following Kyansittha's example, he would not give the throne to his own son and declared the crown prince to be Kyawswar's son, who had been in his mother's womb at the time she became Thihathu's queen. This of course was resented by some of his Shan followers and in 1315 his own son crossed the Irrawaddy river and founded a rival kingdom at Sagaing. He was encouraged to do so also by the sect of forest-dwelling monks, whose ranks had swollen during the chaotic conditions that had prevailed in the kingdom for sometime. They were getting more fond of meat and liquor, and because their adoring worshipers had been impoverished by the war they themselves tilled and sowed their endowed lands. The chronicles even suggested that some of the Ari monks who had fled from Anawrahta's persecution to the remoter parts of the Shan plateau had come back with the Shans. There were riotous scenes at Sagaing; some of these monks became so drunk at victory banquets that they had to be carried back to their monasteries on palanquins.

The new king of Sagaing swore allegiance to his father and with that Thihathu had to be satisfied, although he realized that once he was dead Pinya and Sagaing would become bitter rivals. He followed a policy of restraint, however, and did not punish his son, because of a growing danger from the Shans of the north, known to the Burmese as Maw Shans. They had entered Burma in the extreme north on the eve of the Tatar conquest and were poised to enter the Irrawaddy valley at the slightest sign of weakness on the part of Thihathu. The Maw Shans were more primitive and uncultured and were non-Buddhists. They were watching not only the Shans in Burma but also the Mongols in Yunnan, and secretly they hoped to restore Tai rule to Nan-Chao. Once Thihathu was dead, Sagaing no longer recognized Pinya as its sovereign, and as a consequence sporadic warfare broke out between the two kingdoms.

In 1364 the king of Pinya had a brilliant idea. He would make an alliance with the Maw Shans and then arrange to mount a joint attack on Sagaing. The alliance was accomplished but when the Maw Shans attacked Sagaing Pinya's army merely watched from the other side. The incensed Maw Shans sacked Sagaing and then crossed the river and sacked Pinya also. The whole of Upper and Central Burma thus fell into the hands of the Maw Shans, and they could have held it and established jointly with their cousins of the Menam valley a Tai empire comprising almost the whole of Indo-China. After a short period of occupation, however, the Maw Shans suddenly returned to their own kingdom to the north of Burma; they were perhaps more interested in their plan to restore Nan-Chao. A new Shan leader suddenly emerged in Burma. He was related by blood to the three Shan brothers and the former Pagan kings, but he claimed descent from the Burmese dynasty of the sun race of ancient Tagaung. He abandoned both Sagaing and Pinya and founded a new capital by the name of Ava on the very site where the dowager queen Saw of Pagan had arranged for evil omens to appear to discourage Thihathu. Taking the name of Thadominbya, he strengthened the monarchy and united the whole of Upper Burma into a single kingdom again.

By this time the Mons in Lower Burma had also achieved some unity, and there was now a single Mon kingdom. In the rebellion that broke out in Tenasserim on the ascension of Narathihapati to the throne of Pagan, there was in the ranks of the Mon rebels a Shan mercenary by the name of Magadu. His father was a Tai adventurer and his mother a Mon, and he was born at Thaton. When the rebellion was suppressed he escaped to Sukhotai, where he misrepresented himself as the Mon governor of Martaban and entered the army of the king, who was none other than Rama Khamheng, the great warrior son of the founder of Sukhotai. Because of his experience Magadu became the commander of the elephantry. In about 1280, hearing of the great Burmese defeat in their first battle against the Mongols, he proceeded to win the love of his master's daughter. Then putting the princess on his elephant, he made the long journey to Martaban where he tried to persuade the pro-Burmese Mon governor of Martaban to rebel. When his suggestion was refused, Magadu raised a riot, killed the governor, and declared himself king of Martaban with the title of "Wareru" or "the king who fell from the sky." When Pagan fell in 1287 and the Mon governor of Pegu declared himself king with the title of Tarabya, Wareru accepted him as his ally and they fought together against the Burmese forces led by the second Shan brother. When the Burmese had withdrawn they proceeded to conquer the whole of Lower Burma. Then the two Mon leaders themselves quarreled and in a skirmish Tarabya was captured and executed.

Just as Thihathu, the youngest Shan brother, dreamed of being a worthy successor of the Pagan kings, Wareru endeavored to be a worthy successor of the Mon kings who ruled Lower Burma before the advent of Anawrahta. Accordingly he declared his kingdom of Lower Burma as Ramanna with Martaban as capital. In the meantime he sent his apologies, submission, and tribute to his father-in-law, the king of Sukhotai, so that he would not be attacked from the rear. In 1294 he received from Sukhotai both royal recognition and the gift of a white elephant. Hearing of this, a Burmese force under the three Shan brothers came and attacked Martaban but was again repulsed.

In spite of the efforts of Burmese kings and the influence of Shin Dhammavilasa's law book, the Mons were still confused over the provisions of Burmese customary law, so Wareru appointed a royal commission, which brought out the monumental legal treatise "Code of Wareru." There was another independent Mon kingdom in the east. The Mons in the lower Menam valley near the ancient city of Lavo declared themselves independent of both Burmese and Khmer control and, holding off the Tais, they sought and obtained recognition from China. If Wareru could have won those Mons over to his control Suvarnabhummi would have been restored. But Sukhotai was eying not only that region but Tenasserim itself, and to strengthen his position Wareru also sought and obtained recognition from China. Even the Mons of Lower Burma, as well as those of the Lower Menam valley, looked upon him more as Shan than Mon. In contrast to his contemporary, Thihathu, he was considered a usurper, and when in 1296 he was assassinated by a grandson of Tarabya the Mons applauded his assassination as an act of justice, failing to appreciate the great work Wareru had done in reuniting Lower Burma into a single kingdom and in preventing, both by his skill in diplomacy and by his reputation as a tough warrior, Shan incursions into Lower Burma. His tragedy was that while he endeavored to restore to the Mon people their former greatness, the Mons did not accept him as their national king. Wareru's death caused the Tais of Sukhotai to attack Martaban, and although these attacks ceased after a time the Tais were determined to take over this region of the portage routes sooner or later. Moreover, Wareru's assassination did not permanently restore the throne to Tarabya's line, and there were struggles for power. In the valley of the Menam, the Tai kingdoms were fighting among themselves. Sukhotai itself was in trouble and finally in 1350 a Tai prince took over the lower Menam valley and founded a new kingdom, Ayuthia. In 1356 both Ayuthia and Chengmai attacked the Mons of Lower Burma. Fortunately for them a strong king, Binnya U, was now king of Lower Burma and, although he proved to be no match against the invaders and lost the entire Tenasserim coast, he moved his capital to Pegu and consolidated the territory left in his possession into a well-organized kingdom. He repaired the great Mon shrine, Shwedagon pagoda, and in spite of continual wars against the Tais he restored a sense of pride and nationalism to the Mons.

Another Burmese kingdom that broke away after the fall of Pagan was Arakan. As it was exposed to the advancing Mogul or Muslim rule in India, it had to be on the defensive, and it kept itself aloof from the struggles for power in Central and Lower Burma. It also had its struggles for the throne. It entered into an alliance with Thihathu to protect itself from the Shans, but after Thihathu's death and while Pinya and Sagaing stood as rivals the Arakanese often raided Burmese territory, crossing the Arakan mountains. In 1333 the Arakanese made their boldest raid when they went as far as Thayetmyo, diagonally opposite from Prome on the Irrawaddy river, and took away as prisoner the governor of the town. After the founding of Ava, however, the Arakanese no longer ventured to make raids on Burmese territory. Thus by 1365 chaotic conditions in Burma had become stabilized and now there were three kingdoms, Ava, Arakan, and Pegu, with north Burma held by the Maw Shans, and the Shan plateau held by Burmanized Shans and divided into petty kingdoms. Ava was officially a Burmese kingdom but its dynasty was Burmanized Shan, and the army and the administrative services were filled by Shans. To the southeast the new Tai-Shan kingdom of Ayuthia was becoming swiftly known as the "Kingdom of Shan = Shym = Siam," and it had taken from the Burmese and the Mons the whole region of Tenasserim.

The Burmese had to bear the brunt of Mongol intrusion in southeast Asia because Burma held the back door to China, in the same way that they bore the brunt of the Japanese attack in the twentieth century, and for the same reason. The Tatars, as we have seen, took Nan-Chao in 1253 and Hanoi in 1257, but that was to encircle the Sungs. The Tatar invasion of Burma during the period 1281 to 1287 was part of a far greater encircling movement, namely, to take over the whole of southeast Asia, for in the same period their fleet-borne invasion of Vietnam and the kingdom of Champa on the other side of the Indo-Chinese peninsula took place. However, both the pincer movements failed because of stubborn defense by the natives. Then during the period 1292 to 1293 the pincer movement on the other side was continued, bypassing the Indo-Chinese coast and going on to Java, and then through the straits dividing Malaya and Sumatra. Had the Shan brothers not been so persistent and daring, the pincer movement down the Irrawaddy valley could have been continued, meeting the fleet at Martaban, as the Mons could not have stopped the Tatars.

The Tatar storm that blew over southeast Asia destroyed the balance of power in that region. In the island southeast Asia, once the Tatars had withdrawn, a new balance of power was soon achieved without much conflict, helped by the coming of Islam into the region. In contrast, in mainland southeast Asia, a new balance of power could not be achieved for the next two hundred years because even after the Mongols had withdrawn, their allies, the Tai-Shans, remained permanently settled in the region. The Tai-Shans of course were originally opposed to the Tatars, but after Nan-Chao had fallen they became in effect their followers and then supporters. The Maw Shans to the north of Burma remained truculent, but the Tai-Shans of the Menam valley showed their diplomatic genius by becoming the only racial group in southeast Asia to accept willingly and in gratitude the full measure of vassalage of the Tatars. In the short space of ten years, 1291–1300, in addition to sending five tribute missions, the Tai warrior king, Rama Khamheng, visited Kublai Khan on two separate occasions, making the long and arduous journey just to swear allegiance in person before the great emperor. It was fortunate that after Rama Khamheng's death in 1317 Sukhotai and its ally Chengmai were at loggerheads, for otherwise the whole of mainland southeast Asia would have passed to the Tais.

However, such a strong empire, even of Tais, in southeast Asia was never desired by Kublai Khan. When the newly revived Mon kingdom asked for recognition, Kublai Khan did not hesitate, although he knew full well that Wareru had already accepted vassal status from Sukhotai. When Rama Khamheng, taking advantage of the presence of the Tatar fleet in the adjoining seas, proceeded to take over various small kingdoms of the Malay peninsula, Kublai sent a written order to him, saying, "Do no evil to Malaryu." However, Kublai gave full approval and support to the Tais in their dismemberment of the Khmer empire, whose king he was never able to punish for the execution of his envoys. Obviously, Kublai Khan's main aim after 1293 was to keep the entire region of southeast Asia broken and fragmented with tiny kingdoms warring among themselves. In spite of his ultimate failure to win southeast Asia, his achievement from the point of view of China was in the destruction of the two strong southeast Asian empires. For the Khmers it was the end, but for the Burmese there was to be a resurgence.

V Ava against Pegu; Shan against Mon

Even when Thihathu was generally accepted as the victor over the
Tatars and a worthy successor of the Pagan kings, some Burmese
officials felt that they could not serve under an adventurer and a
barbarian, and so they left with their followers for a small fortified
town in the Sittang valley known as Toungoo or "Hill Spur." They
tried to remain aloof as much as possible from both the Shans and
the Mons, although when raiding bands occasionally came they had
to submit, sometimes even contributing recruits for the raiders.
Secretly, however, they were preparing to fight both the Shans and
the Mons at the first opportunity. After Thihathu died and when
Sagaing and Pinya started to fight each other, more and more Burmese became disillusioned with Shan rule and migrated to Toungoo.
More migrations followed the sacking of those two cities by Maw
Shans. By the time Thadominbya founded the city of Ava, therefore, Toungoo had become strong enough for its ruler to flaunt a
white umbrella and act as if he were a sovereign king.

Thadominbya, in founding Ava, was determined to make it a
worthy successor of Pagan, and his great dream was to unite the
Burmese, the Mons, and the Shans into a single nation as they had
been in the days of the Pagan kings. He at once re-introduced law
and order and tried to purify the Buddhist clergy, which had become hopelessly corrupt. Thus when a monk was found guilty of

misappropriating some gold that a poor widow had left in his monastery for safe keeping during the raids by the Maw Shans, he denounced the culprit in the audience chamber of the palace, cut off his head with his own hands, made a hole in the floor with his sword, and kicked the corpse down the opening. It was a barbaric gesture but it had the desired effect on the clergy. He considered Toungoo to be the main obstacle to the realization of his plan to unite the warring races; declaring the people at Toungoo as rebels, he attacked it repeatedly until Toungoo had to submit.

Although he suppressed the Burmese at Toungoo, at Ava he gave special consideration and favor to the Burmese who served him and was magnanimous even to those Burmese who opposed him. For example, when Ngatetpya, a popular Burmese bandit who robbed the Shans and shared his loot with the poor, was captured, the king in full audience asked him, "Scoundrel, your punishment can only be death, but because you shared the loot with the poor, I will give you this favor. What do you choose, the sword or the spear or trampling by elephants?" The Burmese bandit replied, "I choose your prettiest Shan queen." The king, instead of being angered by his insulting reply, said, "You are a brave man and I spare your life. You may go free." Ngatetpya was so overcome by the king's graciousness that he entered the latter's service and became one of the king's most distinguished commanders. Thadominbya extended full patronage to orthodox monks and encouraged learning among both monks and laymen. But he died in 1368 after too brief a reign of some four years.

Thadominbya left no heirs, and the beautiful Shan queen whom Ngatetpya lightly referred to nearly succeeded in seizing the throne, but the ministers intervened and offered it to a Burmese, the lord of Yamethin, who like all Burmese royal officials of the time was married to a Shan princess, but he declined saying that he was a soldier unused to life at the palace. This lord of Yamethin was respected by both Shans and Burmese alike for his seriousness of purpose and strength of character, and it was even said that throughout his life he smiled only three times. The reason for his refusal, however, was obvious; as he was Burmese, he would have found it difficult to control the Shan lords and their mercenaries. At his suggestion the ministers elected his brother-in-law, "the great lord" Swa Sawkè.

The choice was a very happy one. Apart from the fact that his only rival had suggested his choice, he had the full support of the Burmese because he was descended from both the Pagan kings and the family of the three Shan brothers. As stated above the governor of Prome, who forced his father, Narathihapati, to take poison, was married to the only sister of the Shan brothers. A princess was born of that union and she later married a younger brother of Saw Hnit, who was appointed governor of Thayetmyo by his father, Kyawswar, before he was deposed. The appointment was continued by Thihathu. Swa Sawkè was thus a great-grandson of Narathihapati, a grandson of Kyawswar, and a nephew of Saw Hnit, in addition to being a grandnephew of the Shan brothers. Although only one-quarter Shan, he was given a Shan name and was brought up as a Shan from childhood. He was taken to Arakan together with his father when the whole family was captured after an Arakanese raid on Thayetmyo. Thus he spent his youth as a princeling at the court of the Arakanese king and became popular not only in court circles but with the Arakanese people themselves. Later, when the family was freed, he returned to Burma and entered the service of the king of Pinya, where he won distinction both as soldier and administrator. While in Arakan, he had as his tutor one of the most learned Arakanese monks of the day and thus he had become a scholar in his own right.

In the early years of his reign he considered the Shans in the north to be his most dangerous enemy and therefore pursued a conciliatory policy toward his enemies in the south. He was pleased when Binnya U in 1371 wrote him a friendly letter suggesting a meeting. He journeyed to the frontier where the king of Pegu met him, and together the two kings demarcated the frontier and exchanged gifts. His prestige grew, and the Arakanese sent an embassy requesting the Burmese king to delegate one of his relations to ascend the Arakanese throne left vacant by the death of their king, who left no heir. Accordingly, he nominated his uncle. He also received an embassy from Chengmai assuring him of its friendship. All this time he was watching the situation in the north. The Mongol power in China had rapidly declined, and the final battle between the new Ming dynasty and the Mongols was being fought in Yunnan. In 1371 he was able to win the submission of the Maw Shans at the extreme north of Burma, but in 1373 they again started raiding Burmese territory. In 1381, however, the Ming had completed the conquest of Yunnan and could now turn their attention to the turbulent Maw Shans on the frontier. The Chinese histories claimed that Swa Sawkè sought help from Yunnan, which was given together with Chinese official recognition of Swa Sawkè as the governor of Ava. Burmese chronicles made no mention of any request for help from the Chinese, and even if such request were made it could have been only a proposal for friendly relations and joint action against the Maw Shans. In any case the Maw Shans still continued to raid Burmese territory until 1393, when the taciturn governor of Yamethin inflicted such a crushing defeat that there were no more raids during Swa Sawkè's long reign.

Ava's growing power made the king of Toungoo anxious; as a young man he had received his education and training with the Mons at Pegu and therefore trusted the Mons more than he trusted Swa Sawkè. Swa Sawkè in turn became suspicious and instructed his elder brother, the governor of Prome, to lure the king of Toungoo to Prome on a false promise of marriage between his daughter and the king's son. The king understood the proposal of marriage to be the first step toward joint rebellion against Swa Sawkè; he therefore proceeded to Prome with a strong bodyguard but was ambushed and killed. This act of treachery, so much out of keeping with Swa Sawkè's character, showed that he was merely waiting for an opportunity to attack all his enemies, including the Mons.

After all, he shared his predecessor's dream of making Ava the capital of the whole of Burma. In 1385 Binnya U died and, although his son Razadarit was acclaimed king by the people, the dead king's sister claimed the throne for herself with the support of Binnya U's brother, the lord of Myaungmya. As Razadarit prepared to march on him, the lord of Myaungmya wrote thus to Swa Sawkè:

Glorious king, the ungrateful son, who was a rebel when his father was alive, now has dared to ascend the great Binnya U's throne, assuming the title of "Razadarit." Before he can make his position secure, I beg my lord to attack Pegu both by land and by water. Your humble servant holds Bassein and Myaungmya and shall attack Pegu by water. When you have achieved your great triumph, take all the treasures for yourself; as to your humble servant, grant him only the annual revenue.

The result of Myaungmya's invitation was the forty-years' war between Ava and Pegu.

Swa Sawkè led his army down the Irrawaddy River in 1386 but was repulsed. The following year he led another expedition but was again repulsed by Razadarit. Now the latter turned his attention to his uncle and in a great battle the lord of Myaungmya was killed. His son and two sons-in-law escaped and were given appointments by Swa Sawkè. In 1388 Razadarit entered Burmese territory and was met by Swa Sawkè. The battle was inconclusive and finally Razadarit offered to withdraw from Burmese territory if the Ava king would agree to restore peace between the two kingdoms. Swa Sawkè now had to take into consideration the possibility of an attack on his flank by the Arakanese. His uncle had proved to be a popular king of Arakan but he too died without leaving an heir; again, on the request of the Arakanese themselves, Swa Sawkè nominated his own son, who, however, proved to be a tyrant and had just been driven out of Arakan. Because of these circumstances, Swa Sawkè accepted Razadarit's offer of peace. Until Swa Sawkè's death in 1401, Ava was at peace with its neighbors. In contrast to the short reigns by various kings since the fall of

Pagan, Swa Sawkè's lasted a full thirty-three years, which gave much needed stability to the monarchy in Upper Burma. In spite of his many wars, he was able to accomplish much-needed repairs to the irrigation system, and during long periods of peace his people were able to reclaim much of the arable land that had lapsed into wilderness as the result of the havoc wrought by the Tatars.

The favorite son whom Swa Sawkè carefully trained and appointed crown prince succeeded to the throne only to be assassinated within the year by his tutor. It seemed there was to be again a long struggle for power. There was some fighting, but the ministers were firm and chose as king Swa Sawkè's son by a village maiden whom he had met during one of his campaigns. His name was Minkhaung. The Arakanese, misjudging the situation, raided the Burmese territory. The new king's revenge was prompt. He sent an expedition to invade Arakan and place his son-in-law on the throne. The Arakanese king fled to the Muslim king of Bengal and his son, the crown prince, fled to Razadarit. Razadarit considered this a wonderful opportunity to win the Arakanese as his ally; in order to encourage Arakanese resistance to the Burmese, he sailed up the Irrawaddy river with a huge armada of war boats. Minkhaung was totally unprepared to meet the invasion and ordered all his men to withdraw to fortified towns on the river, allowing Razadarit free passage. Unable to take Prome, Razadarit sailed on to Ava, leaving his son-in-law at a town a few miles below to keep the river open for possible retreat. The governor of Prome attacked the town and drove out the son-in-law, after capturing his wife, Razadarit's daughter. At Minkhaung's request a learned monk met the armada with presents a few miles south of Ava and requested "peace" as his alms. Razadarit withdrew and, meeting his defeated son-in-law near Prome, summarily executed him.

Minkhaung raised Razadarit's widowed daughter to be his queen. Incensed, Razadarit sailed up the river again and made preparations to attack Prome. Minkhaung, with an army of levies from the Shan plateau, came down by land to reinforce Prome. Razadarit

sent raiders right up to Ava and burned the granaries and com-
missarial boats all along the river. Minkhaung now sued for peace
and Razadarit was proving adamant, when two of his queens, sis-
ters, wept before him, saying they longed to see again their father,
a commander, who was now a prisoner-of-war at Ava. The two
kings met at the famous pagoda at Prome and, before the inscriptions put up by Kyansittha telling of his great victories for both
Burmese and Mon alike, they swore to preserve the peace. Minkhaung gave his sister in marriage to Razadarit, who in return assigned to Minkhaung the customs duties and port dues at Bassein.
The stipulation regarding the port dues at Bassein showed that one
of the reasons for this forty-years' war was the vital need of Ava
to have access to a seaport. Even though the region to the north of
Burma was still in turmoil, both the Chinese and the king of Ava
wanted again to open the back door for purposes of trade. Unfortunately the settlement was impracticable because Bassein had
to serve two masters, Razadarit's administrative officials and Minkhaung's revenue officials.

In 1406 Minkhaung declared his eldest son, Minyè Kyawswar,
as crown prince. This disturbed Razadarit because it was popularly
believed that the new crown prince was the vengeful incarnation
of his own son, whom he had executed some seventeen years ago
when he heard reports that his son was plotting rebellion against
him. Razadarit had believed the story because his uncle, the lord
of Myaungmya, who was by that time with the Burmese, was encouraging the young prince to rebel. Moreover, he remembered his
own past, when he himself had rebelled against his own father. He
therefore sent a band of executioners to the town where his son was
ruling as governor. The young prince asked for a few minutes' time
and swore a dreadful oath: "If I am guilty of any treason, by
thought, word, or deed, may I suffer in the fires of the nether regions for a thousand time cycles. If I am innocent, may I be re-born
in the dynasty of Ava kings and may I become the scourge of
Mons." One year later, Minkhaung's chief queen gave birth to

Minyè Kyawswar, and the young prince from infancy was trained as a soldier. He became a commander of a battalion at the age of fourteen and he was already a veteran at sixteen, when he was appointed crown prince. Minkhaung's younger brother and his companion in arms objected to the appointment and challenged Minkhaung to single combat. In the combat the younger brother was defeated and when he was allowed to go free after the combat he escaped to Pegu and entered Razadarit's service. Razadarit's acceptance of his services was regarded as a declaration of war against Ava.

Razadarit decided to open hostilities on a new front. Invading Arakan and killing Minkhaung's son-in-law, he placed on the throne the Arakanese crown prince, who had been in his service since 1403. He brought back to Pegu the widowed queen, daughter of Minkhaung, and made her one of his queens. To revenge this Minkhaung invaded Mon territory both by land and by sea in 1407. Although at first successful, he was finally repulsed. In the following year Ava left the Mons alone because the king was busy driving out the Sawbwa of Hsenwei, a Maw Shan state in the north. His attack on Ava was in revenge for Minkhaung's destruction of two northern Shan kingdoms in 1406. Minyè Kyawswar killed the Sawbwa in single combat but could not take the capital, Hsenwei, because Chinese reinforcements had arrived in the town. As Minyè Kyawswar was laying siege to it, he was recalled to Ava because the Mons were marching on Prome.

In the following year, 1409, Minkhaung marched south again, and the two kings took part in a great battle. Razadarit had a few foreign mercenaries among his troops, but the battle was indecisive. In 1410 Minyè Kyawswar invaded the Irrawaddy delta again but was repulsed. Going over to Arakan, he drove out Razadarit's protégé from the throne, who then escaped to Bengal. He abolished the monarchy and divided Arakan into two governorships. In 1412 the Mons attacked Prome and Minkhaung led an army by river and Minyè Kyawswar another army by land. The Mons were badly defeated and Minyè Kyawswar was on the point of achieving complete victory when he had to rush back to Ava because the new Sawbwa of Hsenwei was approaching Ava. The Maw Shans withdrew on learning that Minyè Kyawswar was on his way. In 1413 there was another raid by two Maw Shan Sawbwas, and Minyè Kyaswar chased them back to their own kingdoms and sacked the towns. As the Sawbwas had fled to Chinese territory, he brought back their families as captives to Ava.

In 1414 Minyè Kyawswar again invaded Lower Burma. He inflicted a series of defeats, capturing one of Razadarit's finest commanders, whom he sent back to Ava as a prisoner-of-war. In the meantime a Chinese army arrived at the gates of Ava, asking for release of the families of the Shan Sawbwas. When Minkhaung refused, the Chinese commander suggested that the issue be decided by single combat between a Chinese champion and a Burmese champion. The Mon commander whom Minyè Kyawswar had sent back offered to fight for Ava. In the combat the Chinese champion was killed and the Mon hero was taken into Minkhaung's service. This was the version given by the Burmese chronicles, but the Chinese histories said that Minkhaung was severely reprimanded by the Chinese for his incursions in the northern Shan kingdoms. Meanwhile Minyè Kyawswar was poised to give the final blow to Razadarit, who had now fled to Martaban.

Becoming impatient and impetuous, Minyè Kyawswar, after another victory, chased the fleeing Mon soldiers into their own lines, with the result that his elephant was wounded by a hundred spears. In great pain, the animal threw off his rider and Minyè Kyawswar's leg was trampled by the elephant. Seriously wounded, he was captured and taken before Razadarit, who said, "Prince, my son, I will cure you of your wounds, if you will but promise to enter my service and serve me well." "My lord," replied Minyè Kyawswar, "I have fought the Mons throughout my life, and I would rather die than accept medicine and food from my enemies." He died the same night. According to Mon chronicles, he died of his wounds, but according to Burmese chronicles he was executed by Razadarit. His death was lamented by soldiers on both sides and their hearts were no longer in the war. There were to be only two more campaigns, fought half-heartedly by both sides. In 1416 the Mons sent a small expedition to Toungoo and, although Toungoo was considered an unfriendly kingdom by Ava, Ava could not allow it to fall to the Mons. So the new crown prince, Minyè Kyawswar's younger brother, came and drove the Mons out. In the following year the same crown prince in a lightning raid captured and held the port of Dagon for a few weeks. That was the last battle, and four years later Minkhaung died. One year after Minkhaung's death, Razadarit also died.

At Ava the crown prince Thihathu ascended the throne without incident, but at Pegu the ascension of the crown prince was followed by separate rebellions by his two younger brothers, one of whom invited Thihathu to intervene. The arrival of Thihathu's soldiers caused consternation in the delta region. Finally one brother fled to Martaban and disappeared; the other brother submitted to the king and was declared crown prince. Thihathu contributed his share to this happy conclusion, and in gratitude the Mon king and the crown prince gave their only sister, the Lady Shin Saw Bu, in marriage to Thihathu. She was a widow with two children, but only twenty-nine years of age, and was a lady of charm and distinction. Thihathu raised her to the rank of queen. Unlike his fiery brother, Minyè Kyawswar, Thihathu did not consider the Mons to be his enemy and followed a policy of friendship and conciliation toward Pegu. He feared that not only the Maw Shans but the chieftains of the Shan plateau were plotting his overthrow. As he suspected, one of the chieftains of the Shan plateau led a raiding party into his territory in 1425; going out to meet the raiders, he was killed by an arrow, after a reign of only four years. His son, who succeeded him, was poisoned by Shin Bohmai, the Shan queen, after a reign of three months. The queen put her lover, a Shan lord, on the throne but a Burmese lord chased him out and made himself king. But to get Shan support, he had to make Shin Bohmai his junior queen.

He founded a Burmese dynasty and made great efforts to rally the Burmese from all over Burma. But the Burmese at Toungoo spurned his overtures, considering him to be a mere puppet of the Shans. On the other hand, the Shan officials under him would not give him their full loyalty because he was Burmese. His dynasty lasted from 1427 to 1527, but it was a continuous period of difficulty and decline for Ava. Arakan regained its independence and Prome broke away. Both from the north and the east Sawbwas often came raiding; these enemies could never unite, so when one chief was attacking Ava, another would come to Ava's support. Another reason why the dynasty did not fall quickly was because the army, consisting mainly of Shan mercenaries and Burmese officers and organized into a ruthless fighting machine by Minyè Kyawswar, remained stable and strong.

Although the Chinese in Yunnan were still interested in opening the back door to southeast Asian trade, they did not seem to be doing much about it. This absence of a firm policy on the part of the Chinese, combined with Ava's weakness, encouraged the leader of the Maw Shans, Thohanbwa, to make a determined effort to re-establish the kingdom of Nan-Chao. In 1441 he sent a raiding army into Ava's territory while he himself led his main army into Yunnan. The Chinese suffered three separate attacks by Thohanbwa before they sent a strong army under the command of the president of the board of war to the frontier. Thohanbwa retreated only to be captured by the Burmese and taken to Ava. The Chinese forces, after defeating the Maw Shans, now demanded that Ava surrender Thohanbwa. When Ava refused, the Chinese invaded but were driven out with heavy losses. In 1446 another strong Chinese army besieged Ava and, as the king was wavering, Thohanbwa committed suicide. The king welcomed his death as a solution to the problem and gave the dead body to the Chinese, which action, in his opinion, did not really constitute the acceptance of the Chinese demand "because a dead body was not a live fugitive." However, the Chinese considered it as Ava's recognition of Chinese overlordship.

The Chinese then seemed to lose interest in keeping the back door open, and the Maw Shans again invaded Ava in 1507, and Ava surrendered a piece of territory in order to gain time to get the help of Toungoo. In spite of repeated rebuffs, Ava had been wooing Toungoo, trying to convince its king that out of a sense of nationalism he should support the Burmese dynasty at Ava. Now the king of Ava gave his niece in marriage to Minkyeenyo, king of Toungoo, together with the precious Kyaukse district. Minkyeenyo gratefully accepted the bride and the gift but would not come to Ava's rescue. In 1524 the Maw Shans under Sawbwa of Mohnyin occupied the frontier forts and sailed up and down the Irrawaddy at will. In 1527 he came again and sacked Ava after a terrific battle in which the king of Ava was killed. Most of the Burmese who had clung to Ava as the national capital now fled to Toungoo.

Sawbwa of Mohnyin's son, another Thohanbwa, became king of Ava. Deciding that Ava should now become a Shan city, he instituted a reign of terror directed against the Burmese. He broke open temples and seized their treasures; he ordered all Burmese monks to come to the palace and when they arrived he burned them alive; he burned or destroyed whole libraries containing priceless manuscripts. But he could not do without some Burmese officials to help administer the kingdom, so he retained the services of one Burmese minister, Mingyi Yannaung, who used his influence to protect Burmese fugitives and arrange for their evacuation to Toungoo. He continued to keep the trust of the Maw Shan king until 1543, when he assassinated Thohanbwa. He was offered the throne but declined; saying that his work was done and the Burmese had been avenged, he became a monk and disappeared from history. As only a few Burmese officials were left at Ava, a Shan Sawbwa was elected as king. By that time, Ava had ceased to be a kingdom and was a mere principality.

This period in Ava, in spite of its wars and insurrections, was a romantic time in Burmese history and a golden age of Burmese literature. The Shan brother Thihathu was a great admirer of the Burmese and their way of life and institutions, and because of this admiration and also because of his burning desire to be recognized as successor to Pagan kings he encouraged the retention of Burmese traditions all over his kingdom. Many Burmese, who were reluctant to serve a Shan king and equally reluctant to leave their homeland and go to Toungoo, took to religion or the pursuit of learning as a way to escape the stress and strain of the period. The Burmese language in the inscriptions of the Pagan period was matter-of-fact and prosaic; in contrast, the Burmese in the inscriptions set up in the Ava period was smooth, flowery, and lyrical, as the following extract will show:

Commit this to thy memory, O Commander, O man-at-arms. When those great kings who founded the country of Burma and established the great religion therein disappeared from the scene, there was a great disunity and events of great terror and great destruction occurred. The king of the gods, the guardian of our religion, carefully scanned the ranks of humanity and looked for one who would bring back the great religion. Then he saw the conqueror of the great Khan, the mighty soldier who pierced the ranks of the Tatars, the lord of the white elephant, whose name was Thihathura, the lion among heroes.

Possessing neither the wealth nor the prestige to carve their poems in brick and stone as their predecessors of Pagan had done, Burmese scholars now wrote their poems with a stylus on a palm leaf, and thereby a vernacular literature suddenly came into being. Minkhaung's reign was especially rich in poets. Apart from poems dealing with religious themes, they wrote two types of poems that were immensely popular. One was the lullaby and the other was the epic. The lullaby was actually a long lyrical poem, dealing mainly with court life. The epic was really a long marching song, dealing not only with the glories of war but with the distress and suffering it entailed. This same Shan dynasty inspired the contemporary Arakanese to develop a Burmese literature of their own. After the

Shan dynasty had passed and Ava started to decline, the fact that a Burmese dynasty was on the throne encouraged Burmese scholars to remain at Ava instead of fleeing to Toungoo. Great religious poems resulted, and two famous monks appeared, Shin Maha Thila Wuntha and Shin Maha Ratta Thara, who in spite of their great learning in Pali chose to use Burmese in their writings. The first monk was originally a simple villager, who acquired his learning and his skill in writing in a remote village monastery, whereas the second monk was a scion of a noble family, who acquired his learning and skill in writing in the shadow of the palace. The kings of Ava gave their patronage to all writers, and in the court circle itself there were both men and women poets.

The period of the Shan dynasty was an age of romance and chivalry. Kings and lords married many wives, and the queens took lovers and plotted intrigues against their husbands. For example, Ngatetpya the bandit tells of one Shan queen who was so beautiful that all men desired her. There was another Shan queen, Shin Bohmai, Minkhaung's favorite, who played king-maker and was the wife of five successive kings. There were many romantic warriors too, for example, the Shan brothers themselves; Ngatetpya, who robbed only the rich; the lord of Yamethin, who seldom smiled but ever hammered the invading Maw Shans; and Minyè Kyawswar, who spurned the love of many women and spent his time either fighting or carousing with his soldiers, drinking pot after pot of toddy wine. There was also the Mon commander Lakun-Ain, who, when his king stooped to treachery, fearlessly shouted a warning to the Burmese; who crept into Minkhaung's camp, but would not kill the sleeping king and merely took away his sword of state; and who, mortally wounded and cradled in the arms of Minyè Kyawswar, refused to accept food because he did not want to die with an undischarged debt of gratitude.

Kings and commanders fought in chain mail, with spear, sword, and bow, riding on horses and elephants. Single combats were the order of the day, but in such combats kings fought only kings,

princes only princes, lords only lords, commanders only commanders, and soldiers only soldiers. Kings and commanders brought
their wives to the wars and often during a retreat it was quite
common for a queen to fall from a baggage train of carts and to be
picked up and made queen by the enemy. By mutual consent every
campaign ended when the first monsoon storm broke because the
men in any case would desert and go back to till their farms. There
were many acts of chivalry and some of treachery. When the death
of Minyè Kyawswar was announced, both armies wept and mourned
the loss of so great a commander, so brave a warrior, and so young
a prince. When Razadarit heard of Minkhaung's death, he lamented,
"My brother, my enemy, my rival, my companion, life is empty
without you."

As Ava declined, both Arakan and Pegu prospered. While
Ava and Pegu were busy fighting each other, in the islands of southeast Asia, under the impact of Islam, trade was recovering its
momentum after a period of disturbance due to the Mongol intrusion. Muslim Malacca soon became the center of southeast Asian
trade. In Arakan, as Ava became powerless to interfere, the prince
who had been driven away by Ava forces now came back after a
long period of service under the Muslim ruler of Bengal. He showed
his gratitude by bringing back Muslim ideas and introducing coinage with Arabic words engraved on it. His brother who succeeded
him even took the Muslim title "Ali Khan." He made a formal
peace with Ava. Benefiting from trade with Bengal and Malacca,
Arakan became so prosperous and powerful that in 1459 its forces
seized the Indian port of Chittagaung.

At Pegu the dynasty was strengthened by the return of the
Lady Shin Saw Bu. When her husband, the king of Ava, was killed
she was kept a virtual prisoner by his successors because she was considered a valuable hostage to ensure good behavior from the Mons.
Perhaps she was not so beautiful and not so frivolous as the Shan
queens, for later kings had no desire to marry her. She took to
the study of the scriptures and was allowed to have as her tutors two

Mon monks who had come to study at the great monastic universities at Ava. One day the two monks stole a sailing boat and, taking the Lady Shin Saw Bu with them, they fled down the river. The king of Ava sent a flotilla of war boats in hot pursuit, but the fugitives arrived safely at Pegu after a number of narrow escapes. She was warmly received by her brother, the king, and later on, amidst squabbles for the throne, she kept a cool head and was able to play the part of conciliator between her brothers and her nephews. She was the power behind the throne, and her gracious personality won her the love of the people. She had a son by her first marriage, which was to a royal cousin, and he became king. Finally after her nephews had reigned and died, she herself was prevailed upon to ascend the throne, and she ruled from 1453 to 1472. Daughter of a king, wife of a king, sister of two kings, aunt of two kings, mother of a king, she was now "king" herself.

She followed a policy of peace and her great ambition was to make Pegu not only a center of trade but also a center of Buddhism, as Pagan had been before. She was sympathetic toward Ava and its problems, and she encouraged the kings of Ava in their efforts to keep the religion pure, appreciating that their task was not easy because the influence of the forest-dwelling monks was still strong, and the Shan-Tais were always overfond of magic and sorcery. For example, in 1467 the king of Siam procured the services of a Burmese forest-dwelling monk and sent him to his enemy, the king of Chengmai, to wreak havoc by magical means. Shin Saw Bu and her brothers were able to pursue a policy of peace and develop trade with Malacca only because the Tais in the Menam valley were having their share of troubles. Sukhotai had become strong and independent again, and together with its ally Chengmai frequently attacked the kingdom of Siam. Muslim Malacca was also driving out the Siamese from southern Malaya. Thus, Siam was unable even to challenge the Mons holding Martaban, which was now a center of trade between the kingdom of Pegu and the Muslim southeast Asia. Pegu itself was still accessible by sea, although its harbor was getting shallower because of the silt of the Pegu river; in addition, for trade with Arakan and Bengal there were the ancient port of Bassein and the rapidly developing port of Syriam, below Dagon. The Mons were rapidly becoming prosperous, as could be seen by the great benefactions to the Shwedagon pagoda made by her second brother and by Shin Saw Bu herself. The pagoda was raised to a height of 302 feet and covered with gold from top to bottom. She exchanged religious missions with Ceylon and threw her ports open, making sea passage available so that similar missions could be exchanged between Ava and Ceylon. She retained as her tutors the two monks who rescued her from Ava. She was known to be pious and she was getting old, but a touch of scandal gave spice to her life and made her even more popular with her adoring subjects, who insisted that the two monks were her lovers.

One day, as she was riding across Pegu on her elephant and her guards were clearing the streets for her passage, a man protested, "This old woman is always going from one place to another. When will she learn to stay at home?" The queen laughed and shouted to the man that he was absolutely right. She now thought of retiring, but there were no more males left in the family and she considered her daughter to be too gentle to rule. Her thoughts went to her lord monks, her tutors, Dhammazedi and Dhammapala. But both were of the same age and of the same seniority as monks, and both were equally learned, equally pious. So she chose two large alms bowls and filled one with the choicest food and the other with royal regalia. Then she invited the two monks to come to an alms-giving ceremony in the throne room before a glittering array of courtiers. The two monks came and were offered the two bowls. Dhammazedi happened to choose the bowl with the regalia and was elected king. He was prevailed upon to leave the order, marry the queen's daughter, and accept the throne. Both Dhammazedi and Dhammapala passed into legend and folklore as romantic figures and masters of the occult.

Dhammazedi reigned from 1472 to 1492 and during this period the Mons in Burma reached the height of their achievement. Although he had spent the best years of his life in the monastery, he proved to be a very able administrator, and throughout his reign law and order prevailed. He requested one of his learned monks to translate the Code of Wareru into Burmese so that the kings of Ava could use it. He himself passed important judgments in suits involving Burmese customary law and published them in a collection. He rose above narrow racialism. He did not make any distinction between Mon and Burmese and always attempted to unite them as fellow Buddhists and as co-heirs of the glories of Pagan. According to him, the two races were tied to each other by the silken bonds of a common religion and a common heritage.

Dhammazedi's crowning achievement was the re-establishment of Theravada Buddhism not only in Burma itself but in mainland southeast Asia. He sent a mission to Buddha Gaya as the great Kyansittha had done before him. Twenty-two monks sailed in two great boats with gilded hulls and silken sails to the king of Ceylon, and they took with them precious gifts for the Temple of the Tooth at Kote, for the great monks of Ceylon, and for the king. Although learned abbots themselves, they took their Ordination again at the ancient Ordination Hall on the Kalayani river and then came back to Burma with sacred relics and return gifts from Ceylon. Dhammazedi then built a replica of the Kalayani Ordination Hall at Pegu and invited monks from Lower Burma, Arakan, Ava, Toungoo, Shan kingdoms, Sukhotai, Chengmai, Siam, and even Cambodia to come and take their Ordination again. All the unorthodox sects, by force of public opinion, had to take the Ordination again or leave the Order and become laymen. All the kings of Buddhist southeast Asia applauded Dhammazedi's master stroke in purifying Theravada Buddhism all over the region.

Even at Ava, under the last kings of the Burmese dynasty, the flame of religious enthusiasm burned bright again. There was a final display of splendor when a bridge of gilded boats connected Ava and the town of Sagaing on the opposite bank of the river on the occasion of the enshrining of relics received from Ceylon in a temple built in that town; over this golden bridge walked kings and queens, Shan chieftains and Burmese lords, farmers and workmen, in gay procession of pilgrimage. And the noble city of Ava, a full fifteen miles in circumference and containing temples, palaces, and humble dwellings, glittered and shone in the sunlight until men whispered that the glory of Pagan had returned, although, alas, only for a day.

Men realized that the days of declining Ava were numbered, but they did not realize that the glorious kingdom of Pegu was also doomed to perish soon. The Shans around Ava were too preoccupied with quarreling among themselves, and saintly Dhammazedi flinched at making war. All this while, Toungoo was getting stronger and stronger. Since its inception it had been a militarized state, for its inhabitants had ever to be prepared to repulse the raids from the Mons, Ava, the Shans, and from even Siam. They were now eager to share in the prosperity of the Mons. They had no access to the Irrawaddy for a share of the internal trade, and no access to the sea for a share of the external trade.

Commerce in southeast Asia was reaching a point never dreamed of before, for Europe was hungry for the spices, the perfumes, the silks, and the precious stones of Asia. Even during the time of the romantic wars of Ava and Pegu, a Venetian traveler and merchant, Nicolo de Conti, had visited Ava, Arakan, and Pegu, taking note of commercial possibilities of these kingdoms. In 1496 a merchant from Genoa, Hieronomo de Santo Stefano, had come to Pegu and sold his wares to the king, Shin Saw Bu's brother. Although he had to wait eighteen months for payment, finally he made a handsome profit and bought a number of rubies. In 1503, during the reign of Dhammazedi's son, a merchant from Bologna, Ludovico di Varthema, visited Pegu and met the king. He gasped at the magnificent city, and also at the priceless rubies worn as necklaces by the monarch. He noted that the king received an enormous amount of revenue as customs duties on the export of shellac, perfumed wood, silk, and rubies. Being a shrewd trader, he sold some of his coral to the king and was paid in rubies.

The Italian merchants of Europe and the Muslim merchants of southeast Asia were soon replaced by the Portuguese Roman Catholics. They came to spread the Roman Catholic form of Christianity and also to capture the trade of southeast Asia. Burning both with religious zeal and the profit motive, they had sailed around Africa and found a new sea route to the spicy East. They were not mere traders, but soldiers in the service of God, and also of mammon; in 1510 they captured Goa on the western coast of India and turned it into a fort to guard their long line of communications between Portugal and southeast Asia, and also into a capital for their far-flung commercial empire. In 1511 their admiral, Don Alfonse de Albuquerque, captured Malacca. The Portuguese considered all Muslims to be their mortal enemies but were tolerant of Buddhists, and accordingly Albuquerque sent embassies to Siam and to Pegu assuring them that their trade with Malacca would continue. Albuquerque's representative duly saw the king of Pegu, and the interview was so fruitful that the Portuguese opened a trading station at Martaban in 1519. In the next fifteen years the trade of the Mon kingdom increased by leaps and bounds, and the Burmese at Toungoo felt that the time had come for them to strike a blow for glory and for trade.

VI *The Second Burmese Empire*

For two full cenuries after the fall of Pagan the Mons, the Shans, and the Tais looked upon Toungoo as an up-start little kingdom—barren, with no natural resources, without any access to the Irrawaddy valley or to the sea, and exposed to raids and attacks from all four directions. But to the Burmese it was not only a haven of refuge from warring barbarians but also an inspiration and a hope for the restoration of the Burmese empire, which had fallen under the arrows of Tatar horsemen. Until the decline of Ava the rulers of Toungoo were kings only in name; they survived because of both military prowess and diplomatic skill, for when they lost a battle they usually submitted, playing for time. They submitted often to Shans from Ava, to the Mons from Pegu, and the Tais from Ayuthia, and equally often they declared their independence.

Toungoo's first real king was Minkyeenyo, who, coming to the throne in 1486, built a wall around the city. He was an able ruler and Ava, Pegu, and Chengmai tried to win his support by recognizing him as a sovereign king. As has been stated above, the king of Ava gave him a princess to be his queen together with Kyaukse district as dowry, which strengthened not only his prestige but also the economic base for his kingdom. When Ava fell to the Maw Shans and Thohanbwa massacred all Burmese at Ava, Minkyeenyo swore revenge and prepared to attack Ava. However, he suddenly died in 1531, leaving as his heir a mere child of fourteen years. But this son was already famous throughout Burma. When he was born in 1516 men said that, although his birth was during the dark hours before dawn, swords and spears in the royal armory shone brightly, which they considered to be an omen that the child would be as great a warrior as Minyè Kyawswar of Ava. The proud father, the king, felt so certain of his son's greatness that he at once named him Tabinshwehti or "Solitary Umbrella of Gold." Because of this widespread belief that the young prince was a man of destiny and because of the great work done by Minkyeenyo as an administrator, Tabinshwehti ascended the throne and assumed command of the army without challenge from any quarter.

Before he could be crowned, however, it was necessary for him to take part in the Ear Piercing ceremony and the Initiation ceremony, with which a Burmese boy entered the Buddhist Order as a novice for a short period of time. He was determined that he should begin these ceremonies at one of the four great national shrines, the Shwezigon at Pagan, the Shwesandaw at Prome, the Shwedagon at Dagon, or the Shwemawdaw at Pegu; his obvious choice was Shwemawdaw, because it was only about a hundred and twenty miles away from his capital. He selected five hundred from among his most skillful horsemen and then rode at their head into enemy territory all through the night, reaching Shwemawdaw at sunrise. Inside the city walls the Mons thought the horsemen were the vanguard of an invading army and, hastily closing the gates, they waited and thus lost precious time. When they realized that only some five hundred Burmese soldiers were inside the temple, they came out of the gates and surrounded it. The ceremony was nearly over, and the royal astrologer was just at the point of piercing the king's ears when the sentry shouted, "The Mons are coming." Tabinshwehti calmly remarked, "Make the holes perfect, for my ears are more important than the Mons." When the ceremony was completed he led his horsemen through the ranks of the surrounding Mon troops, who were so awed to see Tabinshwehti in person that no one attempted to stop the Burmese horsemen. Tabinshwehti rode home in triumph and news of his audacity spread all over the country, heartening the Burmese and frightening the Shans and the Mons. It was a bold stroke of propaganda on the part of the young king.

During this adventure a young commander had ridden at the king's side. He was a young princeling by the name of Shin Yètut, who, although just a few years older than the king, was an experienced soldier already famous for his deeds of valor and for his strength of character. He became the constant companion and adviser of the young king. One day it was discovered that he had been having a romance with the king's sister, which under Burmese law constituted an act of treason. The courtiers held their breath because they remembered the break in the friendship between Anawrahta and Kyansittha under similar circumstances, and some even suggested to the young commander that he should mutiny. Replying that although it was no crime for a young man to love a young woman, it was an unpardonable crime for a soldier to break his oath of allegiance, he submitted to arrest. The king deliberated at length with his ministers and finally came to the conclusion that the young commander should be awarded the princely title of Kyawhtin Nawrahta and given his sister in marriage. This decision of the king made him more popular with his people and won from his brother-in-law a love and a loyalty without parallel in Burmese history. A few years later, after a great battle that was won only through Kyawhtin Nawrahta's military skill and unflinching courage, the king conferred upon him the new title of Bayinnaung or "King's Elder Brother."

Tabinshwehti's strategy was to subdue the Mons as quickly as possible so as to capture some of their ports and thus obtain the much-needed funds to pay for the services of Portuguese mercenaries, without whose muskets and cannons the walled towns of Pegu and Martaban could not be taken. He feared no attack from the Shans at Ava because they were as always disunited and incapable of concerted action. Prome was now independent of Ava's control, and its king, although half Burmese and half Shan, was a brother-in-law of the Mon king and therefore his ally. Tabinshwehti, however, took a calculated risk, hoping that the armies of Prome would not leave their walled capital exposed to attack him from the rear. For the next four years, therefore, he concentrated on gradually conquering the delta region and soon won the port of Bassein, which not only gave him an outlet to international commerce but also enabled him to threaten Pegu and Martaban from the sea. In 1534, feeling that he was ready, he attacked Pegu but was forced to retreat on the outbreak of the monsoon. He attacked Pegu again in 1535 and 1536 and was again repulsed.

The Mon king, although a grandson of the great Dhammazedi, did not have the same strength of character; knowing that people from all over Burma were going over to Tabinshwehti's side, he became suspicious of his own ministers, especially the two ablest among them. The essential weakness of his character could be seen from the fact that these two ministers had been his tutors since childhood and were absolutely devoted and loyal to him. Learning of this state of affairs, Tabinshwehti sent a secret messenger with a letter addressed to the two ministers, purporting to be a reply to their letter. Signed and sealed by Tabinshwehti himself the letter said, "Trusted and valued friends, I accept your offer with great pleasure and after my victory with your help I shall give you the rewards that you desire." The messenger, under Tabinshwehti's instructions, allowed himself to be captured by the Mon guards, who at once seized the letter and took it to the king. Without making any inquiry the king ordered the execution of the two faithful ministers. The king's foolish action had a profound psychological effect on the Mons, who now felt certain that Pegu was doomed.

Tabinshwehti waited two more years to strengthen his army, and in 1538 he marched on to Pegu. The Mon king lost his nerve and fled with his army to his brother-in-law in Prome, allowing Tabinshwehti to take Pegu without much effort. The remnant of the Mon army did not follow their king to Prome but fled to Martaban. Tabinshwehti now sailed up the river to Prome with his flotilla of war boats and Bayinnaung with some light troops advanced by land. The Burmese army was smaller than the combined armies of Prome and Pegu, and also inferior in arms and equipment, for they were still without Portuguese mercenaries. On the other hand, the Burmese army was better disciplined and enjoyed far better morale. The Burmese strategy was to meet and defeat the Mon and Prome armies before they took shelter inside the walls of Prome.

The combined enemy armies came down the river valley by land to await the arrival of Tabinshwehti and give him battle. Bayinnaung with his light troops now arrived on the opposite bank and decided to cross the river and attack. The Mons had acquired all the available boats, so Bayinnaung crossed the river in darkness in make-shift rafts, which he immediately destroyed. His officers protested, "But, my lord, how shall we retreat if the battle should go against us?" "There will be no retreat," replied Bayinnaung calmly, "for we shall surely win or die." A runner from Tabinshwehti now arrived, bringing instructions that Bayinnaung should wait his coming with the main army before making contact with the enemy. "Tell His Majesty," replied Bayinnaung, "that we have not only contacted the enemy but routed him." As his officers stared at him in surprise, Bayinnaung smiled and said, "If we win, the king cannot blame us, and if we lose and die, the king cannot blame us either." Bayinnaung then attacked the combined armies of Prome and Pegu, and under his inspired leadership a great victory had been won by the time Tabinshwehti arrived on the scene. After offering his felicitations to Bayinnaung, the king sailed up to Prome and defeated the combined flotillas of Prome, Pegu, and Ava. Ava had realized that it was next to be attacked by Tabinshwehti and therefore sent a flotilla to the assistance of Prome.

Feeling that Prome was now incapable of attacking him from the rear, Tabinshwehti returned to Pegu to consolidate his position over the Mons. He offered a general amnesty to all Mon officials if they surrendered, and when many did they were not only pardoned but re-appointed to their old positions. Following the example set by the kings of Pagan, his aim was to rule over the Mons and the Burmese as one nation. At long last the Shans of the north and the east realized the necessity to unite and fight Tabinshwehti, and accordingly all the Shan Sawbwas came down with a huge combined army to Prome, intending to invade the delta and place it again under the Mon king. Unfortunately for them, the king was killed in a hunting mishap. The Mons at Prome were disheartened by his death and, preferring Tabinshwehti to the prospect of a possible Shan rule over Lower Burma, decided to take advantage of the offer of amnesty by Tabinshwehti. The Shans, disappointed, returned to their homes.

Tabinshwehti had hoped that his conciliatory policy, together with the death of the Mon king, would result in the peaceful surrender of Martaban. However its governor, who was also a brother-in-law of the deceased king, now declared himself as the king of the Mons, feeling certain that Portuguese ships in its harbor and Portuguese mercenaries inside the walled town would prevent Tabinshwehti from approaching Martaban. In fact Martaban's position was so strong that perhaps the governor would have declared its independence of Pegu even if there had been no Tabinshwehti. The governor sent no help to the Mon king before his death, and obviously the latter never trusted him for, as has been stated, he fled to Prome rather than to Martaban. The governor's action angered Tabinshwehti and he made preparations for an attack on Martaban. By this time, with a natural human desire to back the winning side, and also attracted by the high salaries the Burmese king was offering, many Portuguese had enlisted in Tabinshwehti's armies. Tabinshwehti besieged Martaban, but for seven months he could make no headway. The town was built on high ground and the attackers were mowed down by Portuguese guns mounted on the city walls and by the guns from the seven Portuguese ships in the harbor. The governor of Martaban now offered to surrender, provided he would be allowed to remain as the governor, paying a yearly tribute of thirty thousand viss of silver bullion and other valuable presents. But Tabinshwehti demanded unconditional surrender, pointing out that the governor had already rejected Tabinshwehti's general offer of amnesty. The governor now asked for safe-conduct out of Martaban for himself and his entire family, together with his treasures. This request was also rejected by the Burmese king.

In desperation the governor appealed to the Portuguese viceroy at Goa for assistance, offering to become a vassal of Portugal in addition to an outright gift of half the amount of his treasure. Goa was interested and a Portuguese captain listed the treasure as consisting of two shiploads of gold and silver and twenty-six chests of precious stones. In addition, the gold to be looted from the gilded pagodas of the city would fill four ships. However, the Portuguese feared Tabinshwehti's vengeance and wavered between greed and prudence. In 1541 Tabinshwehti made a final assault on the city, sending down the river first fire rafts, which destroyed Portuguese and Mon ships in the harbor, and then rafts with bamboo "towers" built on them, from which the musketeers fired into the city. Martaban fell, and Tabinshwehti captured a great amount of booty. He ordered the execution of the governor, his entire family, and all the gallant defenders, for he considered that they were not entitled to any mercy, having previously refused to accept the general amnesty. The Mons at Moulmein and adjoining regions, learning the bitter lesson of Martaban, submitted to Tabinshwehti and were duly pardoned.

Prome remained adamant, however, relying on the strength of its walls and assistance from the Shans. So in 1542 Tabinshwehti marched on to Prome both by water and by land. The inhabitants were now mostly Shans and Mons because, except for the king's own immediate circle, the Burmese had fled to Tabinshwehti's side. The king of Prome, as a last desperate measure, sent his sister to the king of Arakan to be raised as his queen, seeking Arakanese assistance. Arakan had become very powerful with its navy and its army bolstered by many Portuguese mercenaries, and now that Martaban had fallen it wanted to remain without any powerful rival in the region. Accordingly Arakan sent an army through the Ann pass and her navy by sea. Bayinnaung met the Arakanese army as it came out of the pass opposite Prome and wiped it out. The navy took Bassein but, learning of the disaster that had befallen the army, it hastily retreated. Tabinshwehti then took Prome and put to death the king and his defenders for the same reason he had executed the governor of Martaban. Then Bayinnaung went north and put to flight the Shan army, which was hastening toward Prome. Re-equipping themselves at Ava, the Shan Sawbwas now came down the Irrawaddy in boats so as to bypass Bayinnaung's army. Their boats presented an easy target to Tabinshwehti's cannons, which he had obtained from the Portuguese. The Shans were now completely routed and Tabinshwehti marched to Pagan, where he was crowned in the full ritual and ceremony of the great kings of Pagan. Returning to Pegu, he was again crowned, in the ritual and ceremony of the great Mon kings. He raised a Mon princess to be his chief queen and, wearing his hair in the Mon style, he appointed Mons to the highest offices both at court and in the army.

Soon after his coronation Tabinshwehti was tempted to interfere in a dynastic crisis in Arakan; the king had died and was succeeded by his son, to the dissatisfaction of the king's brother, who invited Tabinshwehti to invade Arakan. Bayinnaung with a Burmese army entered Arakan by land, and Tabinshwehti with a Mon army went by sea. They met at Sandoway and its governor, the late king's brother, welcomed them. Together Tabinishwehti and Bayinnaung marched north to the capital of Mrohaung, which was very well fortified. The Burmese pierced the outer defenses but failed to take the city. The king of Arakan then released the flood gates and the Burmese had to retreat to higher ground. Tabinshwehti was unprepared to make a long siege. He was anxious lest the Tais should give him trouble, because they would naturally sympathize with the Shans, who had been so soundly defeated by him, and now news was arriving of Siamese attacks in the region of Tenas-serim. So, hastily making peace between the king and his uncle of Sandoway and without loss of honor and prestige to himself, Tabinshwehti returned to Pegu.

Tabinshwehti had been able to achieve so much partly because the Tais had been busy fighting among themselves without noticing the rise of a new power in Burma. The kingdom of Siam had aggres-sive designs on its neighbors, Chengmai and Laos,[1] and had been interfering in their dynastic disputes and power struggles, and also Siam itself came to have its own dynastic problems. The king who had been interfering in the affairs of the neighboring kingdoms was poisoned by his queen, who also killed her own son when he suc-ceeded to the throne. There was a long and bitter power struggle, and finally she and her lover, whom she had placed on the throne, were assassinated and the younger brother of the poisoned king ascended the throne in 1549. To enhance his prestige the new king attacked the Burmese frontier. Siam was full of Portuguese mer-cenaries at the time and felt itself strong enough to defeat Tabinshwe-hti. The Burmese king, however, was by no means a blood-thirsty tyrant, but to keep the newly conquered Shans quiet he wanted assurance from Siam that there would be no more raids on the fron-tier. Tabinshwehti wanted to complete his work of uniting the Mons, the Burmese, and the Shans into a single nation, and he was tired of war. He wanted a peaceful settlement with Siam and so de-manded from the king of Siam the tribute of a white elephant. This was the Burmese diplomatic way of issuing an ultimatum.

Siam naturally felt that it could not become a vassal state of the Burmese even in name and refused to comply with the Burmese demand. So in 1548 Tabinshwehti invaded Siam from Martaban through the Three Pagodas pass. Tabinshwehti realized the serious-ness of his task but thought that his army was strong enough to subdue the king at Ayuthia. During its long march to Ayuthia, the Burmese army was exposed to constant guerrilla attack, and the de-

---

[1] For ease of reference, the modern name of "Laos" is used here.

laying tactics of the guerrillas gave time to their king to fortify at leisure the already well-defended city of Ayuthia. Some 400 Portuguese mercenaries in the army of Tabinshwehti were loyal to him, but the 1,000 Portuguese at the Siamese capital were equally loyal to the king of Siam. Tabinshwehti, finding Ayuthia impregnable, considered besieging it, but because his army was not large enough to lay an effective siege he decided to make an orderly retreat, avoiding further losses. The Siamese, noticing that the Burmese were in retreat, became bolder, and thirsty for victory the king himself led an attack. The Burmese army counterattacked, inflicting heavy losses on the enemy and capturing the king's son, the king's brother, and the king's son-in-law, which forced Siam to sue for peace. Tabinshwehti readily granted peace on receipt of two elephants, other valuable presents, a promise of an annual gift of thirty elephants, a token sum of money, and certain customs duties. Tabinshwehti was never a merciless commander nor a discourteous opponent, and he treated the royal captives with honor and consideration; nor did he press for dishonorable peace terms which Siam would have to accept since he held such precious hostages. The gifts were given both as ransom and as tribute, and thus he had won a technical victory that would ensure that the Tais would not interfere in the Shan states of Burma for some years to come.

Tabinshwehti was now thirty-two years of age, and for the last twenty years he had been fighting. He had realized his father's dream and united Burma into one kingdom again. Both Arakan and Siam were at peace with Burma and although he had not reestablished Anawrahta's empire he felt that he could now rest on his laurels. He wanted the country and the three main racial groups to recover from the wounds of war. But this policy of peace was misinterpreted as a sign of weakness by the more fiery among his Mon subjects, who while sharing in his bounty would not forgive him for destroying their kingdom. For the first time in his life, Tabinshwehti relaxed and with a Portuguese companion he went on long hunting trips. His companion was an expert in manufacturing

wine from various kinds of Burmese fruit, and in no time Tabinshwehti became inordinately fond of the new drink. There were
whispers that the young king had become a common drunkard and
was no longer capable of ruling the country. The ministers, both
Mon and Burmese, met secretly and unanimously offered the crown
to Bayinnaung, who declined it, however, promising that he would
try to win back the king to his old sense of duty to his own kingdom. Giving a substantial bribe, he prevailed upon the young Portuguese to leave the country. But the scandal had already done its
work.

At Syriam a half-brother of the last Mon king of Pegu, who
had been living as a monk, left the Order and raised the standard
of rebellion. Bayinnaung, before leaving Pegu to proceed to Syriam,
left a strong personal bodyguard to protect the king, but during his
absence the Mon governor of Sittang arrived to invite Tabinshwehti
to an elephant hunt. Tabinshwehti summoned Bayinnaung's younger
brother, the viceroy of Toungoo, to come and guard Pegu. Then
he accompanied the governor of Sittang to the elephant hunt, and
while he was asleep one night the governor assassinated him. On
hearing the news, Bayinnaung's younger brother returned to Toungoo and declared himself an independent king. The governor of
Sittang now declared Pegu an independent kingdom with himself as king. But the Mon ministers refused to accept him and placed
the rebel from Syriam on the throne. Bayinnaung returned to Pegu
and marched around the city, and although the gates were shut in
his face no Mon dared to come out and attack him. He marched
to Toungoo but again the gates were closed in his face. The viceroy
of Prome also declared himself independent. However, all was not
lost to Bayinnaung. He held not a single fortified town, but his well-
disciplined army was still intact and loyal to him.

Among the rebellious Mons themselves there was a struggle
for power, and when the governor of Sittang was assassinated by the
new Mon king, the followers of the governor thirsted for revenge
and would not join hands with the king's followers. Above all, none

of the newly independent kings dared to come out and fight Bayinnaung. One thing was certain; Bayinnaung would never submit to any rebel king. He returned to the delta and conquered for himself most of the territory there. He was held in such great regard even by the Mon lords that many joined the ranks of his army. Then he sent for the Portuguese captain who had been Tabinshwehti's follower and his companion-at-arms. This captain, Diogo Soares de Mello, was honorable and loyal, unlike the average Portuguese mercenary; considering himself still bound by his oath of allegiance to Tabinshwehti and refusing to be bribed by the Mons, he fought his way out with the regiment under his command and answered Bayinnaung's urgent summons. Bayinnaung now marched to Toungoo, passing right under the walls of Pegu, and at Bayinnaung's approach the entire army of the king of Toungoo ran out of the city and joined Bayinnaung. The king of Toungoo surrendered but was pardoned and re-appointed governor of Toungoo. Feeling grateful at this unexpected treatment, with Bayinnaung's approval he marched with his army to Prome and soon won it back for Bayinnaung. Bayinnaung was again magnanimous, but the king of Prome attempted to escape to Arakan and was executed.

Bayinnaung now laid siege to Pegu, and the new Mon king at least had the courage to come out in person at the head of the army in an attempt to break the siege. Riding on a war elephant, he shouted an open challenge to Bayinnaung to single combat. When this was reported to Bayinnaung he ordered his guards to make way so that the Mon king could approach him. The king was fiery but proved no match for Bayinnaung and, suddenly losing courage, he turned and fled. The Mon army broke and Bayinnaung took Pegu with no great loss of life. The Mon king was later captured and executed. After his victory and coronation as king of Burma, Bayinnaung declared a general amnesty and restored most of the Mons to their old positions. But he appointed only his own younger brothers to the important governorships of Toungoo, Prome, and Martaban.

Ava still held out, and all the Shan chiefs remained independent. Bayinnaung saw that unless the Shans were brought into the fold of Burmese culture they would always be a source of danger to the Burmese. He also realized that the Shans with their feudalistic pattern of society would not easily fit into the general administrative system of the Burmese kingdom and would resent direct rule. On the other hand, unless some kind of direct control were exercised over them, the Sawbwas would always act as the stormy petrels of Burmese politics. While pondering the problem, in 1554 he sent out an army under the command of his own son and a flotilla under the command of one of his brothers, but they were unable to take Ava. In the following year the governor of Sandoway again quarreled with his overlord of Arakan and sent a tribute and an invitation to Bayinnaung to interfere, but Bayinnaung was wise enough not to accept the invitation, as the conquest of Ava was a vital necessity. He did, however, give recognition to the governor as a sub-king of the Burmese empire. He then led both the army and the flotilla in a siege on Ava. The king of Ava escaped in disguise from the city but was captured and then pardoned, but he was not appointed governor. Leaving his youngest brother as governor of Ava, Bayinnaung proceeded to conquer the Shan states to the north. After two more campaigns in 1555 and 1557 Bayinnaung's conquest of the Shan states both in the north and in the east was complete.

The Tai state of Chengmai was perturbed at Bayinnaung's victory over the Shans and sent agents to stir up rebellions among the Shan Sawbwas; therefore in 1558 Bayinnaung crossed the Salween river and conquered Chengmai. However, the capital was not sacked nor the inhabitants massacred. The king was re-appointed as the sub-king but a great number of artisans, especially workers in lacquer, were taken to Pegu and re-settled there. This conquest of Chengmai by Bayinnaung served as a general signal for all the Shan chiefs on the Burma-China border to submit, and even some chieftains within Yunnan itself swore allegiance to Bayinnaung. By then Bayinnaung's prestige was so high that not only did China not protest, but the Raja of Manipur on the Indian border sent tribute to the Burmese king.

For the next four years Bayinnaung concentrated on solving the Shan problem. The Shan states were reduced to the status of governorships but the Sawbwas were permitted to retain their royal regalia and ceremonies and their feudal rights over their own subjects. The office of the Sawbwa still remained hereditary, but now the incumbent held office at the king's pleasure and could be removed for gross misconduct; the king's choice of the successor, however, was limited to members of the chief's own family. Bayinnaung also introduced into the Shan states Burmese customary law, so far as it was compatible with customs and practices of Shan feudal society. He also introduced the Burmese system of weights and measures. Above all, he introduced Theravada Buddhism. The Shans had gradually absorbed Buddhism since the thirteenth century but the few monks who resided in this large region were not learned, were lax in their general conduct, and monasteries were not many. In addition, ancient animistic practices were continued without abatement; for example, at the funeral of a Sawbwa his war elephant, his charger, sometimes even his favorite slaves, and hundreds of domestic animals, were killed and offered as sacrifice.

Bayinnaung prohibited all human and animal sacrifices, built hundreds of monasteries all over the Shan region, and encouraged monks from Burma itself to go and reside therein. He distributed thousands of copies of Buddhist scriptures and made it compulsory for villagers to congregate and study the scriptures on sabbath days. So that the Shans should not complain, in Burma itself he suppressed the worship of the thirty-seven gods, but like Anawrahta before him he was not successful. His general edict prohibiting animal sacrifice, however, including the slaughter of cattle by Indian Muslims, was honored throughout the kingdom. Bayinnaung also encouraged intermarriages between Shans and Burmese, and he restored the custom of installing a Shan princess as queen by a reigning king. He also required the sons of Sawbwas to reside in the

Burmese king's palace as pages: they served a double purpose—
they were hostages for good conduct of their fathers and they received valuable training in Burmese court life. Bayinnaung's enlightened Shan policy was followed by all Burmese kings right
up to the final fall of the kingdom to the British in 1885.

In conquering Chengmai, Bayinnaung became involved in the
power struggle among the Tais. The warlike king of Laos, Settatirat,
was an ambitious adventurer who had before interfered in the affairs of Chengmai and again he invaded the kingdom; to rescue its
sub-king, Bayinnaung had to rush back and drive out Settatirat.
The latter then set up a confederation of his own state with some
Shan states, and Bayinnaung had to break it up. The following year,
1559, Settatirat made a formal alliance with his traditional enemy,
Siam, and moving to a new capital he fortified the city so it could
withstand a siege by Bayinnaung. All these preparations made it
necessary for Bayinnaung to see that Siam would not join forces
with Settatirat and some dissident Shan Sawbwas in an attack on
Burmese territory. Taking into account that Siam had sent tribute
to Tabinshwehti, Bayinnaung demanded the gift of a white elephant. Upon hearing of this demand, which usually was an ultimatum of war, the king of Siam had a long conference with his
advisers, most of whom counseled peace and compliance with
Bayinnaung's request, in view of the strength of the Burmese army
and the military skill of their king. The crown prince himself advocated conciliation, pointing out that it was merely a matter of giving
a token tribute, but his younger brother and the minister Paya
Chakri disagreed, remarking that Bayinnaung would not be satisfied
with a formal gift but would gradually take over the whole country. They were of course thinking of Bayinnaung's virtual annexation of the Shan states. The king himself desired to fight and readily
accepted the minority view. But he sent a very carefully worded
reply, with a faint suggestion of recognition of Bayinnaung as supreme king of the region:

Royal Friend, White elephants come only to those kings who are sovereign lords, and who rule over their subjects with justice. The king of Burma is a great and powerful sovereign lord, and as he rules his kingdom with justice there is no doubt that in due course of time he will become the proud possessor of white elephants.

Bayinnaung was not satisfied with the letter, and in 1563 he crossed the Salween again and made preparations to march on Ayuthia. The sub-king of Chengmai now turned against Bayinnaung, but not daring to fight openly he resorted to subterfuge and secretly encouraged guerrilla attacks on the Burmese and Mon armies. None the less Bayinnaung proceeded into Siamese territory and easily conquered the key towns of Kampengpet and Sukhotai. The Siamese king's son-in-law, the governor of Pitsanulok, surrendered but was allowed to retain his post. As during Tabinshwehti's campaign, a delaying action by the Siamese guerrillas gave ample time to the king to perfect the defenses of Ayuthia. Bayinnaung decided to make a frontal attack and from specially constructed high wooden towers his army fired cannons and muskets into the city. The Siamese troops, realizing the desperate nature of their position, came out and counterattacked, but they were driven back by Bayinnaung's cannons. Finally the Siamese surrendered.

Again Bayinnaung refrained from sacking the city and there was no massacre of its inhabitants. The Siamese king, together with his queens, the younger prince, and the minister Paya Chakri, were taken prisoners. Bayinnaung accepted as tribute all the royal white elephants, together with much treasure. The Siamese also undertook to make an annual tribute of thirty elephants, a token amount of money, and certain customs dues: in other words the same annual tribute that was given to Tabinshwehti. Bayinnaung placed on the throne the Siamese crown prince who had advocated peace and removed Siamese artisans, craftsmen, musicians, dancers, and writers for re-settlement at Pegu. Preceded by palanquins carrying golden statues of the Buddha and hundreds of ox-drawn carts carrying countless treasures, and followed by two thousand elephants and regiment after regiment of cavalry and infantry, Bayinnaung, in an open carriage drawn by royal prisoners of war, made his triumphant return to his capital of Pegu and received the acclaim of his people.

In the Menam valley old Settatirat remained on the warpath and encouraged the sub-king of Chengmai to flaunt the Burmese garrison stationed there. Bayinnaung found the conquest of Chengmai troublesome, and during the period from 1564 to 1579 eight separate expeditions commanded by his son or one of his brothers, and occasionally himself, had to be sent to Chengmai. Although he had conquered even Laos, Settatirat always managed to escape, only to re-appear later attacking the Burmese garrisons in Laos, Chengmai, and Siam. During one of Bayinnaung's absences in Chengmai, the Shan and Tai prisoners settled in the environs of Pegu mutinied, and burned down the palace. The rebels, although they numbered ten thousand, were easily captured, for it was more a riot than a rebellion. Bayinnaung, on his return to Pegu, felt disappointed that his generosity and leniency had aroused no real sense of loyalty on the part of the prisoners, and he ordered their immediate execution. But the abbots of Pegu pleaded on their behalf and, except for the ringleaders, they were pardoned.

The former king of Siam had been permitted to enter the Buddhist Order and he now requested permission to return to Ayuthia to visit its temples for the last time, as he was getting old. After he swore an oath of allegiance and promised to return to Pegu, Bayinnaung chivalrously allowed him to go. The moment he arrived at Ayuthia he became a layman again and plotted with his son, the sub-king appointed by Bayinnaung, to free Siam from Burmese rule. Encouraged by Settatirat, he attempted to win over his son-in-law, the governor of Pitsanulok, who however refused to enter the conspiracy; he maintained that as a man of honor he was bound by his oath of allegiance to the Burmese king. Furious, the former monk declared himself king of Siam and proceeded to attack Pitsanulok.

Bayinnaung invaded Siam in 1568 for the second time. On this occasion he entered Siamese territory from Martaban and then marched straight on to Pitsanulok to relieve the beleaguered city. The Burmese and Mon armies were probably larger than those of the first campaign, although Burmese chronicles stated that the armies numbered 546,000, some 54,000 less than the armies in the first campaign. According to the Venetian traveler Caesar Fredericke, who was present in Pegu at the time of Bayinnaung's triumphant entry after the first campaign, Bayinnaung's armies contained 500,000 soldiers. According to Siamese chronicles, the number in the first campaign was 500,000 and in the second campaign, together with levies from Chengmai and Laos, the number was 900,000. Whatever the correct figures were, Bayinnaung commanded the largest army that southeast Asia had ever seen and it also contained over 1,000 Portuguese veterans, well equipped with muskets and cannons. Relying on this great superiority in numbers, Bayinnaung as in the first campaign made a frontal attack, but his troops were mowed down by the gun fire of the Portuguese mercenaries on the Siamese side. His losses were so heavy that he reluctantly decided to besiege the city. After ten full months the city showed no sign of surrender.

Then Paya Chakri, who was anti-Burmese in 1563 and had been a prisoner at the Burmese court since that time, came to the conclusion that only Burmese rule could bring peace and prosperity to his war-torn country. One night, pretending to have escaped from his Burmese guards, he appeared before the gates of Ayuthia, which were thrown open to receive him. By that time the Siamese king, the former monk, had died and his son gave to Paya Chakri the command of a particular portion of the city's defenses. Paya Chakri secretly but skillfully weakened the defenses under his charge and then signaled to Bayinnaung, who rushed in with his troops and took the city. The sub-king was executed and the governor of Pitsanulok, Maha Dhammaraja, was appointed in his place. Bayinnaung marched on to Laos but failed to capture the source of all his trouble, Settatirat. After dismantling the walls of Ayuthia and taking away with him half the population of the city for re-settlement in his own kingdom, Bayinnaung returned to Pegu. Some years later, learning that Ayuthia, without any defenses, was continuously being raided by Cambodians, Bayinnaung generously permitted the building of a new wall around it.

By all accounts Pegu was a glorious capital, whose splendors were noted by two European observers, Caesar Fredericke and the English merchant Ralph Fitch. Apart from its magnificence and beauty, the city was a great center of commerce; notwithstanding the wars that both Tabinshwehti and Bayinnaung had to fight, the trade route from China down the Irrawaddy river remained open during most of their reigns, and the seaports of Martaban, Syriam, and Bassein were able to take advantage of the commercial activities of southeast Asia, whose seas were under the dominion of the Portuguese and whose products were carried to far Europe on Portuguese galleons. The richness of the kingdom's commerce was reflected in the richness of the king's palace. It was the creation of artists and craftsmen from all the capitals of the empire; each of its twelve gates represented a particular tributary kingdom and its roof was covered with solid gold plates.

Bayinnaung's court had an atmosphere that could be compared to that of the English court under the great Queen Elizabeth. It teemed with courtiers who were both soldiers and poets. For example, there was the minister Nawaday, who was also a great commander, and on the eves of battles he would sit in his tent, far into the night, composing poems of singular beauty. There was the Mon lord Binnya Dala, who on the encouragement of Bayinnaung, and notwithstanding the many complex duties of his high office, composed a biography of the Mon king Razadarit. There was also Shin Dwayhla, a lady-in-waiting to the queen, who entertained the court with her love lyrics. Inspired by Siamese music and dance, the courtiers, both Mon and Burmese, developed new styles in their own music and dance. Bayinnaung's reign was also a great age of legal scholarship. A commission of twelve monks produced a compendium of Burmese legal writings and other jurists wrote a number of commentaries on Burmese customary law, which had become the law of the land. Bayinnaung himself passed a series of brilliant judgments, which were later collected and published. His aim was to unite all the races of the kingdom by a common system of law, a common literature, and a common system of weights and measures and commercial usage.

Tabinshwehti, perhaps because of his youth, was not greatly interested in his religion, although he made his pilgrimages to famous pagodas of the country and made extensive donations to the Shwedagon and Shwemawdaw pagodas. Bayinnaung, in contrast, considered it his duty to act as the champion of Theravada Buddhism in southeast Asia as Anawrahta and Kyansittha had done before him. He built a number of temples and monasteries all over the country and, surrounded by a glittering retinue of kings and princes, he made state pilgrimages to the temples of Pagan. At the Shwezigon pagoda he donated a large bronze bell cast by his many artisans, and following the example of Kyansittha he engraved on the bell an account of his victories and achievements in Pali, Mon, and Burmese. Whenever he toured the Shan states, in war or in peace, he built temples and monasteries. He considered it also his duty to prevent the loss or destruction of the sacred Tooth and the Alms Bowl of the Buddha belonging to the Sinhalese kings and to preserve them for posterity.

In achieving this end Bayinnaung showed great diplomatic skill. Ceylon was going through a period of strife and disintegration due to Portuguese intrusion. Kotte was the ancient capital, but the island had broken up into a number of kingdoms, the most important of which were Kotte, Kandy, and Jaffna. At Kotte was situated the Temple of the Sacred Tooth, which also contained the Alms Bowl. Apart from their sacredness as relics of the Buddha, they had a political value because the Sinhalese people believed that "he who holds the Tooth and the Bowl shall hold Ceylon." The Portuguese had built the port of Colombo, a few miles from Kotte, and were exercising control over the young king and the regent. To his people the young king was Dhammapala, a patron of Buddhism and the guardian of the Temple, but to the Portuguese who had secretly baptized and trained him he was Don John, the faithful vassal to the king of Portugal. When the king came of age the regent lost favor with the Portuguese and fled to the Tamil kingdom of Jaffna in the northern part of the island. Before he escaped he had entered the Temple in the king's name and stolen what he believed to be the sacred Tooth but which was really a replica, for the abbot in charge had hidden the relic. Some months later the Portuguese raided Jaffna and captured not only its king but also the fugitive regent of Kotte. Finding the replica of the Tooth and thinking it to be genuine, they took it in triumph to their capital in the east, Goa in India. When Bayinnaung heard the news he chartered a Portuguese ship and loaded it with treasure. It then set sail for Goa carrying a commercial mission from the king with full authority to buy the Tooth at any cost. The prestige of Bayinnaung was so high that this ship flying his flag and known to be carrying treasure was not molested in any way on the high seas, which were infested with Portuguese and pirates of other nationalities.

The viceroy of Goa was greatly tempted to accept the offer of the Burmese mission to buy the Tooth, especially because his treasury had become empty. But the archbishop of Goa wanted to prove to the heathen Buddhists of Ceylon and southeast Asia that their great relic could not withstand the might of the Roman Catholic church. The Portuguese captains and commanders naturally supported the viceroy, but the archbishop, when outvoted in the administrative council, scolded the viceroy for his greed and threatened to excommunicate him. The following morning, in front of the great cathedral in the city square, and in the presence of a huge congregation of people including the members of the Burmese mission, the archbishop solemnly lifted up the Tooth and then ground it into powder. The Burmese were not impressed, for already spies from the chief minister from Kotte had whispered in their ears the information that it was merely a replica, and also had issued an invitation to come to Kotte and worship the genuine Tooth.

The Burmese mission duly visited Kotte and established friendly relations with the king and his chief minister, the real power behind the throne. Bayinnaung then sent an embassy, with gifts to the temple and to the king. An alliance was made with the king of Kotte, whom Bayinnaung considered to be the only legitimate king of Ceylon. The chief minister seemed to have truly valued Bayinnaung's friendship because as a devout Buddhist he felt sad that his own king, a Roman Catholic, could never really be a patron of Buddhism. He must have been torn between his gratitude to his own king, who trusted him so much that his daughter had been adopted into the royal household with the full rank of a princess of the blood, and his admiration of Bayinnaung as a Buddhist emperor. When the rebel king of Kandy joined hands with other rebels and laid siege to Colombo, on the request of the king and the chief minister Bayinnaung sent a contingent of his best troops, who impressed both friend and foe with their prodigious physical strength and courage. After the siege the king and the chief minister in gratitude sent to Bayinnaung the adopted princess together with the Tooth and the Alms Bowl.

Later the king of Kandy sent an embassy to Bayinnaung, informing him that what the king of Kotte had sent was merely a replica and offering to sell the genuine relic, which he claimed to hold. Bayinnaung refused to give audience to the mission, pointing out that the king of Kandy was neither a genuine king nor a genuine Buddhist. The king of Kandy, undaunted, built another Temple of the Tooth in his capital and exhibited the relic there. The archbishop of Goa did not seem to have understood the psychology of the masses. Even if what he had destroyed had been the genuine relic, the average Sinhalese villager and his Burmese counterpart would not have believed that the genuine Tooth of the Buddha could ever be destroyed by human agency. In any case, the weight of evidence showed that it was a replica. However, as to the Tooth presented to Bayinnaung and the Tooth seen at the temple in Kandy, the Burmese naturally held that the Tooth in their possession was the genuine one whereas the Sinhalese would maintain that it was merely a replica. It is logical to say that a Sinhalese king would never part with the genuine Tooth, but it is equally logical to point out that the king who gave it away to Bayinnaung was a Roman Catholic, who was also in sore need of financial assistance from the Burmese king, and the chief minister who advised him to make the gift was a devout Buddhist, anxious to see that the precious relic should remain in Buddhist hands. It must be remembered that no one questioned the genuineness of the Alms Bowl that Bayinnaung received.

Bayinnaung was always correct in his dealings with neighboring foreign powers, as well as with their subjects and ships coming to his ports. Pegu itself was accessible from the sea and came into direct contact with foreign merchants. At every port there were eight royal trade representatives, and port dues and customs duties were found reasonable by all foreign shipping. He sent an embassy to the court of the Indian emperor Akbar, but perhaps it went only to his viceroy at Calcutta because Akbar's court records did not mention the arrival at Delhi of a Burmese embassy. Nonetheless the letters and presents carried by the embassy were addressed to Akbar by name, and replies and presents given in return were in Akbar's name. He appreciated the military skill and courage of his Portuguese mercenaries but he kept himself aloof from them, never forgetting that the arrangement with them was merely a matter of business. He paid them high salaries and showered upon them rewards after each victory, but he kept them at arm's length and imposed upon them the same strict discipline that he imposed upon all ranks of the army. Thus when, during his absence in Chengmai, some Portuguese mercenaries at Martaban flaunted his authority and paraded in the market square flying Portuguese flags and blowing trumpets and bugles in protest against the killing of some of their comrades in a drunken brawl, he fined and imprisoned them on his return. Only Captain de Mello won his regard and trust. In the Thai states that he conquered he always allowed the civil servants and military officials to retain their posts, and he gave strict instructions to his military garrisons to show tolerance and consideration to the local inhabitants.

On the other hand, he re-introduced into those regions Burmese religious customs and practices, such as the observance of sabbath days and the initiation ceremony of a boy. He grafted the principles of Burmese customary laws on existing native laws, but in such a way as to prevent native societies from being obliterated, and he re-introduced the Burmese calendar and the Burmese Era. He was doubtlessly a despot but he was enlightened; long after the Tai kingdoms had thrown off the yoke of Burmese rule they remembered with admiration and affection the personality of Bayinnaung and enshrined it forever in their folk-tales and legends. Even Siam, which had bitter memories of successive Burmese invasions, retained the Burmese Era until 1887 when it adopted the European system. There is no doubt that throughout his reign the personality of Bayinnaung dominated the whole of the Indo-Chinese peninsula, winning the awe and admiration of its various racial groups. However, just as it is unfair to judge who was the greater, Anawrahta or Kyansittha, it would be unfair to ignore Tabinshwehti when considering the achievements of Bayinnaung. Tabinshwehti was a dreamer whose dreams were realized in the reign of his brother-in-law, but without Tabinshwehti there could have been no Bayinnaung.

VII The Decline of Bayinnaung's Empire

When Bayinnaung died in 1581 at the age of sixty-six, outwardly all was well with his empire. The governors of all the provinces of Burma were his brothers and nephews. The king of Siam was a follower of proven loyalty and his son and heir, the young prince, had grown up at Bayinnaung's court and was considered a blood brother of his sons. At the request of the king of Siam the young prince had been sent back to his country and was appointed the governor of Pitsanulok. He was now sixteen years of age and he had spent nine of those at the Burmese court learning their military tactics and organization, but all the while he kept a dream of freedom hidden in his heart. At Pitsanulok, away from his father's influence, he surrounded himself with ardent young men and argued and discussed how to throw off the Burmese yoke.

The new king, Nandabayin, had taken part at the age of thirteen in Tabinshwehti's invasion of Siam and was considered in later years to be a worthy deputy of his father; in fact, he had led many campaigns himself. He ascended his father's throne amid acclamation from both the army and the court, and the young Siamese prince, Pra Naret, came all the way from Pitsanulok to pay homage to the new king. But trouble came from an unexpected quarter. The governor of Ava, Bayinnaung's younger brother, plotted to gain the throne of Pegu and secretly wrote to his brothers, the governors of Prome and Toungoo, seeking their help. They were furious at this treachery and passed on the letters to Nandabayin, who immediately led an army to Ava, where his uncle came out and fought a duel on elephants. The uncle lost and escaped with the remnants of his troops toward the Chinese border, but he became sick on the way and died. This easy victory over the first challenge to his authority enhanced Nandabayin's prestige but the sense of security it gave him proved to be false.

Before he marched toward Ava he had ordered each province of the empire to send a contingent of troops to assist him in his campaign. Pra Naret took this as a heaven-sent opportunity to free Siam from Burmese rule. Instead of a mere contingent, he gathered a huge army. His plan was to follow Nandabayin from a distance and if Nandabayin was defeated he would attack the retreating Mon and Burmese armies; if Nandabayin should win, he would march quietly back to Siam and wait for another chance. His plans became known to Nandabayin, who left instructions that the Siamese prince should be permitted to come into Pegu, where he would then be arrested. But some Mon officials, thinking that Nandabayin would be defeated at Ava, sent a warning to the Siamese prince as he was crossing the Sittang into Burma. Realizing that his treacherous plans had become known to Nandabayin, he accused the Burmese king of a breach of faith in secretly ordering his arrest, immediately declared Siam's independence, and marched on to attack Pegu. With surprise, he received news of the swift victory achieved by Nandabayin over Ava and at once changed his plans. He collected some ten thousand Siamese subjects who had been re-settled around Pegu and sent them back to Siam as he slowly retreated. A contingent of Nandabayin's troops stationed at Pegu chased him, but he managed to cross the Sittang and ambushed the Burmese troops as they started to cross the river; partly because of his marksmanship and partly through good fortune, a shot from his musket hit the Burmese commander and killed him on the spot. The small

Burmese force gave up the pursuit and Pra Naret returned to Siam as a national hero, taking leadership of the Siamese nation although his father, the king, was still alive.

Knowing that Nandabayin would soon come in pursuit, Pra Naret frightened and cajoled various Siamese governors to side with him. When two refused he smashed the defenses of their towns and then executed them. He ordered all the inhabitants of the region between Chiengmai and Ayuthia to move to the latter city, a tactic equivalent to the twentieth-century "scorched earth" policy. When Nandabayin came, the Siamese prince and his army remained inside Ayuthia, whose fortifications had been restored through the graciousness of Bayinnaung. Nandabayin had only a small army and since he was unprepared to lay siege to the fortified city he withdrew. The Siamese prince was prevented from following the retreating army because of an attack on his territory by Cambodia. Cambodia considered Siam to be its mortal enemy; at the height of Bayinnaung's power Cambodia sent one or two tribute missions to the Burmese, but there was never a formal alliance or understanding between Cambodia and the Burmese king. However, at a sign of the slightest weakness on the part of Siam, Cambodia always sent an "official" expedition or an "unofficial" raid.

The wars of Bayinnaung had been popular wars in that both the Burmese and the Mons were eager to fight under the banner of Bayinnaung, for glory and also for reward; defeat in battle was almost unknown. Moreover, except during the second invasion of Siam, losses suffered by Bayinnaung's troops were never heavy. By Nandabayin's time many of Bayinnaung's commanders had grown old and were no longer in service. After the failure of only the first invasion of Siam by Nandabayin, his troops were disheartened and the people were no longer enthusiastic. Nandabayin should have given up the idea of re-conquering Siam, or at least should have waited until his kingdom had recovered from its first defeat in many years, while allowing Pra Naret to exhaust his youthful energy and spirit in fighting against Cambodia. But Nandabayin was stubborn and he led two more expeditions into Siam, in 1585 and 1586. Both the invasions failed, with heavy losses, and his Burmese and Mon subjects began to murmur and protest. Many young men entered the Buddhist Order to escape conscription, and Nandabayin, giving the excuse of purifying the clergy, unfrocked the monks. The abbots, disapproving of this high-handed action, publicly prayed for the downfall of Nandabayin, who responded by exiling the leaders among the abbots to the remoter regions of Upper Burma.

In 1584, after the first defeat in Siam, Bayinnaung's brother at Toungoo died and his son was appointed governor in his place. In 1588 Bayinnaung's brother at Prome died without an heir, and Nandabayin appointed his own younger son as governor in his place. Nandabayin had never been sure of his uncles' loyalty, and in his opinion these two replacements would never dare to claim the throne from him. Feeling certain that conditions in the kingdom were well under control, in 1590 Nandabayin invaded Siam again and was repulsed as before. In 1592, with a massive army recruited in the teeth of opposition from his people, he made his fifth invasion. The advance guard under the command of Nandabayin's elder son, the crown prince, went too far ahead and was attacked by a strong Siamese army under Pra Naret, who at his father's death had become king with the title of Naresuen. The crown prince and the Siamese king engaged in combat on elephants, and the crown prince was killed. Disheartened, Nandabayin retreated. Narasuen felt both happy at the defeat of the enemy and sad at the killing of his friend and playmate of happier days at Bayinnaung's court; he built a small temple on the site of the combat and returned to Ayuthia. From Ayuthia, learning that Nandabayin's army had melted away, he sent a contingent into the extreme south of Burma and it easily occupied the Tenasserim coast. Naresuen now dreamed of annexing the whole of Lower Burma; to first secure the rear he invaded Cambodia, drove out the king, and returned with thousands of Cambodian captives for re-settlement in Siam.

As the result of heavy losses suffered during the five invasions of Siam, the rich fields of Lower Burma remained untilled, and adding to the trouble was a plague of rats, which destroyed the small amount of rice produced. In 1593 a group of Mons broke out in rebellion; using this as an excuse, Nandabayin ordered wholesale arrests and executions of all Mons suspected of plotting treason. In protest the Mon lord of Moulmein not only rebelled but called for assistance from Naresuen, who was only too ready to come into Lower Burma. The Mons rushed to join him and a combined Siamese and Mon army besieged Pegu. Reinforcements were faithfully sent by governors of Prome, Toungoo, and Chengmai, and without joining battle Naresuen withdrew, taking with him thousands of Mon volunteers. In addition to Tenasserim he continued to hold both Moulmein and Martaban. For Nandabayin yet more trouble came from an unexpected quarter: his own son, the governor of Prome, declared his independence, obviously to save his territory from the general ruin that was befalling his father's kingdom. Furious and anxious, Nandabayin demanded hostages from the governors of Toungoo, Chengmai, and Ava, although the governors of Chengmai and Ava were the king's own brothers. They all refused to comply and declared their independence. Learning of the difficulties Chengmai was facing, the Laotians invaded the principality and the newly independent king had no choice but to send a plea for help from Naresuen, who promptly came, drove out the invaders, and declared Chengmai as part of his dominions.

As his power dwindled Nandabayin became more tyrannical and finally his cousin, the governor of Toungoo, came to the conclusion that he must race Naresuen to Pegu and thus save Burma from the conquest of the Siamese. He looked for an ally and found Arakan to be most suitable. Since the invasion by Tabinshwehti, Arakan had swiftly developed into a powerful kingdom. It continued to hold Chittagong and at the same time kept up its friendly relations with the Muslim rulers of India. However, the Arakanese remained nationalistic and proud of their Burmese origin. Their magnificent capital of Mrohoung had become not only a great fortress but also a center of commerce and culture; it was a worthy rival of Pegu. Bayinnaung's enlightened policies with regard to commerce, religion, and culture were closely copied by the Arakanese king. Its ports were busy centers of international commerce, its royal court produced brilliant poetry and prose in Burmese, and its jurists compiled and produced works on Burmese customary law. Although because of Muslim influence Arakanese women were kept secluded, the kings were proud of their Buddhist faith and extended their patronage to the Buddhist clergy and the Buddhist temples. In addition to a powerful army it had developed a powerful navy also, and thousands of Portuguese and "half-Portuguese" mercenaries served the Arakanese king. Some of them had served in Nandabayin's armies but had wisely left the "sinking ship." The Arakanese were indeed valuable allies to the king of Toungoo, who took into consideration not only their might but also the fact that Arakanese were interested only in the loot and not in the occupation of Pegu.

In 1599 an Arakanese fleet stormed and seized Syriam as the army from Toungoo began their siege of Pegu. Another Arakanese fleet arrived bringing an army, which joined the Toungoo troops at the walls of Pegu. The siege was found unnecessary, however; Nandabayin had been abandoned by his soldiers and the city was not only undefended but almost deserted, as even the inhabitants had fled since the fall of Syriam. The two armies simply walked into the city and calmly discussed the division of the loot. The gold, silver, and precious stones were equally divided, the great bronze statues that Bayinnaung had seized at Ayuthia went to the Arakanese, and the images of the Buddha found in the palace became Toungoo's share. In addition the Arakanese took Nandabayin's daughter and Toungoo obtained the custody of the fallen king. The white elephants became the property of the Arakanese, and in return they allowed the Toungoo army to break open the relic chamber of the pagoda that Bayinnaung had built and to take away the Tooth and Alms Bowl given by Ceylon. The king of Toungoo did not take possession of Pegu but returned quickly to Toungoo. It is difficult to understand his action, because his main purpose in attacking Nandabayin was to take over the throne of Lower Burma. Perhaps he did not feel strong enough, perhaps he was afraid of having to fight Naresuen in unfriendly country surrounded by Mons, or perhaps he was asked to do so by his Arakanese allies. The Arakanese army methodically stripped the palace and the city of their treasures and fittings and set fire to the whole city. Then with the princess, the white elephants, and the loot, they boarded their ships.

It had really been a close race, for Naresuen now arrived with a huge army and found Pegu in ruins. Then he went to Toungoo and demanded the surrender of the captive Nandabayin, for he wanted to be his successor and occupy Lower Burma. But the king of Toungoo replied that he was under no obligation whatsoever to accede because he was as sovereign a king as Naresuen himself. Thinking that the Arakanese were gone, the Siamese king laid siege to Toungoo. Their ships were still in the harbor of Syriam, however, and the Arakanese soldiers now left the ships and destroyed the long line of communications that Naresuen had to maintain between his attacking army and the coast. Soon his army's food supply was depleted, and the Arakanese attempted to close the route back to Siam. Caught between the Toungoo and the Arakanese forces, Naresuen had to make a hasty retreat, but before he could reach the shelter of his frontier he suffered heavy losses. As he retreated he took away with him thousands of Mon refugees who could not withstand the ravages of the Arakanese soldiers. But it was the end of his dream to conquer Lower Burma.

Three other men began to dream the same dream—de Brito, the governor of Syriam; the king of Ava; and Natshinnaung, who had succeeded his father as king of Toungoo. When the Arakanese finally sailed away from Syriam they left behind as their governor one of their Portuguese mercenaries, Philip de Brito y Nicote. He was the typical Portuguese adventurer in southeast Asia, courageous, unscrupulous, and greedy. From a poverty-stricken home in Lisbon he came out to southeast Asia as a cabin boy in a Portuguese ship, and after many vicissitudes of fortune he enlisted as a gunner in the armies of the king of Arakan; by skill, courage, and charm he rose to the rank of commander. It was 1600 when the sun of Portuguese rule over the commerce of southeast Asia was beginning to set. A hundred years before, when the Portuguese stormed their way into the trade lanes of southeast Asia, they were interested only in establishing small fort-factories and had no desire to conquer and settle large sections of territory. However, the acquisition of Ceylon by the king of Portugal, through the will and testament of Don John Dhammapala, encouraged some of the Portuguese mercenaries fighting in the armies of the warring kings of southeast Asia to discard their role of king-maker and try for a throne for themselves. In Cambodia in 1599 a Portuguese mercenary, together with some Spanish comrades, nearly won the kingdom for themselves and for Phillip II, king of Spain and Portugal. South of Chittagong on the Arakanese coast, Portuguese mercenaries in the service of the king of Arakan, while flying his flag, had turned the port of Dianga into their stronghold and their base of operation for piracy and slave raiding. When occasion demanded they sought shelter behind the name of either the viceroy of Goa or the king of Arakan, but they owed allegiance to neither.

De Brito, inspired by such examples, became ambitious and with the help of his lieutenant Salvador Ribeyro he improved the defenses of Syriam by constructing a wall and a moat around it as if it were a royal capital. He had only fifty Portuguese with him, but using them as a nucleus he built up a strong army by obtaining recruits from among the Mons of the delta. Pegu was in ruins and Syriam swiftly took her place as the commercial center of Lower Burma. Then de Brito on a trumped-up charge expelled the Arakanese royal official who was with him. Both the king of Arakan and the king of Toungoo realized that de Brito was engaging in treasonable activities against the king of Arakan, so an Arakanese naval expedition and an army from Toungoo converged upon Syriam. De Brito ambushed the Arakanese navy and captured its commander, the crown prince himself. Using the crown prince as a hostage, he achieved the withdrawal of all Toungoo and Arakanese forces. Only on the receipt of an enormous ransom was the prince finally released. The Mon leaders now approached de Brito to be their champion and to rule over Syriam as king. De Brito then sailed to Goa and obtained not only recognition as king of Syriam and great vassal of the king of Portugal but also received the viceroy's daughter in marriage, appointment as a captain general of Portugal, six warships, and 3,000 soldiers. The Mon governor of Martaban, owing allegiance to Siam, made an alliance by marrying his daughter to de Brito's son by a former wife. Although Bassein refused to recognize him, de Brito became the overlord of Lower Burma.

Now that his position was secure, de Brito showed his true character. He cast greedy eyes on the port of Dianga and flirted with the Portuguese pirates there. The king of Arakan became so worried over the possibility of de Brito's joining hands with the pirates that he sent an expedition to Dianga and in a surprise attack massacred six hundred Portuguese residing there. One of the pirates, Sebastian Gonzales Tibao, escaped and took over another island, declaring himself king. The governor of Chittagong, quarreling with his brother the king of Arakan, joined hands with the Portuguese adventurer. Tibao welcomed him with open arms, raised his sister to be his queen, and then poisoned him, taking all his treasures and all his men. Both the Muslim viceroy of Bengal and the king of Arakan were now out to get his head. Then the Muslim viceroy and the Arakanese king fought each other and the latter was forced to accept the Portuguese adventurer as his ally. Tibao repaid him by inviting the commanders of the Arakanese fleet to a conference, then killing them and seizing the entire fleet. De Brito was heartened by all this but at the same time he was shrewd enough to know that all good things would finally come to an end; therefore he started to make money as quickly as possible. He forced all the Mons in his kingdom to become Roman Catholics, and, on the plea that idolatry must be suppressed and with the full approval of the friars representing the archbishop of Goa, he looted all the Buddhist temples of their ornaments and treasures, melted down all the golden images, and cast the bronze from the bells into cannons. In the short space of thirteen years he accumulated a personal fortune of thirteen million gold coins.

Natshinnaung, the new king of Toungoo, was somewhat of a Renaissance figure. Learned in the scriptures, he was indeed a strange Theravadian scholar, for his approach to the Buddhist religion was mystical and deeply metaphysical, and he spurned its moral teachings as merely for ordinary folk. He was a brilliant polo player and had been a soldier since childhood. In 1593 when Nandabayin's son, the crown prince, was killed by Naresuen, he had been with him on another elephant, although he was only fifteen; he gallantly requested permission of Nandabayin to ride on his charger back to Pegu to tell the widow of her husband's death. She was Raza-Dartu Kalayani, who was a princess of Toungoo and a most famous beauty. She was at least some six years older than he and a cousin of his mother's. As he sang the praises of the dead hero, he watched her eyes growing dim with sadness and then sparkling with pride at the glorious death of her husband. He fell in love with her. For the next three years he wrote poem after poem declaring his love for her until she finally succumbed to his protestations and returned his love. She was also a poet herself. Nandabayin, however, refused to permit the marriage because of the disparity in ages, and Natshinnaung became obsessed with one idea only, to make the lady queen of Burma with himself as king.

In the meantime, when he was away on a campaign on Nandabayin's service, another cousin forced the attractive widow to marry him and Natshinnaung felt convinced that Nandabayin was behind it all. He took part in the sacking of Pegu, and without the knowledge of his father he stole into the prison quarters of Nandabayin and hacked him to death. The love poems and the philosophical poems that he wrote until he became king are generally considered to be some of the most beautiful poems in Burmese literature. The first thing he did on his father's death was to marry Raza-Dartu Kalayani and together they were crowned king and queen of Toungoo. But their kingdom was only Toungoo, and he was determined she should be the queen of Burma. Together with the king of Prome he was starting on a campaign against the king of Ava when a group of Mons seized the throne of Prome. Natshinnaung then decided to win the friendship of de Brito with the purpose of using him to extend his own territory and undoubtedly hoping to drive him out sooner or later. He visited Syriam and in a banquet highlighted by merry-making and wine the two kings swore to be blood brothers.

Their defeat, through the efforts of the king of Ava, was slowly taking form. At the time of the breakup of Nandabayin's empire the governor of Ava, who declared himself king, was a younger brother of Nandabayin. He was known to Burmese history as the lord of Nyaungyan, a position he held before he was appointed governor of Ava; accordingly Burmese chronicles divided the period of the second Burmese empire into two sub-periods, the period of Toungoo and the period of Nyaungyan. When Nandabayin fell from power Naresuen incited the Shan chieftains to rebel, which they did, but as usual they started to fight each other. The king of Ava improved the defenses of the city but kept it aloof from both the fighting in the lower Irrawaddy valley and on the Shan plateau. Prome and Toungoo resented this, but when Prome was seized by Mon rebels the Burmese from that principality fled for protection, not to Toungoo, but to Ava. Strengthened by these reinforcements, the king of Ava proceeded to re-conquer the Shan states one by one. The Shans looked to China for succor, but when a Sawbwa who had escaped to Yunnan was meekly surrendered by its governor on the demand of the Burmese king, they turned to Naresuen, who duly came to their rescue.

Both the king of Ava and the king of Siam died in 1605 during the campaign, but whereas the son of the Ava king was young, warlike, and enthusiastic, Naresuen's successor, his younger brother, was old, hated war, and could not understand why Siam should be fighting a campaign for the Shans. Anaukpetlun was indeed a young man in a hurry, and even before his father's obsequies were over he had made all the ministers and commanders swear allegiance to him and at once proceeded to continue the campaign. The Shans surrendered everywhere, and Ava found itself with a huge reservoir of men and material whereas the small kingdoms of Lower Burma remained weak and without reserves. In 1608 Anaukpetlun took Prome and in 1610 he took Toungoo but re-appointed Natshinnaung as governor. Anaukpetlun had assumed the role of a patron of Buddhism, and he swore a mighty oath that he would drive away the archenemy of Buddhism, de Brito, into the sea. De Brito was not perturbed, however. Anaukpetlun wanted to make victory certain, so he returned to Ava for further preparation, taking with him from Toungoo the sacred Tooth and the Alms Bowl. Then Natshinnaung, bitter against Anaukpetlun for reducing his status, secretly wrote to de Brito to come and take Toungoo. De Brito and his Mon ally, the governor of Martaban, attacked Toungoo, but Natshinnaung's plan to welcome them went awry because his younger brother refused to submit to a Portuguese or to a Mon and inflicted heavy losses on the invaders before he was killed. De Brito and the governor of Martaban in a spirit of revenge, and perhaps incited by Natshinnaung himself, burned the palace and destroyed the fortifications. Then they withdrew and Natshinnaung accompanied his blood brother to Syriam.

In 1613 Nandabayin's grim avenger, Anaukpetlun, laid siege to Syriam. According to Portuguese accounts, de Brito was doomed from the beginning because the messenger whom he sent to Bengal to buy gunpowder misappropriated the money and never came back. If this was really true, de Brito must have been careless and callous, because Anaukpetlun had been threatening to attack Syriam for at least two years. Anaukpetlun had no Portuguese mercenaries in his army as he distrusted them, and his cannons were too small to bring down the walls de Brito had so carefully constructed. De Brito's ally, the Portuguese adventurer on the Arakanese coast, had his hands full fighting the Arakanese, so no help came from that quarter. For some unexplained reason Goa delayed sending some ships to relieve the besieged city. The siege continued for three months and de Brito anxiously scanned the horizon for a ship bringing him reinforcements. The Mon inhabitants themselves regarded Anaukpetlun as their savior. As the siege dragged on, Anaukpetlun offered to let de Brito and his family sail back to Goa if he would surrender Natshinnaung, but de Brito rejected the offer. Unknown to de Brito and Anaukpetlun, five relief ships sent by the viceroy of Goa were only a few miles away. Anaukpetlun then ordered his troops to secretly dig a tunnel under the walls, and when the tunnel had been dug the Burmese troops rushed in. There was a fierce battle and the city was taken.

When de Brito and Natshinnaung were brought before him, the king looked at Natshinnaung and pitied him, and offered to pardon him if he would take the oath of allegiance. Natshinnaung replied that he had already taken baptism and was ready to die with de Brito. Anaukpetlun then said, "You prefer to be the slave of a foreigner rather than serve the king of your own race," and ordered his execution. De Brito himself was impaled, the usual punishment for a pillager of temples under Burmese law, and he died after three days of agony. His queen, the viceroy's daughter, and other members of the household were sold as slaves. Some Portuguese soldiers with their families were re-settled in a village in Upper Burma and were permitted to retain their Roman Catholic faith. Mon members of de Brito's civil and military services were pardoned. The following day, not knowing that the port had fallen, the five relief ships entered the harbor and the king's ships captured four of them. The fifth, which was still outside the harbor when the battle developed, was able to make its escape. The curtain on the Portuguese dream of founding a kingdom in Burma for themselves was lowered in 1615–17, when the Arakanese king, encouraged by the defeat of de Brito and with the help of the Dutch, repulsed a Portuguese raid and, counterattacking, destroyed the island kingdom of de Brito's comrade, Sebastian Gonzales Tibao, in spite of efforts made by Goa to save it.

The victory over de Brito restored international prestige to the Burmese, but Arakan and Siam were alarmed at the growing power of the Burmese king. Anaukpetlun, however, had no ambition to restore Bayinnaung's empire, realizing that his resources were limited. He was determined only to restore the kingdom of Burma. After de Brito had been defeated and Anaukpetlun had shown both might and magnanimity, the governor of Martaban submitted without Anaukpetlun's having to fire a single cannon. He took back some of the southern territory from Siam but could not take Tenasserim itself because it was well defended by a regiment of Portuguese mercenaries. Anxious lest Siam should rouse the Shans to rebellion, he conquered Chengmai, making it a wedge between the Shans and the Tais. He wisely refused to go onward to Laos and returned to Burma with a desire to give the country a long period of peace.

Anaukpetlun treated all three racial groups with equal consideration, never forgetting that the Mons, groaning under de Brito's misrule, welcomed him as their champion. In front of his palace he installed a brass bell that could be rung by anyone who felt he was a victim of injustice. He forgave the Arakanese king for his part in the sacking of Nandabayin's Pegu because later on he proved to be a great patron of Buddhism in Arakan and sent a mission of Arakanese abbots, at the request of the king of Ceylon, to give the Ordination again to Sinhalese monks. By that time the Temple of the Tooth had been well established at Kandy and the Buddhist Order in Ceylon, after the deprivations of the civil wars and Portuguese persecution, needed purification. According to Portuguese records, Anaukpetlun sent an embassy to Goa, and its purpose is the subject of controversy among modern historians. Some think that

Anaukpetlun feared a joint attack from the Portuguese and the Arakanese, and others think that he wanted Goa's help to fight the Siamese. In actual fact, however, all that he wanted was a resumption of trade. He realized too well that Portuguese power was waning in southeast Asia, and he never had any ambition to conquer Arakan or Siam. The Portuguese records also noted that when Goa sent a return mission it found Anaukpetlun rather indifferent; probably the mission hinted at some alliance and Anaukpetlun found the proposal unattractive. He exchanged missions also with the Muslim rulers of India and Acheh, the hostile neighbor of Portuguese Malacca. He had no thought of playing Muslim against Roman Catholic; these were all trade missions.

Anaukpetlun, remembering that the glory of Bayinnaung's empire was closely connected with the expansion of Burma's international trade, wanted to make contact with the new commercial powers of southeast Asia, namely the English and the Dutch. When his forces conquered Chengmai they took prisoner a Thomas Samuel, who was in charge of the English East India Company's factory in Ayuthia. He was brought to Pegu with other foreign nationals, all of whom were well treated, but Samuel died. In 1617 the company sent two agents to claim the goods of the company that were held by Samuel at the time of his capture. They found to their surprise that the royal officials had kept a correct and detailed inventory of the dead merchant's goods. The king gave them a friendly interview because he presumed that they had come to open a factory at Syriam or Martaban. Taking advantage of this impression on the part of the king, they did not tell him the real purpose of their visit and started to trade illicitly on their own. Learning of this commerce, he restored the goods and sent back the two merchants with a letter to the company expressing his interest in establishing trade relations. On their way back, however, the two bright young men sold the goods, pocketed the money, and reported that the king was a bloodthirsty tyrant who had treated them badly and seized the goods. They were dismissed later by the company from their posts for misappropriation, but their reports remained on record for later generations of the company's servants to see. In any case, even if the reports had been favorable, the company at that time could not have opened any new factory in Burma because of its financial position and its rivalry with the Dutch.

In spite of this rebuff Anaukpetlun decided to rebuild Pegu and make it both the political and commercial capital of his kingdom as in the days of Bayinnaung. He therefore built a temporary palace on the opposite bank of the Pegu river. One day it was discovered that the crown prince was in the habit of visiting a lady-in-waiting in the private apartments of the queens and Anaukpetlun called for him and said, "Such a breach of palace discipline ought to be punished by boiling the culprit in oil." The crown prince, feeling ashamed at his father's remarks in full audience, stole into the palace that evening and assassinated him. The ministers arrested the prince, but fearing that any trouble in the palace would result in rebellion they elected him king. Anaukpetlun's younger brother, who was on duty at that time in Ava, came down with his army and the ministers re-arrested the crown prince and declared the uncle to be king. The new king arrived, executed the ministers and the crown prince for conspiracy and murder respectively, and ascended the throne in 1629 as Tharlun Min. The assassination of Anaukpetlun was a national disaster of the greatest magnitude. It resulted in no immediate rebellion nor any loss of territory, but it was to lead to the abandonment of the great dream that Anawrahta, Kyansittha, Tabinshwehti, and Bayinnaung had of uniting the various racial groups of the country into a single nation.

Tharlun Min was a strong, just, and able king, but perhaps he lacked the vision that his late brother had. He had spent the best years of his life winning back for his father and his brother the Shan states, and he thought that to keep the Shans subdued and satisfied was more important than anything else. He probably thought also that the Shans were easier to please and befriend than the Mons. On the other hand, he might have been a man of vision

who was made to accept reality by force of prevailing circumstances. For four years he seemed uncertain of his position and
would not accept coronation, spending most of his time in Chengmai
and the Shan states. In 1633 he came down to Pegu and was duly
crowned, but one year later he was distressed by a group of Mon
rebels attacking the palace itself. Although the rising was easily
suppressed, there was another rebellion in the neighborhood of
Moulmein, and when an army was sent there the rebels migrated
en masse to Siam. This migration had started with Naresuen's raids
and it became the policy of all Siamese kings to encourage such
moves. Most of these migrants settled down permanently in Siam,
but some returned in groups to raid and harass the Burmese and
then, when the king's forces came, to go back into Siamese territory
again. Tharlun Min finally concluded that regardless of how liberal
his policy toward the Mons might be it was no longer possible for
him to expect any cooperation from them.

In addition, the Pegu river had become so silted that the city
ceased to be accessible from the sea. Had there been any new developments in commerce perhaps he would have moved his capital
to Syriam. But the British and the Dutch remained uninterested in
developing Burmese trade, and the bitter rivalry between the Dutch
and the English in Siam, the attempts of some of those merchants to
interfere in the internal politics and act as king-makers in Siam, and
the corruption and the intrigues of the merchants of the English
and the Dutch East India Companies made him flinch from dealing
with foreign merchants. To the European merchants the kings of
southeast Asia were petulant, petty, and aggressive. But to the
southeast Asian kings, Portuguese, English, and Dutch traders were
greedy, dishonest, and quarrelsome. The ghost of de Brito still
seemed to walk the ramparts of Syriam, reminding the Burmese
that European merchants were all alike. In addition, the king thought
that in time of emergency it was easier to come down the river
than up, and it was easier to control Lower Burma from Ava than

to control Upper Burma from Syriam. Accordingly in 1634 he moved his capital to Ava and took his coronation again, signifying that he was the king of the Burmese and the Shans rather than the Mons.

It is difficult to say whether Tharlun Min's action in withdrawing inside the shell of Upper Burma was wise or foolish. Within a few years of his withdrawal to Ava the Portuguese were supplanted by the English and the Dutch in southeast Asia, and they ushered in a new phase of commercial development in the region. By leaving Lower Burma, Tharlun Min lost his window to the outside world. On the other hand, who could say that the Burmese empire would have lasted longer had the capital been moved to Syriam? It doubtless would have become a center of international commerce, but equally doubtless it would have become also the center of international intrigue. Even the southern Burmese port of Mergui, which Anaukpetlun could not recover and which Siam continued to hold, became a hotbed of international contention and conspiracy. It was first garrisoned by Portuguese mercenaries, then became a center of piracy led by two Englishmen in the service of the English East India Company, and later became involved in the intrigues of the infamous Greek adventurer, Constantine Phaulkon, who with the support of Louis XIV and the French Jesuits became a king-maker in Siam and nearly succeeded in turning the kingdom into a Roman Catholic protectorate under the French. All this happened merely because the poor king of Siam, Narai, wanted a full share in the commercial activities of the Europeans. If Tharlun Min had been a Narai, with the rebellious and discontented Mons around him, he would have fallen prey to Anglo-Dutch rivalry and his successors would have become exposed to the more bitter Anglo-French rivalry not only for trade but for political supremacy in India and southeast Asia. Tharlun Min in his distrust of Europeans was undoubtedly suffering from what English historians have called xenophobia, but it must be admitted that he became afflicted with this malady only because he became exposed to European mercantile intrigues. Because of the removal of the capital to Ava, the kingdom lasted for another hundred years.

Tharlun Min did not abandon the Mons, nor did he throw them to the lions, so to speak. He continued to appoint Mons to high administrative offices in Lower Burma and remained concerned about their welfare. He kept the trade routes and sea lanes open so that the Mons could carry on their trade with Upper Burma and also with the outside world. A year after the removal of the capital to Ava, the agents of the Dutch East India Company arrived and were well received by Tharlun Min and were permitted to open a factory at Syriam. However when the Dutch, as was their usual policy, attempted to impose a monopoly on Burma's international trade, Tharlun Min protected the interests not only of the Mons but also of the Indian merchants and even Portuguese merchants. The Dutch were dissatisfied and complained that the profits from the Burmese trade were poor. Unable to establish a monopoly themselves, they criticized the king's action in controlling certain articles of trade and noted the high cost of transporting goods to and from Ava and the high rates of customs duties, fixed at 16.5 per cent. They did not mention the fact that in spite of the high costs they were making a profit of some 40 per cent on their outlay. The fact that, in spite of their complaints, they did not close down their factory clearly showed that they found the trade profitable. Burma was a good market for Indian textiles, and in addition to its own products of ivory, gold, cutch, tin, lead, and bronze, Burma exported goods obtained from Yunnan. The Dutch complaint of poor returns was probably meant to hoodwink the English East India Company, which was becoming more and more interested in Burmese trade. In 1647 the English East India Company sent one of their ships, loaded with cargo worth some twenty thousand pounds sterling, to the Burmese ports and also established a factory at Syriam.

Tharlun Min was another great patron of Buddhism; he built the famous Kaunghmudaw pagoda on the opposite bank of the

Irrawaddy river from Ava and enshrined the sacred Tooth and the Alms Bowl received from Ceylon by Bayinnaung. Bayinnaung had enshrined them at a pagoda at Pegu, but the structure was never completed. Natshinnaung and his father broke open the vaults, took away the two relics, and enshrined them temporarily in a small pagoda at Toungoo. They were later taken by Anaukpetlun to Ava and again enshrined temporarily in a small pagoda. Tharlun Min felt that it was a duty he owed to his brother, Anaukpetlun, and to his grandfather, Bayinnaung, to build a permanent pagoda for the relics. So he sent a mission to Ceylon to get the architectural plans of the great temple at Anuradhapura, and using it as his model he built the Kaunghmudaw pagoda. He extended his patronage to those monks famous for their learning and purity, and encouraged all ranks of the clergy to follow the rules of the Order strictly. Once his son seized the palace in a rebellion, and in the confusion Tharlun Min escaped and sought shelter in a nearby monastery. The abbot refused to admit him into the monastery, maintaining that under the rules of the Order a monk was precluded from interfering in politics. The king therefore had to take shelter in another monastery. When the prince was killed and the rebellion suppressed, Tharlun Min held a great alms-giving ceremony in honor of the abbot who gave him shelter, and also in honor of the abbot who followed the rules and would not give him shelter. He encouraged not only the study of the scriptures but also various works on Burmese customary law, which was considered the common cultural heritage for all the racial groups. As a result one of his ministers produced another compendium of Burmese law, which took its place with the earlier Code of Dhammavilasa and the Code of Wareru.

Tharlun Min was one of the great administrator kings of Burma. He realized that a sound administrative system was essential and that such a system could evolve only during a period of lasting peace; he therefore exchanged missions with Arakan and established an alliance. He also sent a mission to the king of Siam, thus assuring him that the Burmese king had no territorial ambitions and in turn

making certain that the Siamese would not incite the Shans to rebellion. He crystallized and precisely defined the powers of the
institution of the Hluttaw, which was both the king's Privy Council
and the Supreme Court. He conducted a revenue inquest all over his
kingdom, thus fixing the rates of revenue payable by property
holders. Monastic and temple lands were also inspected and measured
and the details noted down. Because of experience of the people's
reluctance to serve in the military he established a new arrangement
under which an army could be mobilized within a short time. He
encouraged people, especially prisoners of war, to settle and work
the canals and irrigated fields of the Kyaukse district. They were
then organized into service groups, patterned on the service groups
already in existence since the days of Pagan. But the members of
the new groups were to serve only in the armies in time of war. Up
to his time the closest approximation of a professional army was the
regiment of palace guards, which itself was instituted only in the
later Pagan period by Narapatisithu. Now, the service families of
Kyaukse constituted a standing professional army. As a result, the
ministers at the king's court gradually lost their commands and the
ministers themselves were now professionally trained lawyers and
civil servants. In other words, Tharlun Min not only centralized the
administration but in effect separated the army from the civil service.
In time of actual war, of course, there would be regiments of levies
commanded by their own officers.

In addition, Tharlun Min gradually abolished the provincial
viceroys. Before him, provinces were put in the hands of governors,
who however were sometimes viceroys and even sub-kings, as for
example the governors of Ava, Prome, Toungoo, and Martaban. Under Tharlun all the provincial heads were made mere governors
except the head of the Seven Hill Districts, between the Arakan
mountains and the Irrawaddy river, with its capital at Mindon. It
was considered an important principality because of its historical associations; it was a principality even at the time of the Pyus, when
one of its viceroys, a woman, was included among the "Thirty-

seven Nats," and Kyansittha's son was appointed viceroy of that place. It was also remote and on the frontier, and circumstances often made it necessary for the viceroy to act on his own initiative without waiting for orders from the capital. After the first Anglo-Burmese war of 1824 a governorship was established in Rangoon, and he was given the rank of a viceroy. The gradual disappearance of viceroys was a natural result of the growing power of the Hlut-taw.

Tharlun Min was succeeded by his son, Pindalè. He was a weak king and, unfortunately for him, he became involved in the dynastic struggles of the Manchus to drive the Mings out of China. But complete victory did not come to the Manchus for a long time, and in 1644 the last Ming emperor, Yung-li, withdrew to Yunnan and fought back the Manchus. But he was now more of a fugitive than an emperor, and his desperate men were more robbers than soldiers. They retreated into Burmese Shan states and terrorized the whole countryside, robbing and raping and forcing the men to join them. Pindalè sent an expedition to meet the marauders, but it was a small force and could not accomplish anything. In 1658 Yung-li lost his final battle, retreated into Burmese territory, and pleaded to be given political asylum. Pindalè was in great difficulty. He had no forces with which to drive the Chinese out, and humanitarian reasons and international law prompted him to give the fallen emperor asylum. His mistake however was to allow Yung-li and his retinue of bandits to come right up to the capital. Although the Mings were disarmed and placed in a refugee camp on the other side of the river, the Burmese king's action exposed his kingdom to the remnants of the bandit forces, who still wanted to fight on and invited their leader to come out of Burma. The Burmese king correctly refused permission for the emperor to leave; his supporters then invaded Burmese territory and soon routed a Burmese force sent by Pindalè to meet them. In despair the king summoned a Mon levy from Martaban, which not only deserted but rose in rebellion. Then some six thousand Mons fled into Siam and were given a hearty welcome by the Siamese king. Meanwhile, the Chinese marauders came right up to the walls of Ava, looting and killing.

The Hluttaw, although it was as responsible as the king himself for the troubles, made Pindalè their scapegoat, dethroned him, and elected in 1661 his younger brother, Pyè Min, to the throne. Pyè Min accepted the throne only under protest, and when he treated his fallen brother with courtesy and consideration the ministers promptly executed the dethroned king. Tharlun Min's administrative reforms, in spite of their wisdom, were having an adverse effect on the kingdom because, without a strong king to check them, the ministers of the Hluttaw could wield absolute power. At first it seemed that the change of kings was a fortunate one because the Burmese were able to drive out the marauders. In addition, many Chinese were killed in a riot at a conference between the refugee Ming emperor and his followers, and the Burmese representatives. The Siamese, however, took advantage of Burma's troubles and invaded Chengmai during the absence of the Burmese garrison on duty elsewhere, but the people in Chengmai paid great tribute to the Burmese by driving out the invaders and re-affirming their allegiance to the Burmese king. But still another danger to Burma soon appeared. In 1662 the governor of Yunnan, whose son was married to the Manchu emperor's sister, wanted to make certain that there should be no Ming pretender to the Chinese throne. Accordingly he marched into Burma with a strong force and demanded the surrender of Yung-li. Pyè Min wanted to refuse, but his ministers pointed out that during the time of his great-grandfather the governor of Yunnan surrendered to the Burmese king a refugee Sawbwa. Heeding their advice, the king released Yung-li to the governor of Yunnan, who took him back to Yunnanfu and in the market place strangled him to death with a bow string.

The Chinese were now gone but the kingdom was left exhausted and its trade had been impaired. In 1657 the British closed their factory in Syriam and in 1661 the Dutch noted that their Burmese trade had ceased. The Burmese lay at the mercy of the

Shans and the Siamese, but the Shans were fellow sufferers at the hands of the Chinese marauders and had been brothers in arms with the Burmese in fighting them. Siam was swiftly becoming a pawn in the struggle for supremacy between the English and the French and could not take advantage of the difficulties of the Burmese kingdom. Soon the balance of power in mainland southeast Asia was to be disturbed by the bitter rivalry between England and France. In Burma itself both the king and the people somehow felt that their kingdom was doomed but could not determine from which quarter the final blow would come. As was usual in times of uncertainty people resorted to magic and astrology; they found signs and portents that Pyè Min should build a new capital, but the king did not have the financial resources to do so. Only the strength of the administrative machinery established by Tharlun Min kept the kingdom from disintegrating, and Pyè Min continued his unhappy reign until his death in 1672. His son who succeeded him died after a few months and the Hluttaw elected his cousin as king. Through alarms and fears this new king reigned on until 1698, when his son Sanay Min became king and ruled until his death in 1714.

All these kings were kindly, unambitious, peaceful, and undistinguished, and it was the Hluttaw that ruled the kingdom. But with such weak kings discipline in the ranks of the clergy decayed. In the long years of peace without prosperity, however, people both at the capital and in villages turned toward literature for comfort and relaxation. They abandoned religious themes and took up the writing of fiction, narrative poetry, drama, and lyrics, and just before the fall of the kingdom there was a sudden bloom of literature, comparable to the great age of literature of the Ava period. During the reign of Sanay Min's son, Taninganway Min, who reigned from 1714 to 1733, great works of literary merit were produced throughout the kingdom. Among the famous writers were U Kala, who wrote the first history of Burma in polished prose, and the minister Padetha Raza, who wrote a number of narrative poems charged with emotion and full of lyrical passages, and also the first Burmese court play.

But the expected blows were coming, and from all directions. The Manipuris, knowing that the kingdom of Burma had become weak, had long ago declared their country's independence. As the Burmese kingdom grew weaker, a Brahmin leader among them preached that if they could reach the Irrawaddy and bathe in its waters they would become purified of their sins. They had learned from the Burmese the art of horsemanship, and now they raided Burmese territory right up to the town of Sagaing opposite Ava. They were lightly armed, relying on the swiftness of their horses, and instead of engaging in pitched battles with the Burmese, they appeared in unexpected places. They looted and killed wantonly, and carried away women and children to Manipur. The entire western bank of the Irrawaddy lay at their mercy and finally the king had to send all available troops to the troubled regions. But these troops lacked a supreme commander with an imaginative plan and they took up isolated defensive positions, which the fierce Manipuri horsemen merely bypassed. In the midst of these raids the king died in 1733 and was succeeded by his son Maha Dhammaraza Dipadi.

The people, desperate and ashamed, longed for a new leader, and the countryside came alive with rumors of a mighty man of valor who would rule over the people with god-given lances and demon-given swords. The king took note of these rumors, consulted astrologers, and finally arrested one Maung Aung Zeya, a young man of twenty-two years and a son of the headman of a village called Moksobo on the western bank. He was a tall and handsome person, and his courteous and firm demeanor impressed the court, which accepted his denial of any interest in politics. To add to the confusion, the clergy broke into two sects, orthodox and reformed. The point of controversy was in the manner of wearing robes, the orthodox group insisting that the robes be worn for dignity and decorum, and the reformed sect insisting that they should be worn for comfort. It was a bitter conflict, involving not only Burmese but Mon monks also, for they were all under the primate appointed by the king.

As the Manipuri raids continued unabated and troops had to be kept on the western bank, a group of Gwe Shans who were settled near the capital proclaimed their headman as king of Burma, and joining hands with some Mons in the vicinity they created a riot. The riot was suppressed but it proved to the Mons in Lower Burma that the Burmese king was now without any prestige. Then, before the Mons could revolt, in 1740 the Burmese governor of Pegu declared himself king of Lower Burma, but the people would not support him. An expedition came down from Ava, executed him, and appointed the Burmese governor of Syriam to be the governor of Pegu. This governor, fearing rebellion, took stern and repressive measures until the people themselves rose in rebellion and Pegu, Martaban, and Tavoy became rebel strongholds. The people offered the throne to a former royal official, Maung Aung Hla, who was a Burmanized Shan from Chengmai, but he refused, saying that he was a fighter for freedom with no interest in politics. Accordingly the rebels elected a fugitive prince from Ava itself as their king, giving him a Mon title. He also proved reluctant to take up the throne but finally did so. He was more like a comic opera monarch than a real one. Since his flight from Ava he had been a monk and now found it difficult to adjust himself to the life of a layman, and a king at that. Calling himself "Lord of the Striped Elephant," he was most reluctant to take charge of the government or command an army, and usually he was absent from the capital.

The rebellion of Lower Burma began in 1740, but it was only in 1747 that it actually became Mon in character. The insurrection was begun by the Burmese governor of Pegu and was continued after the governor had been executed and the Burmese governor of Syriam appointed in his place. In 1740 it was not by any means a Mon rising, but just an attempt by the Burmese governor to break away from Ava and rule Pegu as an independent king. The second rebellion again was not a Mon rising, because the people of Lower

Burma, consisting of Shans, Mons, and Burmese, were protesting against repressive measures of the new governor of Pegu. This multi-racial character of the rebellion was emphasized by the selection of a Burmese refugee prince as the new king of Lower Burma. In 1743 the rebel government at Pegu consisted of representatives from the three main races, and they were all against the Europeans, who were to be found mostly in Syriam. In addition to being a busy port, Syriam contained dockyards belonging not only to the Burmese but also the English and French. The English East India Company had established its dockyard in 1709 and the French in 1729 with the encouragement and approval of the king at Ava. In 1743 the rebels finally occupied Syriam; they burned all the European churches and factories and took over all ships lying in the harbor. Soon afterwards Father Gallizia, who had been consecrated as the first Bishop of Ava by His Holiness the Pope, arrived at Syriam, but now that peaceful communication with Ava had ceased he sought and obtained permission from the rebel government to reside at Pegu. Later on he and his priests and a ship's captain, on their way to the palace, were surrounded and killed under orders of the rebel government. Up to this point, the rebels had no definite plan or policy.

It was the French who changed the character of the rebellion. The war of the Austrian Succession was over, but the French general in India, the great Dupleix, realized that another round with the English was inevitable. As governor of Pondicherry, he decided to explore the possibility of intervening in the rebellion in Lower Burma. By helping the Mons he hoped to get Syriam as reward, to be used as a French base. After all Europeans had withdrawn from Syriam following its seizure by the rebels, the French appointed as their agent an Italian of proven French sympathies, one Father Vittoni. Father Vittoni had been in Siam during the days of the French influence there, and coming into contact with Mon refugees he had become sympathetic toward them. He was on friendly terms with the Mon rebel leaders at Pegu, and secretly he must have suggested that they take over the entire leadership of the rebellion and lead the Mons to victory over the Burmese.

The so-called ministers at Pegu were really commanders of rebel units, and the rank of chief minister was given to Maung Aung Hla, who had refused the throne. These commanders quickly got rid of their Burmese colleagues and started to massacre groups of Burmese all over the region. The king, noticing the change in the character of the rebellion, began to fear for his life and collected a strong bodyguard to protect him. After all, he was not Mon nor Shan, but Burmese. On the ground that he had never taken part in any battle, the Mon commanders dethroned him and elected Maung Aung Hla. As the dethroned king fought his way out of Pegu and into Chengmai, the simple fighter for freedom, Maung Aung Hla, ascended the throne taking the Mon title "Binnya Dala" and declaring his intention of restoring Bayinnaung's empire, but under Mon leadership. He appointed his younger brother as crown prince and a Mon commander, Dalaban, as the commander-in-chief.

Father Vittoni, pleased with his handiwork, made further suggestions to the Mons, and as a result in 1750 a Mon embassy sailed to Pondicherry, where it was received with great enthusiasm by Dupleix. To head the return embassy Dupleix selected the ablest officer on his staff, the Sieur de Bruno. Bruno completely won over the Mon leaders and obtained a treaty by which the Mons were to receive military aid from France, and in return they were to give substantial commercial concessions. Bruno returned to Dupleix to make his report while the Mons prepared to advance to the north, at the same time continuing the suppression of the Burmese in Lower Burma. The Siamese king, alarmed at the alliance between the Mons and the French, appointed special officers to give aid and comfort to the Burmese refugees fleeing into Siam and sent an embassy to his ancient enemy, the king of Ava, to bolster his prestige and also his courage. The English in India were equally alarmed, and worrying that the French might take control of Syriam they sent an embassy to the king of Pegu asking permission to open a factory at

Cape Negrais, but the embassy was received with open hostility. Both the Mons and the French decided to act quickly before Siam and the Shans could intervene, and with French equipment and advice two armies marched to Ava, one under the command of the crown prince and the other under the command of Dalaban. Binnya Dala himself followed with a flotilla of boats up the Irrawaddy river. There was no resistance and in 1752 Binnya Dala took Ava; with the captive Burmese king and his family he returned to Pegu in triumph. The crown prince also thought that his presence and that of his army were no longer necessary, so he instructed Dalaban to act as military governor of Upper Burma and he returned to Pegu to celebrate the defeat of the Burmese.

VIII   Alaungpaya and the Third Burmese Empire

Binnya Dala and the crown prince were too hasty in coming to the conclusion that the Burmese had been defeated just because Ava had fallen and the king taken prisoner. They neglected to take into consideration that the fallen king of Ava commanded neither affection nor respect from his subjects, who had been for the last sixteen years looking for a new leader whom they could follow. Dalaban sent out small detachments to the outlying provinces in the north and west to obtain the oath of allegiance from royal officials and village headmen. Already there were two resistance movements; the first was led by a Burmese commander who had deserted with a small detachment of troops when Ava was attacked by the Mons, and the second by the leader of the Gwe Shans, who escaped when his riot was suppressed by the king of Ava. Both these leaders declared themselves king of Ava, and they also were sending out detachments requiring the villagers to swear allegiance to them.

A third potential force was Maung Aung Zeya. Some sixteen years before, he had been called to Ava to explain what were suspected to be treasonable activities; since then he had lived quietly, and now at the age of thirty-eight he was a normal, prosperous villager. His village, Moksobo, was a large one and although the office of headman was not officially hereditary his family had supplied the village with its headmen for many generations. His father had retired and he had been elected to serve in his place. According to an Englishman named Captain Baker, who saw him, he was a handsome man of imposing appearance, five feet ten inches tall, with an air of authority. On receiving the news of the fall of Ava he started to fortify his place. When he learned that the commander and the Shan leader had declared themselves king, he decided that he must save his country not only from the Mons but also from those two leaders whom he considered unworthy of the throne because one was a deserter and the other a common rebel.

Maung Aung Zeya was well known in the region, especially because of the notoriety of his arrest as an alleged pretender to the throne some sixteen years before. He won the support of the forty-six surrounding villages and moved the inhabitants into his village, which was now a fortress. There was a moat around it, and because there was no time to put up a brick wall he made a stockade of toddy palm tree stems, which would withstand both musket and cannon. Then he burned the villages with the full consent of the villagers and filled up all the streams and wells. He cut down all trees and burned the vegetation. Within an area of some ten miles from his village, therefore, the countryside became a desert with no place for shelter for any attacking army. He appointed a council of advisers consisting of himself and the headmen of the forty-six villages, together with some villagers who were outstanding in character and national spirit.

When his scouts reported that a detachment of Mons had arrived in the vicinity to administer the oath of allegiance, Maung Aung Zeya discussed in the advisory council the course of action they should take. Many of them were cautious. Some suggested that in order to avoid a frontal battle they should take the oath of allegiance to the Mons and then attack them from behind after the detachment had left the village; others suggested that because of the superiority in numbers of the Mons they should join forces with the Gwe Shans and swear allegiance to their leader as a temporary arrangement. Maung Aung Zeya replied, "Once an oath of allegiance has been taken, it must never be broken, and if we break our oath after we have taken it, on the pages of history we shall always stand in shame as breakers of oaths. Therefore, the only question is, shall we surrender to the Mons and drink their water of allegiance, or shall we fight them openly?" His answer impressed his companions, and it was unanimously decided that they should fight the Mons under his leadership. That night he went before his parents and, kneeling down, he said, "My parents, my lords, as I think that it is my duty to save my religion, my country, and my people from defeat and misrule, I shall fight the enemy and make myself king." When his mother pleaded caution, pointing out that he had only a handful of supporters to stand against a mighty army, he answered, "In war, my parents, numbers alone do not give victory, and the essential factor is the spirit to win and save one's own nation."

A few days later a detachment of Mon troops arrived at the village and were met with withering fire from muskets. This was the first open challenge to Mon authority in Upper Burma and the first attack on Mon forces since the fall of Ava. But Dalaban did not think the matter to be of any importance and just sent a stronger detachment, which was ambushed and wiped out even before they reached the ten miles of artificial desert around Moksobo. Still Dalaban and his commanders were unconcerned, although this time they did decide to send a whole regiment. It too was wiped out. In the meantime U Aung Zeya was attracting many patriots to come to his village and fight under his banner. All sorts of people came, simple farmers, artisans, writers, soldiers, and even former royal officials, who considered it a privilege to serve U Aung Zeya. But he was wise enough not to become overconfident, for he was hemmed in not only by the Mons but by the forces of the former commander from Ava and the Gwe Shans. Nonetheless he felt that the time had come to declare himself king.

Changing the name of his village to Shwebo or "The Place of

the Golden Commander," he proclaimed himself king of all Burma, taking the title of Alaungpaya or "The Great Lord who shall be a Buddha one day." He claimed descent from the dynasty of the first kingdom of Ava and he declared himself as the successor to the kings of Tagaung, Pagan, Ava, and Pegu. He was determined to create a new age of Burmese greatness, and thus his capital would not be the old cities of Pagan, Ava, or Pegu, but the new city of Shwebo. This bold declaration brought more supporters, and now they came in groups bringing with them presents and arms, including cannons. Even from such a remote place as Mindon, a leader came with a regiment of fully equipped soldiers. There was great enthusiasm and a quiet confidence, combined with a somber realization that the odds were still very much against them. A born leader and a strict disciplinarian, Alaungpaya never became arrogant; he showed consideration and kindness to those who came to fight under his banner, assuring them that the glory of victory would not be the special privilege of his own friends from the Shwebo area but would be for all who shared the dangers. Just as he, a simple village headman, had been raised to the throne, he raised his comrades to the ranks and titles of nobility. But there was never any show of favoritism, and titles and honors were freely showered on those who deserved them by their courage and military skill.

Soon the expected attack from the Mons came. Calling for re-inforcements from Pegu, Dalaban built up a huge army, and after crossing the river from Ava he re-grouped it into four divisions and attacked Shwebo from all sides. Alaungpaya wisely kept his troops inside the stockade. For five whole days and nights, without giving the defenders a pause, the Mons attacked in groups, but the Burmese from their prepared positions inflicted heavy losses. After such slaughter Dalaban decided that the battle should not be pro-longed and the stockade must be taken swiftly at all cost. Selecting 1,500 of his best men he ordered them to climb over the stockade from one side as the rest of the army created a diversion by attacking from the opposite side. The commandos were mowed down and only 50 reached the inside, but before they could open the gates they were killed. After this battle the Mon troops were exhausted and withdrew a short distance from the stockade. Now Alaungpaya himself came out, leading all his troops, and attacked the Mons, who broke rank and ran until they reached the Irrawaddy river, where they tried to float themselves down to Pegu on waiting rafts. Hundreds were drowned but Alaungpaya, exercising caution, would not permit his troops to leave the vicinity of Shwebo. The Mons never attacked Shwebo again, but Dalaban tried to encircle it by keeping an army in the north and by building stockades along the river bank. So Alaungpaya sent detachments to destroy the stockades, and Dalaban withdrew to Ava. Then, leaving the Mons alone, Alaungpaya called upon the former Burmese commander from Ava and the Gwe Shans to surrender, and when they refused he attacked and defeated them.

It was now the end of 1752; when the year had dawned it seemed as if the Burmese had been defeated completely, but Alaungpaya had turned the tables. The whole of Upper Burma including the Shan states was in his hands except the city of Ava, and he needed a breathing period in order to rest his supporters, who had been fighting continuously almost the whole year, and to prove that he was a man worthy to be recognized as a great king. He expanded his village into a city, complete with brick walls, moats, temples, and palaces. He appointed a new primate, who belonged to the reformed sect, and gave him full support to end the controversy and the schism. He encouraged learning and scholarship by giving awards and titles to scholars and poets. He suppressed animal sacrifice connected with spirit worship, which had been revived during the decay of authority that followed the death of Bayinnaung. He prohibited the drinking of liquor, remembering past incidents in which drunken Burmese garrisons of the king of Ava were so easily overcome by Mon rebels. He prohibited the killing of cattle, both on religious and economic grounds, for those plough animals were desperately needed in the rice fields, which were now being cultivated again after the years of rebellion and war. He declared all persons above the age of sixty to be free from liability for service to the king or to village authorities, and the cost of their food, clothing, and travel was made a charge on the king's treasury, provided they kept the Five Precepts and spent their time in monasteries and pagodas. He himself led a life of austerity and went on pilgrimages.

After a year of organization, pilgrimage, and rest, at the end of 1753 Alaungpaya with his army marched on to Ava and laid siege to it. The Mons, deciding not to make an issue of it, withdrew one night down the river in the darkness, and Alaungpaya, to conserve his army, did not interfere. In the morning Alaungpaya entered the city in triumph. He then toured the Shan states, receiving not only the allegiance of the Shan Sawbwas but also Shan levies to swell the ranks of his army. Some miles below Ava he had left an army under the command of his first and third sons, and at Ava he left a garrison under the command of his second son. Learning that Alaungpaya was in the Shan states, Dalaban, the crown prince, and Binnya Dala himself came up the river, routed the Burmese army below Ava, and laid siege to Ava itself. With a huge force Alaungpaya came down and surrounded the invading army. At a given signal his son threw open the gates and attacked the Mons. Caught between two Burmese armies, the Mons were routed and the three commanders barely made their escape to Pegu. In the meantime Burmese refugees, escaping from the general slaughter by the Mons, seized Prome and shut the gates to the retreating Mon army. The Mons laid siege to it only to be driven out by Alaungpaya. The way to Lower Burma was now open and in Lower Burma itself there were many repercussions. Some of the Mon commanders now considered that defeat was certain and tried to work out a plan to save themselves. They despised Alaungpaya as an upstart and feared his vengeance. Preferring the loose rule of a weak king, they attempted to free the captive king of Ava, whom Binnya Dala had brought back in triumph, and put him on the throne of Pegu. The plot was discovered by Binnya Dala, who executed not only the conspirators but the former king himself. This foolish action not only removed from the scene the only possible rival of Alaungpaya but also prompted those who had been still honoring their oath of allegiance to the fallen monarch to flock to Alaungpaya with an easy conscience.

Alaungpaya's victories were having their international repercussions also. "The Lord of the Striped Elephant" was courteously asked by the ruler of Chengmai to leave his principality since his presence might give an excuse for Binnya Dala to protest. So he crossed the frontier into Siam, but the king of Siam did not quite know what to do with him and suggested that he should go to China to get assistance to fight Binnya Dala. The Chinese were not interested, however, so he returned to Chengmai as an unwelcome guest. The king of Siam, who had feared the rising power of the Mons, now feared Alaungpaya's growing might but was still uncertain about the Mons, especially because the French were well entrenched at Pegu. Hoping to kill two birds with one stone, he encouraged "The Lord of the Striped Elephant" to declare himself as king of Pegu and to send out letters to the Mons saying that Binnya Dala was a traitor with no right to the throne of Pegu. "The Lord of the Striped Elephant" was careful to take a new title so as to disassociate himself from the original rebellion whose leaders had elected him as king. Some of the letters fell into Alaungpaya's hands, and he sent a messenger to the ruler of Chengmai and "The Lord of the Striped Elephant" ordering them to say no more on the matter but to come and swear allegiance to him. Both came meekly and Alaungpaya reappointed the ruler to Chengmai but kept "The Lord of the Striped Elephant" a prisoner, although in comfort and honor. The latter was quite happy with the arrangement; spending the rest of his days in the solace of religion, he died a natural death some years later.

Just as Alaungpaya was winning his first victories in 1752, Bruno duly returned to Pegu as the resident representative of the French and became in effect the political and military adviser to the

Mons. The English East India Company was thoroughly alarmed at the influence Bruno had over the Mons, and since further negotiations with the Mons would be fruitless it ordered a strong expedition to occupy Cape Negrais by force and build a factory there. Negrais was an unhealthy place, unsuitable for either a trading station or a naval outpost, but for reasons of both strategy and prestige the English continued to maintain the settlement. By that time Alaungpaya had fully established himself in Upper Burma, and both the French and the English reconsidered their positions, wanting to back the winning horse. Dupleix went so far as to send a present of arms to Alaungpaya, who accepted them but went on regarding the French as his enemy. Accordingly, Alaungpaya sent to the English at Negrais a protest at their occupation of his Burmese territory, but offered to cede it in exchange for arms. However, neither the French nor the English were in a position to spare any substantial consignment of arms to the combatants, for they themselves were poised for battle in India.

In 1755 Alaungpaya came down and attacked the Mons in Lower Burma, who retreated to the two fortified cities of Pegu and Syriam. Bypassing Pegu he took the port of Dagon, and to encourage his followers he renamed it Rangoon or "end of opposition" and held a great victory parade at the foot of the Shwedagon pagoda. His forces detained a number of French and English ships found lying in the harbor, but he refrained from seizing them and called upon the captains to await further instructions, because he wanted to act according to international law and usage although he needed arms and ammunition desperately. He gave an interview to Bruno, who had come from Syriam to see him about the ships, but he became angry when the French ships suddenly weighed anchor and sailed away. Then he detained the English ships but merely to request the captains to sell him some of the muskets and cannons they carried on their ships. The captains had been selling arms to the Mons, but not thinking that Alaungpaya could ever take Syriam they did not want to incur the hostility of the Mons at Syriam by supplying

Alaungpaya with arms. Moreover, whatever their company's view might be, they were personally in sympathy with the Mons.

Alaungpaya thus found himself ill equipped to storm Syriam, and on receiving an urgent report that Manipuri horsemen were again raiding Burmese villages on the Indian frontier, Alaungpaya rushed back to Upper Burma. Soon after, the Mon crown prince and Bruno directed an attack on Rangoon from Syriam, and some English ships in the Syriam harbor, including the notorious *Arcot*, which was one of the ships freed by Alaungpaya and whose captain was a Mon sympathizer, joined in the attack. The siege failed dismally, and fearing Alaungpaya's anger the English settlement at Negrais sent a representative, Captain George Baker, to Alaungpaya at Shwebo to ask for official permission for the East India Company to maintain their settlement at Negrais. Alaungpaya no longer trusted the English but because he was pleased with the cannons and muskets Baker brought he sent back the agent with a promise that he would consider the matter when he came down to Rangoon to take Syriam.

Alaungpaya settled the Manipuri problem by sending a strong punitive force to Manipur, which paid the Manipuris back in kind by looting, killing, and burning their villages. Thousands of prisoners were taken and re-settled in Burma. The captured Manipuri horsemen were forced to serve in Alaungpaya's cavalry, and the Manipuri astrologers who incited the raiders were also brought to the king's capital and made to serve the court by working out astronomical and astrological predictions. In 1756 Alaungpaya again went to Rangoon and directed operations against Syriam. Even before he arrived, the Burmese garrison at Rangoon had already stopped all communications between Syriam and Pegu. The inhabitants of Syriam were starving but the port was still well defended under the direction of Bruno himself. Alaungpaya was in a good mood and granted audiences to the representatives of the English at Negrais. In return for vital military equipment, which they undertook to supply, Alaungpaya gave official permission for the settlement to remain at Negrais and for another factory to be built at Bassein. He also delivered to the English representatives a letter on gold leaf addressed to the king of England conveying his felicitations on the occasion of the first official contact between the king of Burma and the king of England. Then Alaungpaya laid siege to Syriam in earnest, but eight months went by and the city had not fallen. He needed more arms and ammunition, and when his requests were not fully met by the settlement at Negrais he began to suspect that the English were deliberately keeping him in short supply.

In the meantime Bruno was sending message after message to Pondicherry for reinforcements. Alaungpaya became anxious lest French ships should arrive from India to break the siege, and so he called for volunteers. He selected ninety-three out of those who came forward and instructed them to scale the walls. One dark night this company of commandos, known later as "The Golden Company of Syriam," successfully scaled the walls and after desperate hand-to-hand fighting they opened the gates for their comrades. Bruno and his French gunners fought back but were soon overcome. The following morning in the market square Alaungpaya heaped the gold and silver captured in the city and presented it as reward to some twenty survivors of the Golden Company and to the families of those who had fallen. Two or three days later three relief ships with cargoes of arms and ammunition and food arrived, and the Burmese succeeded in capturing two of them. Bruno and a few of his senior officers were executed, and the rest of the French contingent were either impressed into royal service or re-settled at the Roman Catholic villages in Upper Burma, where the descendants of de Brito's followers were living.

Alaungpaya proceeded to Myanaung, a small town below Prome, to consolidate his position before attacking the last Mon stronghold at Pegu. There he received a representative of the English, Ensign Lester, because he was no longer suspicious of the intentions of the English. He granted a document with these stipulations: (1) The king would grant to the East India Company Cape Negrais together with a plot of land in Bassein with permission to build a factory on it. (2) The king would permit the East India Company to trade without any let or hindrance in all parts of the kingdom. (3) The East India Company would present to the king every year a supply of cannons, muskets, and ammunition. (4) The king would permit the company to open a trade center at Rangoon. (5) The king would reimburse to the company the cost of any operation it had to undertake against any enemy of the king. (6) The company would undertake not to assist in any way the enemies of the king. Alaungpaya then started the siege of Pegu. A delegation of Mon monks came out to meet the Burmese and attempted to negotiate a peace between their king and Alaungpaya, who rejected their proposals courteously but firmly. Binnya Dala then started his own negotiations for surrender, sending his only daughter as a peace offering. Alaungpaya was sympathetic and, receiving the princess with great ceremony, raised her to the rank of a queen.

Some of the Mon commanders proved adamant however. Dalaban, disgusted with the power struggle among his own commanders, slipped out of the city into the Sittang region. The no-surrender party among the commanders carried the day; dethroning Binnya Dala, they called back the negotiators, closed the gates, and defied Alaungpaya to do his worst. Soon the city fell, Binnya Dala and his family were captured, and Alaungpaya returned to Shwebo with the royal captives. The whole of Lower Burma now accepted Alaungpaya, but Dalaban fought on until he was captured and pardoned by Alaungpaya. In spite of the harshness shown to the Burmese by the Mons during the period of their supremacy, Alaungpaya's policy was conciliatory, and many local Mon officials were given back their appointments.

Unfortunately for both Burmese and Mons, the Manipuris started their raids again, and Alaungpaya had to lead his armies into Manipur. This time it had to be not a mere punitive expedition but a campaign of conquest. The Mons thought that Alaungpaya was too preoccupied with the Manipuri problem and, in any case, was too far away to come down in person to Lower Burma. So they rose in rebellion, massacred the Burmese all over the delta, and drove out the Burmese viceroy from Pegu. The English at Negrais were indeed involved in this rebellion, as the captured rebels later testified. Just before the rebellion broke out the *Arcot* entered the Rangoon harbor and gave or sold arms and ammunition to the Mons. Alaungpaya rushed down to Rangoon, but his intervention proved unnecessary because the rebellion had been suppressed by the local garrisons. Alaungpaya was embittered by this uprising, which he considered to be an act of treachery and a poor return for his magnanimity toward the Mons. Fearing his vengeance, the Mons in great numbers crossed the frontier into Siam, where they were again welcomed because Siam was now worried at seeing a strong Burma emerging again.

Alaungpaya was also disappointed with the English. The testimony of the rebel prisoners and the presence of the *Arcot* in the harbor on the eve of the rebellion, combined with the fact that he had received no reply to his letter to the king of England, convinced him that the English regarded him as an upstart king who must be got rid of. He considered himself no longer bound by his agreement with the East India Company, as the company itself had broken it; he therefore passed orders to take back Negrais, burn down the factory, and massacre all the servants of the company found therein. Since there was no evidence that the factory at Bassein was involved in the rebellion in any way he gave strict orders that it should not be molested. Alaungpaya was weary and disappointed and would have preferred to spend the remaining years of his life in peace, engaged in the rehabilitation of his country. However, the continued migration of Mons into Siam, and Siam's attitude toward his kingdom, convinced him that unless Siam gave assurances that it would not intervene in Burmese affairs there could be no peace, because the Mons would always be plotting and planning to rebel and win back Lower Burma. Some historians have suggested that Alaungpaya, ambitious and aggressive, wanted to include Siam in his empire because the first Burmese empire of Pagan and the second Burmese empire of Bayinnaung had covered not only Siam but the entire Menam valley. This estimate of Alaungpaya's character is unfair. As the Arakanese did not show any hostility toward him he never invaded Arakan although Sandoway sent him tribute even at the time of his early victories. Even with Siam he was at first patient, merely requesting its king to surrender some of the Mon rebel leaders in Siamese territory.

It was Siam that started hostilities. The king of Siam improved the defenses of Ayuthia and took up prepared positions all along the routes that the previous Burmese expeditions had followed. Then units of the Siamese army attacked the Burmese town of Tavoy in the south, and Alaungpaya led an army to the Tenasserim coast and won back the region, which had been held by Siam since the death of Bayinnaung. Then he crossed the narrow isthmus and marched northward to Ayuthia. He met with no strong resistance because the Siamese armies were massed to the north and west of Ayuthia. He laid siege to it in April 1760, hoping to take it before the monsoon. Alaungpaya sent envoys into Ayuthia, calling upon the king to surrender because he was a man destined to be a Buddha and desired to avoid bloodshed if possible. The king of Siam sent back an insulting reply: "In the lifetime of this present universe, there will appear only five Buddhas. Four have already appeared, and the one who would appear as the Fifth Buddha is now living in the abode of the gods. Surely, there cannot be a Sixth Buddha." As Alaungpaya prepared for an assault on the city, the Siamese king, after reconsidering his position, sent his own envoys to negotiate for peace, but Alaungpaya's terms were found unacceptable and negotiations broke down completely.

As Alaungpaya prepared an assault on the city he suddenly became ill. According to Siamese sources, he was wounded by the bursting of a shell from a battery whose installation he was personally supervising, but the Burmese sources definitely stated that he became sick with dysentery. There is no reason why these sources should attempt to hide the truth, for surely it is more glorious for a hero to

die of wounds received on the battlefield than to die of a common ail-
ment. Moreover, if he had been wounded in full view of the army,
the fact of the seriousness of the injury would have become known
to the whole army, creating consternation and confusion. Only a
handful of top commanders knew the nature of his sickness, however; putting him on a litter, they ordered a general withdrawal, giving the excuse that the king was indisposed. Under the famous
commander Minkhaung Nawrahta 5,000 musketeers with batteries
remained at Ayuthia, and the whole operation was conducted so
efficiently and smoothly that the Siamese did not realize the main
army had retreated. Alaungpaya died when the main army had
crossed the frontier and approached Thaton. The commanders kept
his death a secret for another fortnight and sent a horseman with the
news to Alaungpaya's eldest son at Shwebo, suggesting his immediate
ascension to the throne. Swathed in bandages lined with herbs to
prevent decomposition, the body of the king lay in a curtained litter,
and every sunrise and sunset the commanders came to the litter and
issued the daily orders in his name. Across the frontier Minkhaung
Nawrahta slowly retreated, fighting a brilliant rear-guard action
against the entire Siamese army come in pursuit, and against both
Mon and Siamese guerrillas. With surprisingly small losses he
brought his musketeers to safety.

The death of Alaungpaya at the early age of forty-six and at the
height of his physical and mental powers was a grievous loss to the
Burmese and adversely affected the course of their history. He had
led his people in waging war, but his leadership was still sorely
needed to wage a peace. He had roused his people to the fever heat
of nationalism, but he was denied the time and the opportunity to
calm them down to tolerance and restraint. It would be redundant
to dwell long on his qualities or on his achievements. He reigned for
only eight years, but during that short period what changes had been
wrought! When he seized the throne in 1752 he found a people
divided and broken, humiliated and ashamed, and when he died in
1760 he left to his successors a people united and confident, holding

up their heads again in pride and in glory. The achievements of Alaungpaya and his comrades once more emphasized and illustrated the democratic nature of Burmese society, where all men and women were deemed equal, where there was no hard and fast division into different social classes, where the "aristocracy" was open to talent and character alone, and where the same monastic education prepared the king's son and the farmer's son to

> Raise a ladder to the sky,
> For they are swift and strong and able.

Alaungpaya once casually remarked that he wanted all of his six sons in turn to take his place on the throne, but he made no official declaration or arrangement regarding the succession, for obviously he did not expect to die so soon. His eldest son, Naungdawgyi, of course, was the first heir, but the second son, the prince of Myedu, who was later to become king with the title of Hsinbyushin, was the most fiery of the brothers and did not approve of his elder brother's succession because he, prince of Myedu, wanted to march back to Ayuthia and win the city. He had been taking part in the siege of Ayuthia with his father, and he assumed command of the army on Alaungpaya's death. The prince of Myedu attempted to pressure his commanders into choosing him as king, but the commanders refused to give him support. He had hoped especially for the support of the brilliant rear-guard commander Minkhaung Nawrahta, because Naungdawgyi and Minkhaung Nawrahta had never got on well together as fellow commanders in Alaungpaya's early campaigns.

The army was still in Lower Burma, although the body of the dead king had been carried up the river for cremation at Shwebo. Hearing of the abortive attempt to seize the throne, Naungdawgyi summoned both his younger brother and Minkhaung Nawrahta to the capital. The prince of Myedu obeyed the summons, and through the intercession of the queen mother Naungdawgyi pardoned him. Minkhaung Nawrahta, because of the old enmity between them, was suspicious of Naungdawgyi's intentions and deliberately slowed down his journey to Shwebo, meaning to wait for developments. Naungdawgyi now ordered his arrest, and although he had not been involved in Myedu's conspiracy, he felt sure that he would be stripped of his command and probably executed by Naungdawgyi on some excuse. He had been a simple villager in 1752, and he had fought in all the campaigns, shoulder to shoulder with Alaungpaya. He looked back on the eventful years, the victories that had come his way, and the titles and honors that had been showered upon him by his grateful master. He said to his followers,

I was a common villager, when I drew my sword and said to my lord, "My friend, my comrade, the Mons are winning everywhere, and thou must defeat them. With this sword, I shall make thee king or die in the attempt." But those days are gone and my gracious master, who alone could help me in this crisis, is no more. This is no time for regret or fear, and I must strike, come what may.

So he led his followers into the gates of Ava and took possession of it. Naungdawgyi's troops surrounded the city and Minkhaung Nawrahta fought his way out to the north. He was pursued by royal forces, but he had no definite plan of rebellion—it was merely a gesture of defiance. He was hit by a chance shot from one of his old musketeers and was thus killed. Naungdawgyi was shaken by this tragedy but worse was yet to come.

Alaungpaya's uncle, the viceroy of Toungoo, and some of the senior commanders rose in rebellion, but again it was more a gesture of protest at the treatment given to Minkhaung Nawrahta than a real rebellion. They were easily defeated, but Naungdawgyi, remarking that he was weary and unhappy over these developments, not only pardoned them but restored them to all their offices. Incidentally it should be noted that, following the administrative pattern set by Tharlun Min, Alaungpaya was reluctant to appoint many viceroys and as a result, in addition to the viceroy of the Seven Hill Districts, he appointed only two viceroys, one at Toungoo and another at Pegu, and they were in the nature of special and personal appointments; with the death of the two incumbents, the offices automatically became mere governorships. Naungdawgyi had been a brilliant commander himself, but he was tired of war. Nonetheless he was constrained to send an expedition to Chengmai because the ruler there, although Burmese by race, decided to declare his independence, hoping to get assistance from Ayuthia. The expedition took Chengmai and then marched right up to the Chinese frontier, demonstrating Burmese control over the entire region. Naungdawgyi recalled those troops, being satisfied with the re-conquest of Chengmai, and spent the few months that remained of his reign in pilgrimage to the pagodas at Sagaing, Ava, and Pagan. He died in 1763. As he left an only son barely twelve months old, there was none to dispute the succession to the throne of the militant prince of Myedu, who took the title of Hsinbyushin, "Lord of the White Elephant," and moved the capital from Shwebo to Ava.

Hsinbyushin's aim to conquer Siam was too well known for the Siamese to remain quiet when they received the news of his succession to the Burmese throne. So the king of Siam sent encouragement and assistance to Chengmai to rise in rebellion again, and Hsinbyushin sent an army to re-take Chengmai. The Burmese army easily overran Chengmai and went on to occupy Laos. To counteract this victory the king of Siam sent encouragement and assistance to the Mon governor of Tavoy to declare his independence. Hsinbyushin sent another army to re-take Tavoy, which was done without much trouble or loss. Then Hsinbyushin ordered the Burmese army at Laos to march south and the Burmese army at Tavoy to march north. The army from Tavoy followed a route different from that taken by Alaungpaya, and the army from Laos went down the Mekong by boat. There was no need for surprise, however, because unlike on the eve of Alaungpaya's invasion Siamese preparations to inflict losses on the invaders before they could reach Ayuthia were inadequate. But it took the two armies over a year to reach Ayuthia because they carefully occupied places on their way so as to obtain fresh recruits.

When in January 1766 the two Burmese armies met before the gates of Ayuthia, they had amassed a force of some 50,000, which however was just equal to the force that the king of Siam had collected at Ayuthia. The Siamese king, holding that he had the advantage over the Burmese because his army consisted of experienced soldiers and the Burmese army contained many units hastily recruited in Chengmai and Laos, ordered a frontal attack. The battle began, and the Siamese, concentrating their attack on the right wing of the Burmese army, forced it to retreat. It was however a disciplined retreat, and by no means a rout, but the Siamese thinking that victory was within their grasp pursued the retreating Burmese. The left wing of the Burmese army, bringing in fresh reserves, slowly wheeled round and attacked the Siamese army from behind. Surprised at this maneuver, the Siamese paused to consider what counteraction to take, and that gave time to the Burmese right wing to re-form their ranks and counterattack the Siamese. The Burmese commander of the musketeers then borrowed a page from history; as Kublai Khan's bowmen had done the musketeers fired their shots at the Siamese elephants, which in great pain threw their riders and trampled the foot soldiers. Then the Burmese fired their cannons into the confused ranks of the Siamese army, and the encounter ceased to be a battle and became a carnage. Only a small number of Siamese soldiers escaped the slaughter and reached safety behind the walls of Ayuthia.

The defenses of Ayuthia had been carefully strengthened during the long march of the two Burmese armies toward it, and therefore the Burmese set themselves a difficult task in deciding to besiege the city. It was necessary to guard not only the approaches to the city by land but also the approaches by various streams and canals. Four months went by and as the monsoon broke the Siamese gave a sigh of relief, thinking that the Burmese would be forced to withdraw. But the Burmese commanders had covered every high ground with brick enbankments, on which were mounted batteries that continued to fire salvos in the incessant rain. In addition, the

Burmese soldiers had constructed thousands of boats and rafts, and as if they were on a picnic they sailed over the flooded fields and around the city, preventing any exits or entries. A Siamese prince who had deliberately stayed outside the city collected a force of some 10,000 soldiers and attacked the Burmese, but he and his forces were easily defeated. When the monsoon was over the Burmese constructed mounds of earth around the city, from which they fired over the walls. Within the city itself there was the usual difference of opinion whether to surrender or to fight on. A few commanders, including the famous Pra Taksin, fought their way out of the city in cover of darkness.

The commander-in-chief of the Burmese forces then died of sickness, and at this juncture news was received of a Chinese invasion of Burma in the north. Hsinbyushin sent a message by relays of horsemen, instructing the army to carry on until it had taken Ayuthia, no matter what was happening in Burma itself, for he feared that the Siamese, taking advantage of the situation, might invade Lower Burma. The Siamese king now sued for peace, and the Burmese replied that it was too late for negotiation. In April 1767 the Burmese dug tunnels below the foundation of the walls and, filling them with straw and firewood, set fire to them. When a portion of the walls crumbled, the Burmese troops entered and took the city. Contrary to accounts given in Siamese sources, there were no massacres of the inhabitants but all were taken prisoner, including the king himself and his entire court. The city was stripped of all valuables and then burned; the walls were leveled and the moats filled, and all the prisoners were taken back to Burma. As with Bayinnaung's conquest of Ayuthia, the Burmese took back with them dancers, musicians, artists, artisans, physicians, astrologers, weavers, gold- and silversmiths, scholars, poets, and so on. The result was a renaissance of Burmese literature and art.

China naturally was perturbed at the growing political and military power of the third Burmese empire. To add to this anxiety, Burmese incursions in the Shan states and the Menam valley had their repercussions on the Burma-China border. The remnants of the Gwe Shans, who had been driven out of the Ava region by the Burmese and refused permission by the Sawbwas to enter their states, withdrew to the frontier and crossed and re-crossed it again and again as a roving band of robbers. Some Sawbwas on the outlying parts of the Shan states, when dismissed from their positions by the Burmese, took refuge in Yunnan and pleaded for assistance to regain their lost status. The occupation of Laos had taken the Burmese army right up to the Laos-China border. The wrath of the Chinese fell first on Kengtung, the eastern-most state of the Shan plateau, because its Sawbwa was very loyal to the Burmese.

The Chinese were looking for some excuse to attack the Burmese, when in a drunken brawl between some Chinese and Burmese residents in Kengtung state a Chinese was killed. The Sawbwa and the Burmese authorities offered full compensation to the family of the murdered Chinese and undertook to arrest and punish the person responsible for the murder. But the governor of Yunnan made a demand for the surrender of the culprit to him, which of course was a disguised demand that the Chinese suzerainty over Kengtung be admitted. The Burmese authorities and the Sawbwa naturally refused, and in 1765 the governor of Yunnan invaded Kengtung with a large army. Hsinbyushin always held an army in reserve to meet any emergency in the Shan states, and he dispatched it at once to meet the Chinese invasion. The Sawbwa with his own forces was already pushing back the invaders when the Burmese army arrived, and together the Sawbwa's forces and the Burmese army pursued the Chinese right up to the bank of the Mekong, inflicting heavy losses and killing the Chinese commander. The governor of Yunnan, on receiving news of the disaster, committed suicide.

The emperor of China appointed a new governor with instructions to subdue the Burmese at the border. He soon was able to defeat small Burmese detachments, but he did not realize that the encounters were not battles but mere skirmishes, and the Burmese detachments were merely on patrol duties. He became ambitious and thought that Upper Burma could easily be occupied. He sent back rather imaginative reports, which gradually won the emperor to his view. In approving the proposed invasion of Upper Burma, the emperor gave instructions that the kingdom should be turned into a protectorate with his own Burmese nominee on the throne. The governor accordingly sent a powerful army along the trade route to Bhamo in Upper Burma. Hsinbyushin, on receiving reports from his patrols of the movement of the Chinese army, resolved to lay a trap. He sent one army to Kaungton, a small town on the Irrawaddy a few miles below Bhamo, with orders to fortify the place. The Chinese arrived at Bhamo, which they took without much trouble because Hsinbyushin had placed only a few troops there. Encouraged by this initial success, the Chinese commander accumulated large stores of food so as to overcome the need of a long line of communication, which Burmese guerrillas could cut. Then he stormed the fortress of Kaungton. After two or three days Hsinbyushin ordered a second army to reinforce Kaungton and then to bypass it and attack Bhamo. As the second Burmese army arrived at Kaungton the Chinese commander became alarmed and threw his entire army at the fortress. That was the signal for the second Burmese army to sail up the river and re-occupy the undefended Bhamo. In the meantime, Hsinbyushin had sent a third army by land along the western bank of the Irrawaddy with instructions to cross the river only to the north of Myitkyinna and give battle to any Chinese reinforcements which might come.

The Chinese army was now caught between the second Burmese army at Bhamo and the first Burmese army, which had come out of the fortress, and the Chinese suffered heavy losses both from wounds and through sickness. Then the Chinese retreated toward the east and then to the north, where the third Burmese army was waiting. The other two armies followed and the Chinese army was destroyed almost entirely. The Burmese went on to occupy eight Shan states within Yunnan. The governor of Yunnan, although heartbroken over the disaster, did not lose his imagination. He wrote a report to the emperor saying that Bhamo had been occupied, its Burmese inhabitants had even adopted the Manchu custom of wearing the hair in pig-tails, and the Burmese commander after losing 10,000 of his men had arrived in Yunnan to beg for peace. In view of the need to restore normal trade relations between the two countries, however, he would recommend that the Burmese commander's plea for peace be graciously accepted. The emperor, knowing from his maps that the battles were being fought well within the Chinese frontier, realized the falsity of the report and ordered the governor to come to Peking. On his arrival the governor committed suicide at the emperor's order.

The emperor now appointed his own son-in-law as the new governor of Yunnan and in 1767, when the monsoon was over, the governor sent one army to take Bhamo, and that was a mere feint. He himself led the main army toward the south through the Burmese Shan states of Hsenwi and Hsipaw. After occupying Hsenwi he executed the Sawbwa and appointed his own nominee in his place because he wanted to use the state as a base for his supplies. Leaving his second-in-command with 5,000 troops to remain at Hsenwi and guard the rear, he assigned 15,000 soldiers the task of guarding the line of communication between Hsenwi and the main army. Then the governor marched on in the direction of Ava itself. Hsinbyushin had already sent an army to hold the fort at Kaungton but could not recall it in view of the Chinese threat from the north. Then he sent one army to meet the governor of Yunnan and another to go behind him and attack his line of communication. Both armies failed to achieve their objectives. The second army was merely driven back, but the first army, outnumbered by two to one, was entirely routed by the main Chinese army under the governor. However, the survivors did not retreat but hid in the jungle waiting for reinforcements. The governor now occupied Singu on the river, some thirty miles above Ava.

Hsinbyushin was not a king who would run away from the Chinese. Instead of preparing to defend the city he quickly raised another army and ordered it to march toward Singu. His calmness in such circumstances inspired his troops and they took up positions in front of Singu. It was now March 1768, and the Upper Burmese sun in all its fury beat down on the Chinese soldiers. Near Hsenwi the second army had achieved its objective by destroying the Chinese force of 15,000 guarding the line of communication. Then the Burmese attacked the Chinese garrison at Hsenwi, overcoming it after a fierce battle, and the Chinese commander of the garrison cut his throat and died. Some of the Burmese commanders felt anxious over the Chinese threat to Ava and wanted to return to help in its defense, but their commander-in-chief said, "Our king is a soldier, and he knows what he is doing. His orders were for us to await Chinese reinforcements or the Chinese in retreat. So let us remain here."

The governor, learning that the Burmese troops were behind him, started to retreat, exposing himself to attacks from the third Burmese army. He was now attacked by the second army also, as well as the survivors of the first, who had come out of the jungle to join their comrades. The governor, gallant and able, resorted to defensive tactics, playing for time to enable the Chinese army at Bhamo to come to his relief. The Chinese commander of that army, however, hearing of the initial success of the governor and wanting to have his share of glory, stormed the fortress of Kaungton repeatedly and suffered heavy losses. Then, losing his nerve, he turned and fled until he reached Yunnan, where he was later publicly shamed and executed on the orders of the emperor. Now that the threat from the north was gone, the Burmese commander left a garrison to man the fort and led his army to join the attack on the governor's main Chinese army. Caught between three armies, the Chinese were massacred and only a handful managed to escape. The governor could have escaped with that group; but instead, after he cut off his pig-tail and sent it to the emperor as a token of his loyalty by those who were escaping, he hanged himself.

It was now a matter of honor and prestige for the emperor of

China to make yet another attempt to defeat the Burmese. By this time the Burmese armies, having left garrisons in the Siamese towns, had returned and been demobilized. The commanders were ready for another war, however, for it was obvious to them that the Chinese would try again to win Burma. Toward the end of 1769 the Chinese had built up on the frontier an army of 60,000 soldiers under the command of a famous Manchu general. Their plan was to make three separate invasions at the same time. The first army was to march down the western bank and the second army to march down the eastern bank of the Irrawaddy; a third army was to attack Bhamo. Hsinbyushin assigned the task of defending Kaungton to the same commander who had so gloriously defended it against two previous invasions. Another army was sent to meet the Chinese on the western bank and a third army to meet them on the eastern bank. Realizing from past experience the importance of cutting the line of communication of the Chinese army, Hsinbyushin sent a fourth army charged with the sole task of breaking the line and preventing the Chinese army from receiving fresh supplies of food and arms.

The Chinese commanders from the beginning seemed to have been suffering from a sense of inferiority; they delayed too long on the way and were from the beginning on the defensive. The army that crossed to the western bank re-crossed the river on the approach of the Burmese army. The Chinese army on the eastern bank also did not advance. They probably thought the key to victory was to build a fort as strong as Kaungton and force the Burmese to waste their troops in storming it. Obviously they assumed that it was Kaungton that had inflicted the defeats on the Chinese armies on the previous occasions, and so they had brought with them a full regiment of carpenters. The three Chinese armies made a combined attack on Bhamo, which they easily occupied. Then at the small village of Shwenyaungbin, halfway between Bhamo and Kaungton, they started to build a fortress much larger than Kaungton. The next step was for the carpenters to build hundreds of boats; sailing down the river in those boats, the first Chinese army bombarded Kaungton continuously for many days, while the second army stormed it from the eastern bank. The Burmese army sent to cut the enemy line of communication had now achieved its purpose and was gradually closing in on the Chinese on the Irrawaddy river. Hsinbyushin sent a flotilla of war boats from Ava, which attacked and sank the Chinese boats, drowning almost the entire army. It served as a signal for all three Burmese armies to converge on the Chinese fortress. After a fierce battle the fortress fell, and the survivors ran to join their comrades on the eastern bank who were attacking Kaungton. Desperately they stormed the fort in waves, only to be mowed down by the guns from the fort. The attacks gradually ceased and the Chinese found themselves surrounded by a ring of Burmese soldiers.

Just as the Burmese troops were poised for the kill, urgent orders arrived from the Chinese emperor instructing his commanders to withdraw immediately and return to Yunnan. "The Burmese are guilty of heinous crimes and deserve to be crushed and destroyed," said the imperial communication, "but the great emperor in his magnanimity grants them his pardon and decides to end the war." The Chinese commanders now sued for terms, and the Burmese commanders refused to negotiate until Maha Thiha Thura, the conqueror of Ayuthia, who was the commander-in-chief said, "Comrades, unless we make peace, yet another invasion will come, and when we have defeated it yet another invasion will come. Our nation cannot go on just repelling invasion after invasion of the Chinese, for we have other things to do. Let us stop this slaughter and let their people and our people live and trade in peace." The commanders were not convinced, but Maha Thiha Thura, on his own responsibility and without informing the king, demanded that the Chinese agree to the following terms: (1) The Chinese would surrender all the Sawbwas and other rebels and fugitives from Burmese justice who had taken shelter in the Chinese territory. (2) The Chinese would undertake to respect Burmese sovereignty over those Shan states that had been historically part of the Burmese empire. (3) All prisoners of war would be released. (4) The emperor of China and the king of Burma would resume friendly relations as before, regularly exchanging embassies bearing letters of good will and presents.

The Chinese readily accepted the demands, first because they had no choice, and second because the fourth stipulation gave them a loophole that would save their necks when the time came for them to appear before the emperor. The Chinese had always claimed suzerainty over the whole of southeast Asia, and to them all embassies were tribute missions. Just as the Europeans in the nineteenth century did not realize this Chinese conception of the purpose of embassies, the Burmese commanders never thought that any of the stipulations, more or less extracted from the Chinese army at sword's point, could be misinterpreted or misunderstood in any way. In any case, the Chinese were allowed to depart in peace, although they were later to die in thousands through sickness and starvation on their long way home. The Chinese emperor was not quite pleased with the explanations given by his commanders regarding the fourth stipulation in the treaty, so he did not permit the surrender of the fugitive Sawbwas and rebels, nor the resumption of trade between the two countries. Because the Chinese would not surrender the fugitives the Burmese refused to return the Chinese prisoners they still held as hostages. Nonetheless the treaty ended the war. As for Hsinbyushin, he was furious and tore up his copy of the treaty. Fortunately for the commanders Manipur rose in rebellion, taking advantage of the Chinese invasion, and without waiting for orders from the king they marched to Manipur and suppressed the rebellion, which gave time for the king's anger to subside.

Although Burmese opinion at the time was divided concerning the wisdom of Maha Thiha Thura in making peace with the Chinese, posterity must praise him not only for his wisdom but also for his selflessness. He could easily have destroyed all the Chinese troops and then come back to Ava to receive the acclamations of the king and the people. But, as he pointed out to his commanders, war with the Chinese was swiftly becoming a cancer that would finally destroy the nation. Compared to Chinese losses, Burmese losses were light, but considered in proportion to the population of the country they were heavy. He took the blame entirely on himself, and facing certain dishonor and possible loss of his life under the king's justice he made the peace. Whatever Chinese records may say, the Burmese defeated four massive Chinese invasions within the short space of some four years, and whatever Siamese sources may say, it was the Chinese invasions of Burma that really enabled them to regain the independence lost with the fall of Ayuthia. Just as the Burmese took on their shoulders the full brunt of the Tatar invasions in the thirteenth century, they took the full brunt of the Chinese invasions in the eighteenth; and if the Burmese had failed in the eighteenth century as they did in the thirteenth, southeast Asia would have fallen to the Chinese and the course of its history would have been different.

The immediate effects of the treaty on the Burmese people were unfortunate. There was dissension in the army and also at court over the rights and wrongs of Maha Thiha Thura's action, and the prestige of the king and the commander were lowered to a certain extent. In addition, Hsinbyushin had declared his own son, the prince of Singu, to be his heir although his four younger brothers were still living, but the king's action had the support of Maha Thiha Thura because Singu was married to his daughter. Above all, the Burmese as a nation became drunk with victory and grew arrogant and aggressive. They showed their arrogance especially to the defeated Mons who were still living in Lower Burma, provoking them to rebel in 1773 at the instigation of their compatriots in Siam. The rebellion was put down without undue severity, but thousands of Mons again fled into Siam to swell the forces of Pra Taksin, who had founded a new capital farther down the Menam river and declared himself king of Siam. Since the Mon rebels had conspired to free Binnya Dala to put him back on the throne, Hsinbyushin ordered his execution in spite of the fact that Alaung-paya had spared his life.

In 1775 Hsinbyushin ordered a fresh invasion of Siam in an attempt to capture Pra Taksin. Again the invasion was led by Maha Thiha Thura, but none of the Burmese commanders was now enthusiastic. Knowing that Hsinbyushin was sick and dying and the palace was full of rumors and intrigues, they behaved with arrogance. They were arrogant to the few Mons who were still loyal to the Burmese king, and they were inconsiderate even to the Burmese governor of Chengmai, who could not bear to see his subjects treated with contempt by the Burmese commanders. Hsinbyushin sent order after order instructing them to curb their arrogance, but feeling certain that he was soon to die they took no notice of his instructions. Finally their spiteful behavior drove the governor of Chengmai to join Pra Taksin and to declare Chengmai to be part of Siam. The same arrogance prompted the people of Laos to accept Siamese suzerainty. Maha Thiha Thura himself suffered an initial defeat but took back the northern part of Siam; he repulsed attacks by Pra Taksin and his fellow commander, Pra Chakra, who was later to depose and execute Pra Taksin and seize the throne for himself. Maha Thiha Thura remained as courteous and chivalrous as before, and after a battle in which Pra Chakra fought brilliantly but was defeated he sent a message to Chakra to come and receive his congratulations in an hour of truce. Trusting him, Chakra appeared, and Maha Thiha Thura offered his congratulations, remarking, "You have the bearing of a king. Perhaps you will be king one day." In 1776 Hsinbyushin died and as Maha Thiha Thura was more interested in seeing his son-in-law, Singu, ascend the throne without any mishap, he ordered a general withdrawal of the Burmese forces and hurried back to Ava.

It was his father-in-law's support that made it possible for Singu to ascend the throne, but there were secret murmurs questioning his right and suitability to be king, and intrigues and power struggles continued in the palace circles and among the army commanders. Hsinbyushin had kept his four younger brothers in the background, but the one next to him, the Prince of Amyint, had taken part in the campaigns of Alaungpaya; with the encouragement of some of his old comrades he attempted to find support for an attempt at the throne, and Singu promptly executed him. He exiled the remaining three brothers, his own uncles. He also exiled the other two possible claimants to the throne, Alaungpaya's son by the second queen, the Prince of Sitha, and Naungdawgyi's son, the Lord of Hpaungsar. Reflecting his people's general weariness of war, he demobilized the armies and spent his time on pilgrimages. But he was not by nature religious and soon decided to enjoy life in another way. Surrounding himself with gay, young people, anti-war in temperament like himself, he spent his days at the palace listening to music and poetry, and his nights in drunken bouts in a hideout across the river. He executed or dismissed those courtiers who criticized his conduct. He even dismissed his father-in-law, Maha Thiha Thura, the king-maker, who now looked for a substitute to take the throne.

Knowing of the general discontent with the king at the court, and of the intrigues and plots to dethrone Singu, the lord of Hpaungsar gained entry to the palace one night by pretending to be the drunken Singu and thereby seized it. Hearing of the rebellion, Singu came back and boldly walked into the palace, only to be cut down by Hpaungsar's followers. Hpaungsar recalled Maha Thiha Thura to office and made him the chief minister. Together they recalled Alaungpaya's surviving three sons from exile and placed them under arrest. The fourth son, the Prince of Badon, escaped from prison with the help of some commanders, seized the throne, and executed the lord of Hpaungsar, who ruled for just seven days. The new king, later known to Burmese history as Bodawpaya, attempted to win the support of the old king-maker by confirming his appointment as chief minister. But Maha Thiha Thura could not tolerate Bodawpaya because he was too strong a king, and he therefore conspired to put the prince of Sitha on the throne. Bodawpaya was driven out of the palace but his followers rallied and put down the rebellion. Bodawpaya had no respect for the past and immediately executed the old hero, together with the prince of Sitha and their supporters. Then a follower of Hpaungsar gathered a band of robbers and attacked and held the palace. Again the rebellion was suppressed and the leaders massacred. The fifth son of Alaungpaya then claimed the throne with the help of some commanders, but by that time Bodawpaya had become adept at putting down rebellions and executing the participants wholesale. The Mons in Lower Burma then rose in rebellion and held Rangoon for a time. Bodawpaya used it as an excuse to introduce the sternest measures against the Mons, who fled in thousands to Siam. These blood-baths eliminated Bodawpaya's possible rivals and many of the top commanders of Hsinbyushin's reign. Only one possible claimant to the throne survived, the sixth son of Alaungpaya; however, he was timid, shy, and unambitious and Bodawpaya was quite fond of him. This prince led a quiet life and died a natural death toward the end of Bodawpaya's reign.

Bodawpaya, like all fourth brothers in Burmese folklore, was an eccentric and unpredictable figure, but he was no fool. During the reign of Hsinbyushin and Singu he had cut rather a pathetic figure, lonely and neglected, keeping himself in the shadows to escape notice, arrest, and possible execution. He had no contact with the glorious personages of Hsinbyushin's reign whose names were being written in history. Courageous and physically fit, he had received no military training and was treated with some contempt by his elder brothers and the army commanders. Now that he had gained power beyond his wildest dreams, he was determined that there should be no challenge to his authority from any quarter. He grew into a despot and a tyrant, but he had the full support of his people, who, after long years of war and a period of unseemly power struggle at the royal court, desired peace and stability above all things. The country was fortunate in that there was one who could curb the despotism and wild ideas of Bodawpaya, the minister U Paw U. This minister was a learned scholar as eccentric as his master. He held no portfolios and acted as both jester and adviser to the king, and he saved many lives by his jests at the risk of his own life. When Bodawpaya in the later years of his reign announced that he was a Future Buddha, both the clergy and the people resented his claim. U Paw U first flattered and then jeered the king into realizing that he was unworthy.

Bodawpaya's model was not his illustrious father, Alaungpaya, but Tharlun Min, because his aim was to centralize the government. He had subdued the turbulent army commanders by wholesale executions, and now he was determined to suppress the turbulent clergy by wholesale unfrockings. Alaungpaya had supported the reform sect by appointing a primate from that sect and thus put down the controversy. However, with the death of Alaungpaya the primate had lost his office automatically and Hsinbyushin was too much of a soldier to take an interest in the renewal of controversy among the monks. In any case his reign was but one continuous campaign. Singu appointed a primate from the orthodox sect, but the controversy did not end. Bodawpaya was reluctant to share authority even with a primate and he appointed, instead, a royal commission to consider the point of conflict. The commission heard witnesses and arguments put forward by both sides and then reported in favor of the orthodox sect.

Accepting the commission's report, Bodawpaya proclaimed that all monks must wear their robes in the orthodox manner and the controversy should cease forthwith. No king in the long history of Buddhism, both in Burma and outside, had ever dared to proclaim a *Vinaya* rule for the clergy and there were outcries of protest from all ranks of the clergy. Systematically Bodawpaya disrobed all monks who questioned his authority to make the proclamation. The protests did not cease, and he unfrocked the leader of the reform sect who had been Alaungpaya's primate and ordered him to be taken to Lower Burma. Bodawpaya also gave implicit instructions that at every village on the way the guards should stop the boat, exhibit the unfrocked monk, and recite the following doggerel:

> First guard: With ropes that tightly bound him,
> With swords flashing around him,
> Who is this strange creature?
> Second guard: This black-skinned creature with
> a crooked nose,
> As a scholar of the *Vinaya* he
> did pose,
> His crafty career we now close.

It was a terrible punishment for a learned scholar who had produced so many outstanding works on the religion; it is no wonder that when he was set free at Thayetmyo he made his way to Mindon and died there a few years later, unhonored and unsung. But there was no more protest against the king's proclamation.

Bodawpaya revived the ancient offices of the ecclesiastical censor and the commissioner of ecclesiastical lands. But he soon found out that without the supervision of a primate these lay officers could not function properly. Still refusing to share authority with a primate, he appointed an ecclesiastical council consisting of four abbots, and later, at their request, he increased the number to twelve. The abbots did their best, but without a chairman the council found itself in difficulties over matters of both procedure and administration and finally prevailed upon the king to appoint a primate from among their number. Bodawpaya reluctantly agreed, but to prevent the primate from ever challenging his authority, he made it clear that a decision of the primate by himself was not binding, and therefore the ecclesiastical authority did not rest with the primate alone but with the primate-in-council. The primate-in-council soon took measures as effective but not as harsh as Bodawpaya's and restored discipline and order among all ranks of the clergy.

Bodawpaya encouraged the study of the scriptures by all laymen and laywomen and built pagodas and monasteries. He was so successful in restoring prestige and discipline to the clergy that he became convinced that he was a Future Buddha. But neither the clergy nor the people accepted his contention, and under the jeers of his minister U Paw U he gradually abandoned his claim. In passing, it may be noted that the Hindu cult of the divine king in a modified form with the king as a Future Buddha remained unacceptable to the Burmese people, and only two of the great royal patrons of Buddhism were recognized as Future Buddhas—Alaungsithu and Alaungpaya, whose personalities and characters indeed must have been most unusual.

Bodawpaya then became attracted to a new conception of the Buddha, which probably was a result of contact with Christianity and Mahayana Buddhism. The new theory held that the Intellect or Reason of the Buddha did not die with his body but remained eternal and ever present in the universe. The primate challenged the king as to the truth of this new doctrine, and when the king in anger ordered him to resign his appointment he refused, daring the king to dismiss him. Even Bodawpaya did not dare to do that, although in theory the primate was a royal official and, like all royal officials, he held office at the will of the king. The king now threatened to disrobe him, but the primate questioned whether royal authority ever extended to include the right to unfrock monks. The primate was the king's own choice, and the stand now taken by the monk clearly showed how strong the clergy had become once it had got rid of its nondiscipline and abuses. After some time, however, the primate became weary of the conflict with the king and left the Order to retire as a layman. As public opinion grew strong against him, Bodawpaya announced that he must have been mad to accept the new doctrine; he executed the scholar responsible for its origin and became a contrite patron of the Buddhist clergy.

Bodawpaya took a scholarly interest in the hundreds of stone inscriptions at Pagan and Ava and ordered copies to be made. To preserve them from destruction by weather and accidents of war, he ordered many of the inscriptions to be brought to the new capital of Amarapura, which he had built a few miles above Ava. In making his officials study and preserve the inscriptions, Bodawpaya had another purpose in mind: to check the boundaries and examine the legality of the ecclesiastical lands that had to be exempted from taxation. Like Tharlun Min before him, he held an inquest of all properties and the amounts of taxes payable, and the inquest was so efficiently held that the returns from even the remotest villages were quickly received at the capital. He improved the communications of the kingdom, severely punished any negligence of those who repaired roads, and summarily executed robbers who plagued the highways and waterways.

During his reign the Hluttaw became the center of Bodawpaya's administrative system and its instructions had to be sought regularly by the governors of provinces. The sole viceroy in the whole kingdom, the viceroy of the Seven Hill Districts, was the only person who could act on his own without referring to the capital for orders. Like Bayinnaung, Tharlun Min, and Alaungpaya, he encouraged the study of Burmese customary law and publication of treatises and collections of judgments. During his reign the profession of law became especially popular and, as it was during the time of Queen Elizabeth I in England, some training in the law was considered part of a liberal education; even in the monasteries some law came to be taught, and legal treatises were read as part of literary studies. The growing importance of lawyers showed that with the restoration of peace with China and the improvement of communications under a strong and centralized government, business and commerce had rapidly developed and Burmese life had become complex. The caliber of these lawyers and the regard the king had for the law could be seen from the fact that Bodawpaya was often made a defendant in suits before the Hluttaw involving wrongful seizure of lands.

Letters written by private persons during his reign and that of his successor contained references to Burmese villagers becoming merchants and traveling up and down the river and by road to the north and to the Shan states. The same letters described how villagers from Upper Burma migrated to Bhamo, to the Shan states, and Rangoon in search of quick riches. Rangoon especially was considered to be the place where a man could get rich in a few days by sawing timber in the many dockyards that had sprung up since Alaungpaya changed the name of this ancient port. Thus a villager from the vicinity of Shwebo, signing himself jocularly as Mr. Quester after Silver, wrote to his wife as follows:

Therefore, pulling up my loin cloth with its flowery pattern of light yellow, and loosening it a little, I climb a high sawing platform, and from sunrise to sunset, with sweat from my brow falling on my big toes, I push and pull the saw, up and down, cutting the logs into thin planks. In no time and with no mistake, every hundred planks put twenty Kyats in my pocket; I want to laugh, but merely smile.

The letter was written in 1784, two years after Bodawpaya's ascension to the throne when a Burmese Kyat was valued by the British at two shillings. Since one Kyat at that time in Upper Burma was enough to feed a person for one month, the villager found his wages for sawing timber unusually high. The demand for planks that the villager mentioned was due to the popularity of the use of Burmese teak for ship-building.

Notwithstanding the conflict between the Burmese and the French during Alaungpaya's time and the subsequent execution of the French agent Bruno, the French had to make friends with the Burmese for they had no other place in the east after Mauritius to re-fit and repair their ships, and they had been using Mergui as their repair depot. Mergui of course had reverted to Burmese hands during the time of Alaungpaya. In 1783 the French even sent an envoy to Bodawpaya to get more facilities for their shipping. The British also had established dockyards at Rangoon. Apart from the military need for ships and ship repairs, the East India Company was developing the trade between India and China through their so-called country vessels. These were about five hundred tons in displacement and were built mostly at Calcutta, using Burmese teak.

As profits mounted from trade with China, these vessels increased their average tonnage to one thousand by about 1790. This increase in tonnage meant an increase in amount of teak used by the ship-builders.

According to students of Burmese literature the period of the third Burmese empire, also known as the Konbaung period after the Konbaung dynasty of Alaungpaya, should be divided into two parts, the first part ending with the passing of Singu, because of the new styles and fashions that followed the ascension of Bodaw-paya. From the point of view of history, the first period should be taken as ending on December 13, 1769, with the signing of the peace treaty between the Burmese and Chinese armies, for that period constituted an age of triumph for the Konbaung dynasty. There was a definite change in the temper and outlook of the Bur-mese people after that date, and in spite of the achievements and victories of Bodawpaya's reign the decline of the third Burmese empire began after its great victory over the Chinese.

During the first period of the Konbaung dynasty a number of prose writers and poets appeared and there were two interesting developments. The first was that these writers were all laymen and laywomen, and the second was that the writers as a general rule abandoned the use of the scriptures as their sources. There appeared also a work that could be described as the first novel in Burmese literature. In style and atmosphere it was completely different from the semi-dramatic court romances that were later to appear as a delayed result of the conquest of Ayuthia, and which would be based on the Siamese court romances of *Eenaung* and *Aindarwuntha*, which had their source in the Hindu epic of *Mahabharata*. The novel was entitled *The Jeweled Mirror*. It told of the love of a prince for a princess, and unlike in the later court romances the hero did not fall in love with other princesses. In other words, he was an unromantic hero, loving one woman only. In the court romances there would be no narration, only dialogue, for they would be semi-dramatic in form. In this first Burmese novel, in contrast, there was narration, given in prose, interspersed with dialogue, given in verse. The most famous poet of the period was the minister Letwethondra, who was found guilty of neglect of duty by Hsinbyushin and exiled to a remote village in the north of Burma. He wrote a poem expressing his longing to return to the city and describing the various religious festivals he imagined he was witnessing again. Although the festivals were described as royal ones, actually he was remembering the festivals of his own village. Impressed with the poem, Hsinbyushin recalled him from exile.

The novel and the poem were characteristic of the period in that, under the guise of court prose and poetry, the writers were actually describing the village life with which they were familiar. In other words, up to Hsinbyushin's reign the king's court was not yet removed from the life of the common people, and a certain artificiality that became the keynote in later reigns had not yet crept in. Like the giant Atlas drawing his strength from his contact with the earth, the court under Alaungpaya and Hsinbyushin drew its strength from contact with the people.

IX Burma on the Eve of the English Wars

Bodawpaya reigned from 1782 to 1819, and during this time great changes were taking place in America and in Europe that affected southeast Asia also. In China the Manchu dynasty was on the decline. In island southeast Asia the Dutch were quickly losing their control of the trade. England and France were fighting their last battles for supremacy in India. Siam under a new and progressive dynasty had not only recovered from the Burmese conquests but was again dreaming of conquering mainland southeast Asia. The English were on the eve of establishing their political and commercial supremacy in south and southeast Asia. The age of imperialism was swiftly drawing to a close in the West but a new age of imperialism was dawning in the East. It is a paradox in the history of the human race that the age which saw the spread of liberal ideas and the achievement of freedom by the peoples of America and Europe should also be the age in which the peoples of southeast Asia lost their political and economic independence. British imperialism, overwhelming India, was on the march and it was Bodawpaya's misfortune to have stood in its path.

Bodawpaya was never able to make a good impression on the English. That harsh critic of the Burmese, Captain Hiram Cox, called Bodawpaya and his court "a bunch of clowns," and even Michael Symes, who was more sympathetic toward the Burmese, described the king as "a child in his ideas, a tyrant in his principles, and a mad man in his actions." Bodawpaya's Burmese subjects looked upon him with affection, admiration, and occasionally amusement, but his Arakanese subjects hated him. Although he had no experience of the outside world, he was by nature shrewd. In spite of his eccentricities and natural impulsiveness, his long years as a prospective rival to reigning kings had taught him to act with caution in all matters; he was not quick-tempered as Hsinbyushin had been. One great disadvantage that he labored under was the absence of experienced advisers, for they had died in the power struggles before and during the first months of his reign.

Bodawpaya in 1784 decided to invade Arakan, not because he was aggressive but because he believed that continued lawlessness in that region would encourage intervention by either the British or the French. He doubtless remembered how Portuguese intrusion in Arakanese affairs had resulted in the Arakanese conquest of Nandabayin's Pegu and the establishment of de Brito's kingdom of Syriam. Conditions in Arakan in 1784 were indeed chaotic. The kingdom of Arakan had become powerful through the services of Portuguese mercenaries and pirates. About the time of de Brito's fall Arakan was also helped by the Dutch, who had opened a factory in the capital. It also went on using Portuguese pirates, and with their help Arakan still maintained a powerful navy. In 1660 the king of Arakan became involved in the power struggle for the throne of India, which resulted in Aurangzeb's becoming emperor. Aurangzeb's brother, the viceroy of Bengal, lost the struggle and escaped together with his family and some few hundred followers to Arakan, where he was well received by the king. After some time, however, the king became tempted to seize the enormous treasure brought by the fugitive prince. The prince, sensing danger, tried to return to India, but he and his followers were murdered by an angry mob. Aurangzeb, hearing of his brother's murder, sent an envoy to Arakan, protesting the massacre and demanding the surrender of the three children of the dead prince. The king refused to comply, and when the new viceroy of Bengal sent a rescue mission the king executed the three children together with a number of Indian Muslim residents at his capital. He then ordered his fleet to raid Bengal. In 1666 the viceroy defeated the Arakanese fleet, after the Portuguese mercenaries had changed sides, and he annexed the port of Chittagong. Arakan never recovered from the blow and rapidly declined. The Muslim palace guards now became king-makers and, raiding the treasury regularly, they placed one king after another on the throne. In 1710 the Arakanese people rose against the palace guards and overcame them but their leader, who became the new king, proved himself to be but another pirate. He was assassinated in 1731, but Arakan remained in chaos.

To escape from the continuing chaos, Sandoway made itself part of Alaungpaya's kingdom and invited Alaungpaya to take northern Arakan also. By that time the Mogul power in India had waned, and as there was no danger of foreign intervention Alaungpaya did not march into Arakan. Since Alaungpaya's time the position had become worse, and Bodawpaya clearly felt that unless he acted Arakan would fall to the English East India Company. Moreover, delegation after delegation of Arakanese arrived at Amarapura, pleading that Bodawpaya take over the kingdom and restore law and order. Bodawpaya sent three armies by land together with a flotilla by sea. There was no organized resistance on the part of the Arakanese king, for his authority had broken down years before. There is no doubt that the Burmese conquest of Arakan at the beginning was popular with the Arakanese people. Many Arakanese villages received the invading Burmese troops not with bullets but with drums and pipes and gongs, and the villagers danced with joy as they thought that the years of lawlessness were over. The crown prince, Bodawpaya's son, who commanded the armies, became immensely popular and was greeted as a hero and a savior. It was the arrogance of the Burmese troops that changed the Arakanese attitude. The captured king of Arakan was treated discourteously, and as a result the almost unknown king came to be looked upon as a martyr.

Thousands of Arakanese were forced to widen a mountain pass to enable the Burmese troops to take away the great Mahamuni image of the Buddha. The statue was cast in bronze and was covered with gold. Apart from its intrinsic value, it had deep historical associations and was the pride of the Arakanese people. They could forgive the hours of forced labor, they could forgive the humiliating treatment of their king and of themselves, but they could not forgive this act of piracy. All over Arakan the people wept and men said that the great image itself shed tears. In robbing Arakan of its great image the Burmese army commanders were trying to emulate the exploit of Pra Taksin in taking the Emerald Buddha from Laos to Siam. But they did not foresee the effect their action would have on the Arakanese people. The Emerald Buddha from the beginning of its history was a bone of contention. According to legend it was carved in Ceylon and was gifted to Anawrahta, but because of a storm it reached a portage kingdom and Anawrahta nearly went to war over it. Then it passed from kingdom to kingdom in the Menam valley until it reached Laos. In contrast, the Mahamuni image was a creation of Arakanese craftsmanship, and from the day it was cast it had remained in Arakan as a national treasure. It was a great feat for the Burmese army engineers to have taken this great image all the way to the Irrawaddy River through the mountain passes and then by raft to Amarapura, but Bodawpaya lost a great chance of uniting the Arakanese and the Burmese people. When the Arakanese protested the Burmese army became even more arrogant and started to deport them to Burma for re-settlement there.

In 1785 Bodawpaya invaded Siam. Some would say that the conquest of Arakan had whetted his appetite, but in fairness to him it must be pointed out that Siam, with the help of the Mon refugees, was again raiding the Burmese frontier with a view to winning back the port of Mergui so as to obtain access to the Bay of Bengal again.

Bodawpaya himself took command of the invading army, but because of poor commissariat arrangements on the part of a negligent commander, and because of his own lack of military experience, his forward forces suffered a defeat; although those troops regrouped and marched on, Bodawpaya felt discouraged and ordered a general withdrawal. In the following year he sent another army, which was also defeated; again in 1787 he sent another expedition that saw only defeat. Unlike Burma, Siam was able to buy arms and ammunition from foreign ships including even American ones. Realizing Siam's superiority in arms, Bodawpaya gave up all ideas of re-conquering Siam. In 1791, however, he was again constrained to turn his attention to Siam.

Siam's aim was to re-assert control over as much of the Malay peninsula as possible and thus restore its thirteenth-century domain. In fact, the English East India Company received the island of Penang from the sultan of a Malay peninsula kingdom because the sultan wanted British help against Siam. The sultan also wrote to the Burmese king asking for his intervention. Checked in their expansion southward, the Siamese concentrated on the re-acquisition of the Tenasserim coast. Bodawpaya sent an army to the region, which was able to defeat a Siamese army led by the king of Siam himself. To the end of his reign Bodawpaya kept a Burmese army there. In spite of the successful holding of the Tenasserim coast against Siamese aggression, Bodawpaya's campaigns in Siam not only lowered his prestige but caused more resentment against him in Arakan, because Arakanese levies were impressed for service in those expeditions.

To re-gain his popularity he expanded the irrigation system around the town of Meiktila and the great reservoir there. He also built a number of temples and began the construction of a large temple at Mingun on the opposite bank of the river above Ava. He ordered Burmese, Siamese, and Arakanese craftsmen to work together and cast a great bell for the temple, which still hangs at Mingun. It is the second largest bell in the world, smaller only than the one in the Kremlin; the Russian bell, however, is cracked and could never be sounded even from the beginning. In spite of its great beauty, the Mingun bell was cast without enthusiasm or pride of achievement, for the workers were underpaid. Wages had risen sky-high at Rangoon and at other ports in Lower Burma, but the king insisted on paying the low wages prevailing in Upper Burma. Mingun at the time was also malarial and working conditions were not satisfactory. Learning of the shortage of labor for the king's project, the army in Arakan deported more Arakanese to Mingun. To pay for his project the king raised many taxes. Unlike the great temples of Pagan, the Mingun temple was not a labor of love and its workmen, drawn from all racial groups in the country, started to whisper, "When the pagoda is completed, the great king shall die." It was not a mere protest but a bitter curse.

Although in Upper Burma the peace remained unbroken, Bodawpaya had many anxious moments because the Chinese emperor still remained petulant over the failure of his invasions, and on his instructions the governor of Yunnan occasionally sent threatening and insulting letters to the Burmese king. Bodawpaya was anxious to restore normal trade relations between the two countries. Officially the emperor had refused to honor the stipulation of the treaty of 1769 regarding trade relations, but unofficially, because of prevailing peace conditions, trade between the two countries had resumed to some extent. The Sawbwa of Bhamo and some Chinese merchants from Yunnan were especially interested in the full resumption of trade relations, and they conspired to hoodwink both the emperor and Bodawpaya. They brought a bogus mission purporting to be from the Chinese emperor, and Bodawpaya received it with due honor. When Bodawpaya sent a return mission to Peking, the conspirators arranged that the mission's own interpreter should become separated from the mission on the journey. Then as the mission arrived before the emperor the conspirators explained that the mission was bringing tribute. The emperor was pleased and ordered full resumption of trade. Sometime later the conspirators again brought a bogus mission with three beautiful Chinese girls who were said to be the emperor's granddaughters. Bodawpaya now realized that he had been fooled and put the Sawbwa of Bhamo under arrest. Whether the emperor of China ever found out the truth is not known, but the conspirators did achieve their objective —normal trade relations were restored.

Bodawpaya wanted to exchange missions with Ceylon but that proved impossible in view of the prevailing political situation in the island. The Sinhalese people succeeded in driving out the Portuguese with the help of the Dutch, but the Dutch stayed on as unwelcome guests, occupying the coastal regions they had wrested from the Portuguese. Then during the European wars in the later half of the eighteenth century the British supplanted the Dutch, so that in Bodawpaya's time only the tiny kingdom of Kandy in the central highland remained independent. Buddhism had decayed under colonial rule in the coastal regions, and although the kings of Kandy maintained the Temple of the Tooth and acted as patrons of Buddhism, they were Indian by race and Hindu by religion. Bodawpaya was distressed over the decay of Buddhism in Ceylon and was overjoyed when a Sinhalese abbot, in spite of the geographical and political difficulties of the journey, arrived at Amarapura to seek re-Ordination and to study. Bodawpaya extended his patronage to him, and when the monk prepared to return to Ceylon after a stay of some three years Bodawpaya conferred the title of Royal Teacher on him. With a show of deep devotion combined with pageantry, he escorted the monk in state to his own royal barge and waded into the water to help push it off from its moorings. This monk later founded in Ceylon the Amarapura Sect, which is still held in the highest regard by the people of Ceylon because of its austerity.

Bodawpaya was also distressed because places of Buddhist pilgrimage in India had fallen into neglect and ruin, so he sent religious missions to India with the purpose of repairing Buddhist temples and obtaining copies of various works of Buddhist interest.

201 The English Wars

But such devotion to religion by a monarch whom the East India Company considered to be a merciless tyrant roused the company's suspicion; it therefore accused the Burmese king of using the missions for a political end, namely, to encourage the Indian princes to rise against the East India Company the moment the Burmese attacked Bengal. The Burmese envoys denied this accusation, but the British stopped granting them permission to pass through Bengal. The East India Company was never able to present any evidence in support of its allegation against the missions, and it was not in the nature of Bodawpaya, in spite of his many failings, to resort to subversive activities or to use religion as a cloak to hide his actions.

Since its conquest and the removal of its great image, Arakan had been restless, and the Burmese army did not dare withdraw lest rebellion should break out. But after ten years the Arakanese had suffered so much that even the presence of the army could no longer intimidate them, and in 1794 they rose in rebellion, led by one of their own chiefs. The rebellion was easily suppressed but the survivors crossed the frontier into British territory. A Burmese army unit followed in pursuit and established a forward camp; a British force appeared and requested the Burmese to withdraw. According to European international law, the action of the Burmese army was aggression, but the Burmese had always maintained that a "right of hot pursuit" existed in international usage, and over ill-defined frontiers they had chased Shan fugitives into Yunnan and Mon fugitives into Siam. The encounter fortunately did not develop into a battle, because the colonel in command of the British forces proved sympathetic to the Burmese contention regarding the right of hot pursuit, especially because the frontier between Burmese Arakan and British Bengal had never been defined. When the Burmese commander offered to withdraw if three rebel leaders from among the mixed band of refugees and rebels were surrendered to him, the British colonel complied and the affair ended. Although modern writers on the subject make much of this incident, at the time it was considered a minor incident by both sides. The British never looked upon it as a matter involving the prestige of its rule over Bengal, and the Burmese did not think that the British were weak and fearful of Burmese might. After all, the fugitives involved were not dethroned kings or Sawbwas but mere lieutenants of the rebel chief. The rebel chief himself died sometime later without ever escaping to British territory; the rebellion petered out and the incident at the frontier was soon forgotten.

The British, now at war with Revolutionary France, were anxious lest Burmese ports should become bases for French warships to attack British ships in the Bay of Bengal, and the governor-general of India, Sir John Shore, did not desire to give any offense to the Burmese king. So at the time of the frontier incident he wrote a letter to the Burmese king explaining the British position and attitude toward the frontier incident. The king did not send a reply, probably thinking none was called for because the matter had been closed. Sir John Shore, however, became anxious over not receiving a reply and thought the time was opportune for the restoration of diplomatic relations between the East India Company and Burma, which had ended with the withdrawal of its factory from Bassein in 1762, in spite of Naungdawgyi's request that the British should continue their trade with Burma. Sir John Shore in 1795 appointed Captain Michael Symes to lead a full-fledged British mission to Burma with three assigned tasks: (1) to persuade the king to close his ports to the French, (2) to obtain a commercial treaty, and (3) to explain the British position and eliminate any hostility the king might be feeling toward the British over the frontier incident.

At first the British envoy found Burmese court etiquette rigid and burdensome, and the king was suspicious of British intentions in sending the embassy to him. After some initial difficulty Captain Symes came to understand and sympathize with Burmese views and attitudes, and Bodawpaya began to realize that European diplomatic practice had certain differences from his own. The results of the mission were on the whole satisfactory to both sides. The king emphasized a sovereign country's right to open or close its ports to any ship, but Symes felt assured that the king would never stoop to playing the French against the British, noting that there was no French influence in the Burmese court; if the ports were open to the French, they would equally be open to the British. The king did not agree to the proposed commercial treaty, but Symes was not unduly disappointed for he knew that in 1783 the French had sent an embassy to Bodawpaya to obtain a commercial treaty and had failed. Above all, Symes received from the king a letter in which he agreed to permit an agent of the East India Company to come and reside at Rangoon. In the letter the king also agreed to the new frontier arrangements under which the Burmese, instead of crossing the frontier, would send a request in writing to the British authorities to surrender Arakanese refugees who were using British territory to commit crimes in Burmese territory, and the British would surrender them. The success of the mission was due to the good sense of the king and the patience, good will, and personality of Symes himself.

In the following year, the company appointed as its agent in Rangoon Captain Hiram Cox, who proved to be the first of a long line of British officials who had the greatest contempt for the Burmese, closing their eyes deliberately to every good quality in the Burmese and looking through a magnifying glass at every bad characteristic. Even before leaving Calcutta he was at war with the world because the governor-general refused to grant him diplomatic status, and he was angry with the governor-general, Michael Symes, and Bodawpaya, whom he had yet to meet. On arrival at the king's capital he demanded recognition as an envoy, a status his own government had denied to him. He acted insolently and repeatedly boasted of the might of the British government in India and his influence over it. Such behavior had cost the Tatar envoys their heads, and it must have been quite an effort for Bodawpaya and his court to exercise their patience with the angry young Englishman. It was Captain Cox who lost his patience; speaking ill of the king, the court, and the whole nation, he left the capital suddenly for

Rangoon. The king was annoyed and ordered the authorities at Rangoon to bring Cox back to Amarapura under arrest. Cox, becoming nervous, sent an urgent message to Calcutta asking that a frigate should storm into the port of Rangoon to rescue him. Fortunately the governor-general knew his man and just ignored the request. The angry captain calmed down a little, and Bodawpaya rescinded his order to bring him to the capital. Soon after this the governor-general recalled Cox, sending to the Burmese authorities a letter apologizing for Cox's behavior. On arrival in India, Cox wrote a report defaming the king and his people, and Michael Symes as well, whom he openly accused of cheating his own government by submitting a favorable and false report about the Burmese. Even Sir John Shore was discouraged and did not appoint a new agent for Rangoon. To make matters worse, Sir John Shore retired and Lord Wellesley became governor-general of India, who, without knowing the background, believed implicitly Cox's prejudiced report.

Some three years passed and Arakanese rebels became active again. In 1799 a Burmese force pursued fleeing Arakanese rebels across the frontier and when a small British force intervened the Burmese gave battle and defeated it. The Burmese commander, realizing perhaps that he had acted unwisely, withdrew into Burmese territory, thus avoiding a general conflict. The governor-general was angry but he knew that the Arakanese had been using British territory as the base of their activities, and local British authorities had made no effort to stop the rebels from misusing British territory in that manner. He was, however, determined to uphold British prestige and refused the request received in writing from the Burmese military governor of Arakan for surrender of the rebels. The governor-general would have liked to invade Arakan, but England was now locked in battle with France under Napoleon, and the East India Company was still busy making its final conquests in India. He therefore resorted to subterfuge. Bodawpaya's eldest son, the crown prince, was an able, learned, experienced, and pop-

ular person. Nonetheless his younger brother, the prince of Toungoo, resented his appointment as crown prince and conspired to
rebel. But Bodawpaya, discovering the plot, executed the supporters
and exiled the prince. Lord Wellesley received reports from his
spies that Bodawpaya was dying and Toungoo would again rebel.
As with all spy reports there was an element of truth in them, but
again as with all spy reports they contained more conjecture than
fact, and Bodawpaya was still very much alive.

To Lord Wellesley the reports were most welcome. He decided to offer secretly to the crown prince the services of two
British infantry regiments, a cavalry regiment and an artillery regiment. He hoped that after the suppression of Toungoo's expected
rebellion the British regiments would stay on and turn the kingdom
into a British protectorate. Accordingly in 1802 he again sent Michael
Symes with an embassy. To impress the Burmese king and also the
crown prince with British might, the governor-general, in spite of
remonstrances from Symes, sent an entire regiment of soldiers with
plumes and swords and guns as the envoy's escort. The Burmese
permitted the embassy to come but resented the presence of such
a large force acting as escort, and Bodawpaya for a long time refused to give audience to Symes. The main task assigned to Symes
was to attempt to obtain a commercial treaty. Finally the king met
Symes and gave him a letter again permitting a British agent to
come to Rangoon, and also a verbal assurance that no demand for
wholesale expulsion of Arakanese refugees from British territory
would ever be made.

The governor-general duly sent Lieutenant John Canning to
Rangoon, but he was sent not as the representative of the company
but as the representative of Symes. An envoy's agent was unknown
either in European or Burmese diplomatic practice. His lack of
status proved to be a difficulty and Canning soon returned to Calcutta. For the next six years the governor-general kept a regiment
to guard the frontier, with the result that there was no attempt
made by the refugees to attack the Burmese across the frontier.

Bodawpaya also gave instructions to his commanders in Arakan to avoid conflict with the British. Moreover in 1808 the crown prince died suddenly of an illness and Bodawpaya appointed the crown prince's son in his place, taking precautions lest his wayward son, the prince of Toungoo, should create trouble. In 1809 the British imposed a blockade of the French Indian possession of Mauritius and the new governor-general, Lord Minto, sent an embassy under Canning to Bodawpaya to explain the nature of the British action. Canning was well received but the governor-general did not think it was necessary to have an agent at Rangoon. At the Arakan frontier things were so quiet that the governor-general withdrew the regiment stationed there to guard it.

In 1811 the storm suddenly broke. An Arakanese leader, Chin Byan, who had been a refugee in British territory, collected a force of refugees and Indian sympathizers; armed with the latest British weapons, including cannons, he crossed the frontier, attacked the Burmese forces, and occupied the capital. He declared himself king of Arakan, appealed to the governor-general for assistance and recognition, and offered to rule his kingdom as a British protectorate. There is no doubt that at least some of the local British officials encouraged Chin Byan and turned a blind eye on his preparations to rebel while on British territory. The governor-general, however, rejected Chin Byan's request and hastily sent Canning to Bodawpaya to assure him that the British would prevent the crossing of the frontier in either direction by refugees. Canning was coldly received but he endeavored to explain the British position. However, news arrived that Chin Byan on being defeated by the Burmese forces was back in British territory with his army still intact. Canning returned to Rangoon from Amarapura and for some unknown reason stayed on in Rangoon. Bodawpaya ordered his immediate arrest just to make him leave the country, and Canning boarded his frigate and returned to Calcutta. Although diplomatic relations between the two countries had broken down, the governor-general saw the justice of the king's anger and took measures to prevent

Chin Byan from crossing the frontier again, but he was never captured. Bodawpaya and the Burmese felt certain that the British were
merely playing a game of bluff because they found it difficult to
believe that the British with all the resources at their disposal could
really fail to capture a mere rebel and a fugitive.

Bodawpaya became convinced that the British could no longer
be trusted. In 1813 there was a struggle for supremacy between two
rival claimants to the throne in Manipur, which had been a Burmese
protectorate since Alaungpaya's time. Bodawpaya called the rivals
to Amarapura, but because one refused to come Bodawpaya sent an
expedition to put the other on the throne. In neighboring Assam
a civil war had been raging since about 1750. Its Ahom kings had
long ago lost their Tai and Buddhist connections and had accepted
Indian culture and Hinduism. In about 1700 a new sect called the
Moamarias appeared. They were Hindus, but worshiping only
Krishna they criticized the orthodox sect. In 1750 the king with
the advice of Brahmin priests at his court started a campaign of
persecution against the new sect, which resulted in rebellion and
civil war. Some of the Assamese leaders sought British assistance,
and in 1792 the East India Company sent an observer to see whether
it should intervene. Bodawpaya also had been approached by some
Assamese refugees to intervene, but as long as the British kept aloof
he was not interested. Now that diplomatic relations between the
British and Burmese had broken down, however, and with the British becoming supreme everywhere, he reconsidered his position.

The fall of Kandy in Ceylon to the British and the British
victory at Waterloo in Europe, both in 1815, convinced Bodawpaya
that he must act quickly. In 1816 when Chandra Kanta Singh, king
of Assam, fled to Bhutan and sent envoys to Bodawpaya, he no longer
hesitated; he ordered his armies into Assam. The fugitive king was
again placed on the throne, but the moment the Burmese armies
left the country he was dethroned again, necessitating their return.
As with Arakanese refugees, Assamese refugees escaped into neighboring British territory and then came back to attack the Burmese.

Chandra Kanta himself now thought that the British would intervene out of hostility toward the Burmese; therefore, to save his own
skin, he entered British territory to seek British assistance. The
Burmese chased and captured him, and then brought him back to
Assam. Burma now had a long frontier with British India because
Arakan, Manipur, and Assam adjoined British territory; it became
obvious that sooner or later frontier clashes over refugees and rebels
would develop into an open war between the two countries. Thus
when Bodawpaya died in 1819 he left to his grandson a country
full of rumors of war and disaster.

Bodawpaya's reign was a great age of Burmese literature and
music. As villagers went to Rangoon in search of wealth, they regularly exchanged letters with their families left at home. Although
the average Burmese was literate, he considered that a letter which
was going to be sent over miles of land and water was too important
for him to write alone. He would approach the monk of the village
monastery to compose an epistle for him, giving the monk all the
details of the news and advice that he desired to convey. After
the epistle had been completed it was passed around the village for
all to read and enjoy, and when it was later received by the addressee
it again was passed around. Two monks became famous writers of
these epistles, which were collected and preserved. One of these
two monks was Kyeegan Shingyi, who after the usual studies as a
novice became a lawyer and a courtier and had a gay time at
Rangoon. After some years of moving in legal and official circles,
however, he suddenly grew tired of secular life and re-entered the
Order. His epistles contained vivid descriptions of life in Burma
during Bodawpaya's reign. Another monk, U Awbartha, re-told the
stories of the *Ten Great Jatakas* in lively and effective prose as if
they were not religious writings but novels. The effects of Hsinbyushin's conquest of Ayuthia were now seen. Inspired by Siamese
poets, musicians, and actors, Burmese courtiers wrote court plays
based on episodes from the Siamese versions of the Indian epics
Ramayana and *Mahabharata*. The royal treasurer by the name of

U Toe wrote his *Yamayakan*, in which episodes from *Ramayana* were re-told in prose, using his own native village as background.

Toward the end of Bodawpaya's reign a note of artificiality gradually appeared in Burmese literature. Minister Myawaddy's songs set to Siamese music were elegant and still vigorous, and his court plays still had some village background. Those who followed and imitated him could not reproduce his master touch, though, and their writings became too elegant, too romantic, and too full of sentimentality. Perhaps the pathos that was the keynote of the newly arisen court drama was a reflection of an atmosphere of disappointment and despair that came to pervade the court after the death of Bodawpaya's son, the crown prince; perhaps it was merely a literature of escape, and the lords and ladies who wrote, performed, and watched the plays together with Bodawpaya did so to forget for a few hours the clashes on the distant frontiers.

X *The British Intrusion in Burma, 1824–1852*

Bagyidaw became king at his grandfather's death in 1819 amidst rumors of war and the impending fall of the kingdom. To restore confidence he announced the abandonment of Bodawpaya's great temple and great lake projects, suspension for three years of all taxes payable by the people, and the removal of the capital back to Ava. Having grown up under a domineering but adoring grandfather, he was good-natured but weak, and he allowed his chief queen, her brother Minthargyi, and their relatives to become the powers behind the throne. According to later propaganda the queen, Mai Nu, was an abusive and rowdy fish wife, but in actual fact she was of ordinary village stock and her brother and relations were able and talented people. When a queen had able relatives it was not nepotism but sound common sense on her part to appoint them to high offices, and in Burmese society birth was neither a qualification nor a disability.

The army resented her growing power and one of the senior commanders was the king's brother, the prince of Tharrawaddy. People liked Bagyidaw, but considering him to be an ineffectual angel they could only pray that the kingdom would somehow manage to last until his son could succeed him. This son, the prince of Nyaungyan, was popularly known as the Setkyar Min, or "a king who would come to possess god-given machines of war." Signs and portents and the predictions of astrologers marked him as a great ruler of the future. But it was the British who possessed the mighty machines of war, and the victors over Napoleon's Europe, India, and Ceylon had their colonial appetite sharpened by the acquisition of much territory in southeast Asia. They even occupied the Dutch East Indies during the recent wars, and empire builders like Raffles were disappointed because the islands were returned to the Dutch as an item of the peace settlement in Europe.

Just as the king of Assam had wanted to be on the winning side, the king of Manipur wanted to please the British by breaking his ties with the Burmese. He did not attend the coronation of Bagyidaw nor did he send an embassy bearing tribute, which all vassal kings were under an obligation to do. By not fulfilling this obligation he was making a declaration of independence. Bagyidaw felt that he should assert his authority immediately, before the British could intervene, and he had the full support of the army commanders. Accordingly he dispatched a punitive expedition. The king of Manipur fled into the neighboring kingdom of Cachar, but he proved to be not a mere fugitive, as he proceeded to drive out the king of Cachar, who appealed to both the British and the Burmese to assist him to regain his kingdom. Refugees from Cachar fled into the adjoining kingdom of Jaintia. The British became alarmed that the trouble might spread to Bengal itself. Cachar and Jaintia, in spite of the smallness of their territories, were useful as buffers between Burma, Manipur, and British Bengal, but both were now overrun with refugees and the Burmese in pursuit. The British took swift action and declared both Cachar and Jaintia to be protectorates. The Burmese would not recognize this declaration as legal and continued to chase the rebel-refugees. As in Assam, also, the Burmese continued to meet resistance from rival claimants to the throne. The long Anglo-Burmese frontier from Assam to Bengal was the scene of rebel activities and Burmese pursuits into British territory.

Amid these troubles the king's uncle, the prince of Toungoo, re-belled, and as it was his second attempt at rebellion he was executed summarily.

The crisis occurred in Arakan. The Naaf river was considered to be the boundary by the Burmese, and when some hunters em-ployed by the East India Company came chasing elephants across the river the Burmese promptly arrested them. When the governor-general, Lord Amherst, demanded that the frontier be clearly de-marcated and sent two officers to inspect, the Burmese arrested them. British troops then occupied an island in the river, but the Burmese attacked and overcame them. In January 1824 Burmese troops marched into Cachar and in the following March the British for-mally declared war against the Burmese. Maha Bandula, the com-mander-in-chief with headquarters in Assam, decided on a two-pronged attack, one from Assam and Manipur through Cachar, and the other from Arakan, the two armies meeting in Bengal and together attacking Calcutta, which was the seat of the governor-general. Maha Bandula himself led the army from Arakan. At the battle of Ramu across the frontier the Burmese defeated units of the British Indian army. Bandula used a combination of guerrilla tactics and frontal attacks. Had he marched on to Chittagong, which unknown to him was lightly held, he could have taken it and the way to Calcutta would have been open. Already there was panic in Calcutta among its Indian populace. The army invading through Cachar was being slowed down by the British, however, and Bandula decided to wait, thus losing his chance of at least winning Chitta-gong. The Burmese, because of the disparity in arms, could not have won the war in any case, but had they been able to threaten Calcutta there would have been no naval expedition to Rangoon and the Burmese could have obtained more favorable terms in the peace negotiations later on. While Bandula hesitated, British ships with troops and arms and other equipment were sailing from Indian ports to keep their rendezvous at the Andaman Islands, some miles to the south of Rangoon in the Bay of Bengal, and in May 1824 this armada entered the harbor of Rangoon, taking the Burmese by surprise.

Bagyidaw hastily mobilized two armies and sent them down to Rangoon, which had fallen to the British almost without resistance. The Burmese commanders called to all the inhabitants to leave Rangoon, orders which they obeyed without question. The British were left with an empty town, and as the monsoon rains thundered down they fortified the Shwedagon pagoda. The Burmese armies were awaiting the arrival of Bandula and their task was merely to stop the British from advancing. In the worst of the lashing monsoon Bandula brought his army across the Arakan mountains without any loss of men or equipment. He then made a second mistake, however; instead of using guerrilla tactics he made a frontal attack on the British forts at the Shwedagon pagoda. Probably he thought he could win the battle because his forces outnumbered the British two to one. Combined with the two armies awaiting him at Rangoon his forces numbered some 30,000, of which only 15,000 had muskets. The British had a little over 10,000 soldiers, of which 5,000 were British, the remainder being Indian sepoys. But Burmese muskets dated from the eighteenth century while the British muskets were modern; furthermore, Burmese cannons fired only balls whereas British cannons fired exploding shells. The British waited until the whole line of Burmese soldiers approached the pagoda and then discharged the first volley. The Burmese charged but the British, reloading quickly, fired their second volley. The Burmese in return fired their first volley, but the British charged as they were engaged in the slower reloading of their arms. The Burmese line never broke but they died in thousands, and at the end of the day when Bandula ordered a retreat he found that only 7,000 of his men had survived.

Bandula then made an orderly retreat to Danubyu at the head of the delta, awaiting the advance of the British. When the rainy season was over and reinforcements had arrived from India the British advanced up the Irrawaddy river. The Burmese had taken their positions on the only high ground in the neighborhood, and if they had owned but two cannons of the same caliber as the British cannons, the entire flotilla of British boats conveying the army would have been sunk at the first salvo. But it was the British who had the cannons, and after a fierce battle in which Bandula himself was killed by a bursting shell the Burmese army was routed. The British took Prome and waited for another monsoon to pass. The Burmese attempted to re-capture Prome, and although the first skirmishes were in their favor the final battle went to the British. In this attack on Prome, Shan regiments commanded by Sawbwas with their ladies on horseback showed great courage, only to be mowed down by British muskets.

A Burmese peace mission came to discuss terms with the British commander, but finding his demands too harsh they returned to the capital. The British fought on until they reached the village of Yandabo, only fifty miles from Ava. Another peace mission came from the king, and this time they had no choice but to accept the British terms, which were as follows: (1) The Burmese king would cede to the British the territories of Arakan, Tenasserim, and Assam. (2) The Burmese would recognize Manipur, Cachar, and Jaintia as British territory. (3) The Burmese would pay an indemnity of one million pounds sterling in four installments, the first install-ment to be paid immediately, the second installment within one hundred days from the signing of the treaty, the balance to be paid in annual installments within two years. Until the second installment was paid, the British army would not leave Rangoon. (4) The Burmese would receive a British resident representative at Ava and in return the British would receive a Burmese resident representative at Calcutta. (5) The East India Company and the Burmese king would sign a commercial treaty in due course. Admittedly the British losses had been heavy, but the terms were not only harsh but cruel. The Burmese had to surrender not only the Indian prov-inces of Assam and Manipur, but also two out of their three maritime provinces. The indemnity of one million pounds sterling would have been considered a colossal sum even in Europe of that time, and it became frightening when translated to the Burmese Kyat equivalent of one hundred lakhs, viewed against the fact that the cost of living of the average villager in Upper Burma in 1826 was one Kyat per month.

The outcome of the war was a bitter blow to the Burmese and it was not true, as some historians suggest that the Burmese people or their king had been eager to fight the British or that they ever hoped for victory. A letter written on the eve of the war by a courtier, or at least a person who had access to the court, described vividly the atmosphere of fear and uncertainty prevailing at that time by giving extracts from folksongs being sung in the streets of Ava. The following are examples:

> Dear little miss,
> You will get your gown,
> When the ruined pagoda
> Acquires a halo;
> I will punt the royal boat
> Down to Lower Burma,
> And buy you some silk.

> Dear little miss,
> Let us take soup together
> When the tamarind tree stump
> Shoots out new tender leaves.
> I will go to Lower Burma
> And bring you salted beef.

(All young men will have to go down to Lower Burma soon and fight the enemies and only if impossible things happen will they come back.)

> In my little boat
> I am sailing downwards;
> Mistress Pretty Picture,
> My farewell message is,
> "Marry again! Marry again!"

(All young men will have to go to Lower Burma and fight and get killed, and their wives will become widows.)

> With turbans untidy,
> They turn back from the outer palace.
> When the officials themselves give trouble,
> The axle of the cart must break.

(There are intrigues in the palace; many royal officials go to the palace, not to see the king in his chamber, but to plot with the queen in the outer rooms. How can the kingdom remain intact when the royal officials themselves are disloyal?)

That some even dared to hope for a peaceful settlement with the British is evidenced by the following song:

> There comes an epistle,
> Encased in a lacquer casket;
> Which governor has sent it?
> Written in heavy gold paint,
> It will bring peace to the kingdom.

(Negotiations with the British governor-general in India will be successful and bring peace to the country.)

Although the British achieved victory in the end with the signing of the Treaty of Yandabo in February 1826 their plans went awry. Their colonial policy at the time was to avoid annexing territory as much as possible, preferring to have a line of protectorates with native kings, and they had planned to revive the kingdom of Lower Burma with a Mon king on the throne. They expected that there would be simultaneous risings by the Arakanese and the Mons, but to their disappointment they found these peoples lukewarm. In Arakan the British succeeded in raising an Arakanese battalion to cooperate with the main British forces to defeat the Burmese garrison Bandula had left under the viceroy of the Seven Hill Districts, who was fighting a brilliant holding action. But once the garrison had been forced into retreat the Arakanese only wanted the British forces to leave their province. The Mons who were in Lower Burma at that time were those who had chosen to throw in their lot with the Burmese after thousands of their compatriots had fled to Siam, and they resented the British intrusion as much as the Burmese did.

The Siamese approved of the British attack on the Burmese kingdom, and although Siam was specifically mentioned in the Treaty of Yandabo by the British as "our good and faithful ally," it acted more as a silent partner except for some raids on Kengtung and Tenasserim, which it had long desired to possess. In other words, it was only the British who really wanted the war. When only the events on the Anglo-Burmese frontiers are considered, it appears that the Burmese provoked the British, but when the events in the whole region of southeast Asia are viewed together it becomes clear that the British would have taken control of the Burmese coastal regions even if Bagyidaw and his court had acted with docility, humility, and humbleness, for the period of the first British intrusion in Burma coincided with the period of the British struggle to acquire and hold the island of Singapore. The East India Company already possessed Penang, and with the acquisition of Singapore in 1819 it became necessary to obtain possession of the Burmese coast to turn the Bay of Bengal into a British lake.

In September 1826 the governor-general sent a mission to discuss the signing of the commercial treaty. It was headed by one John Crawfurd, who proved to be a worthy successor to Hiram Cox, for he had but the greatest contempt for the Burmese. He came not as an envoy but as a conqueror, and his general behavior, to say the least, was insolent. He was angry when the Burmese court would not agree to his proposal that the Burmese should export rice and silver. The country was still recovering from the effects of the war, the fields remained untilled, and so there was no surplus of rice at the time; to export it would have caused famine in the country. As to the silver, the Burmese had just paid two installments of the huge indemnity, and to enable the king to meet his obligation under the treaty the people had voluntarily contributed their little savings; even the queen had contributed all her gold and silver and ornaments. In such circumstances it was good common sense and sound economic planning to place an embargo on the export of silver. After browbeating the king and his court, Crawfurd obtained a commercial treaty with the following provisions: (1) The king would allow British merchants, and the East India Company would allow Burmese merchants, to trade and travel freely in their respective domains. (2) The king would draw up a schedule of flat-rate port dues for all ships, classifying them according to their tonnage. (3) The king would permit entry and render all assistance to British ships in distress, and in return they would pay all dues and charges.

Crawfurd was instructed by the governor-general to discuss the matter of the exchange of resident envoys. As he found the Burmese court rather suspicious of the proposal to appoint resident envoys, he recommended in his report that there should be no exchange of envoys. Crawfurd must be given credit as the innovator of the campaign of defamation and calumny against the Burmese, which, continued by others, led to the second Anglo-Burmese war of 1852. Crawfurd's pattern of arrogant behavior toward the Burmese was followed by British officials in other parts of Burma. In Manipur the British extended the frontier right up to the Chindwin river, which gave them a substantial piece of Burmese territory in addition to the territory actually ceded under the treaty. In Tenasserim the conduct of the British officials provoked the populace, both Burmese and Mon, to rebel. When the insurrection was put down the rebels fled to Burmese territory, and the British, following them in pursuit across the river, burned down the port of Martaban itself. The British officials were proving themselves more arrogant than the Burmese in Arakan had ever been, and such a flagrant breach of international law the Burmese commanders had never committed. Even in Arakan, where they were first welcomed, they behaved in such a high-handed manner that the Arakanese also rebelled.

There was a change of governor-generals in India; the new man, Lord William Cavendish-Bentinck, like Raffles was imbued with a new philosophy of colonial rule, having been influenced by the liberal ideas that the American Revolution, the French Revolution, and the Napoleonic Wars had produced in European thought.

He regretted the unsympathetic attitude the British envoy had shown toward a people who had just suffered a crushing defeat, and he wished that Crawfurd had taken some measures "for gradually removing from the minds of our opponents the sore and angry feelings left there by defeat, assuring them of the sincerity of our desire of cultivating friendly relations. . . ." He appointed new commissioners for Arakan and Tenasserim. Both officials were liberal and attempted to preserve not only Burmese social customs and conventions but also Burmese customary law and administrative practices. In 1830 the governor-general sent Major Henry Burney as the first resident envoy to Ava. Burney was an able and experienced diplomat, having led a mission to the king of Siam in 1825. He was also a fine scholar, although his scholarship did not keep him from occasionally indulging in diplomatic bargaining and political intrigue. A man of liberal principles, he was very sympathetic toward the Burmese until thwarted ambitions soured him. Burney had a pleasant personality and the king and the court, believing him to be another Symes, gave him their full trust. At first his advice was sound. On his suggestion the king sent a mission to the governor-general, although Bagyidaw would have preferred to send a mission directly to the king of England. Burney earned the gratitude of the king for prevailing upon the governor-general to re-demarcate the Manipuri frontier and restore to the Burmese the territory taken from them unjustly.

Burney also gained the friendship of the king's younger brother, the prince of Tharrawaddy. This prince was a commander under Bandula both at Rangoon and at Danubyu; after the death of Bandula he rushed back to Ava and, establishing a peace conference at the court, advised Bagyidaw to sue for peace, as the British with their modern weapons would merely slaughter all Burmese troops sent to meet them. The queen and her brother opposed all proposals to end the war, and the prince of Tharrawaddy never forgave them, holding them responsible for the further loss of some 20,000 men. Burney mistakenly thought Tharrawaddy to be pro-British; his peace proposals were made not because he loved the British but because as a commander he realized the effectiveness of British muskets and cannons. Burney on the other hand was not quite honest with the Burmese; for example, when Bagyidaw sent his mission to Calcutta, Burney advised the king to require the mission to travel overland to Arakan, and then he appointed his younger brother, Captain George Burney, to act officially as escort but secretly as spy. George Burney carefully noted the details of the route, in case it might become necessary for British troops stationed in Arakan to attack the Burmese kingdom by way of the Arakan mountains. In addition, he opened and read not only the official reports but also private letters written by the members of the mission to their families at Ava.

Burney dangled Tenasserim like a carrot before both the Burmese and the Siamese, doubtless assuming them to be as dense as donkeys. The Burmese could not pay the last installment of the indemnity for some time, and Burney in effect threatened and cajoled them with Tenasserim until in fear that the province would be given to Siam, and in hope that it would be given back to them, the Burmese paid the balance of the indemnity at a great sacrifice in November 1832. Poor Bagyidaw continued to believe that both Arakan and Tenasserim would be returned to him. Although the cost of administration of Tenasserim and Arakan proved a heavy charge on the resources of the East India Company, the British would never permit these coastal regions to go back to Burmese control because Penang and Singapore would become isolated. The Siamese with their diplomatic acumen soon realized that Burney was merely playing a game, but Bagyidaw went on hoping until he lost his sanity. Burney was not displeased with this turn of events because he believed that the regency council, consisting of the queen, her brother Minthargyi, and the prince of Tharrawaddy, would be easier to control. Since Bagyidaw, in gratitude for his services in connection with the Manipuri frontier, had appointed him a member of the Privy Council with the rank of a junior minister, he was present at all official discussions of affairs of state and kept his ears and eyes always open for information regarding palace plots and conspiracies.

Taking advantage of the stipulation of the commercial treaty giving British merchants the right to enter Burmese territory at any point and travel in any direction, Burney sent his assistants on spy missions to the far north to Bhamo and to the far east up to the Karenni states. There was a British spy ring in the country then, and although British records would suggest that its headquarters was in the office of the commissioner of Arakan, obviously the operations were directed by Burney himself. Doubtless Burney was one of the first people to know of the plot headed by the queen and her brother to oust Tharrawaddy from power. The three had been at loggerheads for some time, and the conspiracy was to place Bagyidaw's son Setkyar Min on the throne, which would have won the approval of the people. It is not known which side Burney supported. Tharrawaddy was supposed to be pro-British, but by this time Burney must have discovered the true attitude of Tharrawaddy toward the East India Company. In 1837 Minthargyi ordered the arrest of Tharrawaddy for treasonable activities, but the prince successfully evaded arrest, fled with his followers to Shwebo, and raised the standard of rebellion. Burney was invited by the queen to play the role of peacemaker and won from Tharrawaddy a promise to avoid bloodshed. Relying on that promise made to Burney, the queen and Minthargyi surrendered. Tharrawaddy became king and his first action was to execute the queen, Minthargyi, and the Setkyar prince. Tharrawaddy kept Bagyidaw in custody but assigned him lords-in-waiting and allotted a privy purse for his needs. Some of his supporters, maintaining that he had recovered from his illness, plotted to restore him to the throne, and Burney seems to have been involved. Tharrawaddy, learning of the conspiracy, removed Bagyidaw to a safer place under heavy guard. Burney's great dream to play king-maker in Burma ended abruptly, and a rift developed between the king and the envoy.

Tharrawaddy as a former commander was interested in the

procurement of modern arms, especially cannons and shells, and he proceeded to order them from the foreign merchants, mostly English, who thronged the port of Rangoon. These English captains delivered shiploads of arms and ammunition at exorbitant prices and then calmly reported to Burney that Tharrawaddy was preparing for war against the British. Tharrawaddy needed those arms to restore law and order in the kingdom, and also to meet the advances that the Siamese armies were making in Burmese territory. He was too experienced a soldier to think of attacking the British when he was not sure of his own position as king and with the British holding the Bay of Bengal as their domain. Burney was angry and asked the king to stop buying cannons; the king was angry also and asked Burney to stop his allies, the Siamese, from raiding Kentung. Burney accused the king of going against the spirit of the Yandabo Treaty, and Tharrawaddy replied that the treaty no longer bound him since the British had broken it already by not stopping their allies from attacking his kingdom. Tharrawaddy, in spite of his annoyance, continued to accord all honors due to the envoy, but the position was becoming intolerable and Burney returned to India. His assistants acted as his successors, but one by one they left, until no representative remained and the residency closed down in 1840.

Tharrawaddy never demanded that the envoy or any of his staff should go and gave the residency all courtesies, but he did not hide his joy when all left, for he considered the presence of a British envoy at the capital a badge of shame because the envoy was the governor-general's representative and not the representative of the king of England. He was always prepared to exchange envoys with the Court of St. James's, but not with a mere governor-general's court at Calcutta. In celebration of the closing down of the residency, Tharrawaddy came to Rangoon in state at the head of an army with his son the crown prince accompanying him and heading another army. He made many offerings at the Shwedagon pagoda, turning Rangoon into a field of gold cloth and holding feasts and festivities. The governor-general, expecting an attack on Arakan and Tenasserim, sent troops to both regions. But the crisis existed only in the minds of the British officials in the two maritime provinces and the king of Siam, who wrote to Calcutta offering to act jointly with the East India Company should the latter decide on war. Tharrawaddy himself had no plans to attack the British. The position eased with the return of the king to Amarapura, which had again become the capital of the kingdom.

Some of the more fiery commanders were not satisfied because they desired revenge for the disastrous defeats of 1824–1826, but Tharrawaddy restrained them. He had the loyal support of his eldest son, the prince of Pagan, the crown prince, who had been given the command of the armies. The younger son, the prince of Prome, did not approve of his father's peace policy, however; his attitude was that, as the British would attempt to conquer the whole kingdom sooner or later, the Burmese should "strive to reach the golden pinnacle or fall into the grave in a blaze of glory." He was supported in a plot against the king by the Lady Myagalay, the junior queen, who as a musician, songstress, and poet was not only the favorite of the king but also of the court. She was the daughter of a minor Mon official in a small delta town and had captivated Tharrawaddy, then a dashing young army commander, by her vivacious personality and great poetical gifts. The plot she and the young prince were planning was discovered, and both were executed. As the executioner pulled Lady Myagalay's hair to steady her head before striking with the sword, she shouted in anger, "Let go of my hair, for only the king should caress it. I know how to die." Then, singing a song in which she reminded "all those in power, of the vicissitudes of life," she waited for the executioner's sword to fall on her comely neck. Tharrawaddy, already afflicted with fits of insane melancholia, never recovered from the shock of her death and totally lost his reason. The Pagan prince tended him and ruled in his name. Tharrawaddy died in 1846, a few months after Bagyidaw's death. Pagan's two younger brothers, the prince of Mindon, religious and ascetic, and the prince of Kanaung, second in command of the army, gave their full support to the new king.

In the first year of his reign Pagan proved to be an able monarch. He took a Shan princess as his queen and won the gratitude and support of the Sawbwas. He repaired the irrigation system at a district called Sagu and built temples and monasteries. He wanted to turn his army into a strong, peace-keeping force in the kingdom, and following the precedent set by his father he engaged European experts to assist him in casting better cannons and bought quantities of the latest weapons from the gun-running English captains. His great ambition was to remove the sting from the Treaty of Yandabo by exchanging envoys with the king of England. Suddenly he became disillusioned, however; leaving the conduct of the government to his ministers, he sought solace in drink and games. The British were now poised for war; they had overcome all obstacles in India. They had refrained from declaring war against Tharrawaddy because at that time on the northwest frontier of India they were taking measures against a possible Russian threat from that direction, and because they were fighting the Opium War against China.

China had now been forced to open her ports to all nations, but because Britain's rivals, France and the United States, also were taking their share in the Chinese trade at that end the British became interested in the back door to China through Burma. It was as if the deltaic coastline of Burma was an eyesore on the British maps because it was not colored red, emphasizing the fact that there was still a small gap in the long coastline of the Bay of Bengal, which had become British territory. The port of Rangoon was rapidly developing, and the British merchants turned their greedy eyes on its potentialities. The American Baptist mission, which had been more or less expelled from India by the East India Company, was proving to be its loyal ally in Burma, for the missionaries identified themselves with the all-conquering Englishmen. Above all, the new governor-general, Lord Dalhousie, was an imperialist of the deepest dye, who longed to extend his Indian empire at the cost of the Burmese, about whom he wrote thus: "Among all the nations of the East, none is more arrogant in its pretentions of superiority, and none more pertinacious in its assertion of them, than the people of Burma." However, Pagan was no Tharrawaddy, and in spite of the most violent propaganda that merchants and missionaries spread against the Burmese there was no threat nor provocation from the monarch at Amarapura, and the East India Company was hard put to find a cause for war.

In 1851 the governor of Rangoon, finding conditions in the port so chaotic, started to take measures to suppress the flaunting of port rules and regulations, smuggling, and evasion and tardy payment of port dues and customs duties. The British merchants and ship captains immediately complained to Calcutta of the harsh and oppressive actions of the Burmese. Toward the end of the year the captains of two English merchant ships were found to have defrauded the Burmese customs and were fined the usual nominal amount in such cases. They insolently refused to pay and were arrested and kept in custody until a fine of 100 pounds sterling was paid. Under the circumstances this punitive fine itself was not unusually high. The captains immediately sailed back to Calcutta and drew up a list of damages they had suffered at the hands of the Burmese and claimed a compensation of 1,920 pounds. Lord Dalhousie considered the matter to be a serious one involving the prestige of the East India Company and decided to take stern action against the Burmese kingdom. However, even he found the captains' claims so unreasonable that he reduced the claim by one thousand pounds. Then he chose a fiery, irresponsible, but well-connected naval officer, one Commodore Lambert, to head a mission bearing a demand for compensation and the punishment of the governor of Rangoon. How peaceful Dalhousie's intentions were could be guessed by the fact that Lambert was instructed to take with him a squadron of well-armed frigates.

Again, following the precedent set by Crawfurd, Lambert behaved like a conqueror rather than an envoy. He acted against his instructions by delivering the letter demanding compensation and punishment to the governor in a contemptuous manner, which violated all rules of protocol. Even Dalhousie was annoyed and the other two members of the governor-general's council wrote minutes censuring Lambert's behavior and breach of protocol. It may be mentioned that when all papers relating to the dispute were later submitted to the parliament in London, the remarks of those members were expunged. Doubtless to the disappointment of Commodore Lambert, the Burmese king showed diplomacy and restraint; he agreed to recall the governor of Rangoon and to pay the compensation to the aggrieved captains after the usual formal inquiries by the new governor of Rangoon. The king especially mentioned the grand friendship that existed between the two nations. The crisis seemed to have passed, but when the new governor of Rangoon arrived Lambert publicly insulted the governor by sending a delegation consisting of some of his officers and a local missionary to proceed on horseback right to the governor's door. Courtesy and protocol demanded that even royal princes dismount on entering the courtyard of the Rangoon governor, who had the special status of a viceroy, and the presence of the local missionary was meant to be a slap in the face of the governor, who had just taken his post and could not be accused of being harsh or insolent.

The governor naturally refused to see the delegation and Lambert demanded a public and abject apology from him. Finally Lambert seized a ship belonging to the king, thus committing an act of piracy worthy of de Brito and his comrades some two hundred years before. As Lambert sailed out of the harbor with the king's ship as prize, the Burmese shore batteries fired on the British squadron, which returned the fire with its superior guns, destroying all the Burmese batteries and Burmese ships and setting the foreshore aflame. Dalhousie condemned Lambert's action and held him responsible for the hostilities committed by both sides. But he never dismissed Lambert nor called upon him to explain his conduct. Lambert was never even court-martialed, and Dalhousie's adverse remarks upon his action were expunged when the papers were submitted later to parliament. One may therefore wonder, did Lambert have secret instructions to behave so lawlessly? Was he an agent provocateur? Or, for that matter, was not Crawfurd an agent provocateur also? Leading a mission to Siam before he went to Burma, Crawfurd was normal, courteous, ordinary, yet a few years later, how changed he was. Dalhousie, in spite of his recorded disapproval of Lambert's action, deliberately ignored a letter from the governor of Rangoon offering to pay the demanded compensation to the captains in full and pleading that his side of the story of the encounter with Lambert be heard also. Dalhousie proceeded to make full preparations to take Rangoon before the advent of the monsoon and issued an ultimatum to the king at Amarapura with the following demands: (1) The king would dismiss the new governor of Rangoon from his post. (2) The king through his ministers would offer a formal apology to the East India Company for the insult to the delegation of British officers, disavowing the action of the governor of Rangoon in refusing to receive it. (3) The king would pay an indemnity of 100,000 pounds sterling to cover the payment of compensation to the two captains, damage to the property of British subjects in Rangoon in the fire caused by the shells of Lambert's squadron, and the cost of preparation for the war. (4) The king, conforming to the provisions of the Treaty of Yandabo, would receive an envoy of the East India Company to be resident at Rangoon. Except for the fourth item the demands were unjustified, cruel, and nothing less than diplomatic blackmail.

At Amarapura the king felt distressed that his conciliatory attitude remained unappreciated at Calcutta and that Lord Dalhousie was bent on war. He realized too late that his dead brother, the prince of Prome, and the Lady Myagalay were right; the British would not rest content until the whole kingdom had fallen under their rule. His brother and heir-apparent, the prince of Mindon, recoiled at the prospect of war, for he was a devout Buddhist, gentle and humanitarian. He believed that all matters could be solved by patient negotiation and that the British would react favorably to humility and humbleness. "Let us sue for peace," he argued, "and the British will relent." The youngest brother, the prince of Kanaung, wanted to fight but felt that the Burmese army was still unready and should be further equipped with modern arms. Pagan was adamant. Had he not offered the olive branch to Dalhousie and had he not been spurned? Had not his concessions been met by fresh demands for more concessions? It was true that the army was still ill-equipped, but would the British ever permit it to become fully equipped? If the golden pinnacle was beyond his reach and the reach of the people, should not the king and the people strive for death in a blaze of glory?

No one answered the king's bitter arguments, and Pagan instructed his troops to fight to the death. In a concerted move General Godwin, the British commander-in-chief, attacked Martaban while the Siamese attacked at various points along the frontier. Martaban fell and a counterattack by the Burmese to regain the port was repulsed with heavy losses inflicted on the attackers. Lambert's squadron was able to bombard Rangoon at will because the Burmese shore batteries had been silenced long ago, during his piracy of the king's ship. However, for three weeks Godwin could not land. Then the port fell and Godwin attacked and gained the Burmese stockades on the slopes of the Shwedagon pagoda. But his losses were heavy, and in a fit of pique he looked for the governor of Rangoon everywhere in order to have the pleasure of capturing and then hanging him. The age of chivalry was indeed dead. Burmese troops, obeying the call of their king, fought on desperately. Lambert's squadron took Bassein, the last of the Burmese ports, in May 1852. As Lord Dalhousie had so carefully planned in advance, the delta region was in British hands before the monsoon began. Dalhousie himself came to Rangoon to direct the final operations. In the following June, Pegu fell, although the Burmese staged a series of fierce counterattacks. The British marched on to Prome, their last objective in this campaign, but could not hold it because of Burmese counterattacks. The monsoon was now beginning to hamper the operations and the British waited for it to end. In the following October they took Prome and in December the Burmese made their last counterattack. At Amarapura, Mindon was appalled at the wanton wastage of Burmese lives in the counterattacks and advised the king to open peace negotiations. Pagan's commanders ordered the arrest of Mindon and Kanaung, and the two princes fled to Shwebo, where they soon collected an army to fight against the king. At this point the Hluttaw intervened. Recalling all the troops in Lower Burma to the capital, it elected Mindon as the new king.

Dalhousie had only an academic interest in these developments at the capital, for they could not affect his plans and schemes regarding the newly acquired territory. He knew very well that Pagan was not an aggressive monarch, and his fall was of no importance to him. In any case, the war had been won and he had gained, as he had schemed, the rich province of Pegu, containing the fertile lands of the delta, and all three Burmese ports. He now controlled the Irrawaddy river, along which trade with China could be conducted. Without any access to the sea but through British territory, Burma and the Burmese people now lay at the mercy of the British. Dalhousie resolved also that there should not be another Treaty of Yandabo for the Burmese to debate and dispute. He boldly proclaimed that Pegu was now the third province of British Burma. In making the proclamation Dalhousie gave a stern warning that if the Burmese should misbehave "it must of necessity lead to the total subversion of the Burman state and to the ruin and exile of the king and his race."

Such a method of acquisition of territory by brute force alone without negotiation, without a treaty, and without a declaration of peace was not in keeping with the expression of liberalism repeatedly made by European political thinkers and statesmen of the period,

and the second Anglo-Burmese war was a war of "naked imperialism" in the fullest sense of the term. The Burmese who were most
arrogant in the first half of the nineteenth century had been humbled
enough in the second half, and both the king and the people, unlike in the first Anglo-Burmese war, were innocent victims of aggression. But perhaps to Commodore Lambert and Lord Dalhousie,
it seemed only fitting that the tragedy of Burmese Pegu should begin with an act of piracy by Lambert and close with an act of
piracy by Dalhousie. No writer could ever hope to surpass the great
British liberal statesman, Richard Cobden, in summing up the nature
of this second war:

Lord Dalhousie begins with a claim on the Burmese for less than a
thousand pounds; which is followed by an additional demand of an
apology from the Governor of Rangoon for the insult offered to
our officers; next, his terms are raised to one hundred thousand
pounds, and an apology from the king's ministers; then follows the
invasion of Burmese territory; when, suddenly, all demands for
pecuniary compensation and apology cease, and his lordship is willing to accept the cession of Pegu as a compensation and a repa-
ration.

Bagyidaw's and Pagan's reigns were a time of blood and tears
for the Burmese people, yet it was also a time of great literary activity. At the court, especially through the continuing influence of
Siamese literature and court ritual, life had become more formalized
and ceremonial in tone and atmosphere, and as a result the note of
artificiality that had begun to appear earlier became more pro-
nounced. Just as the ordinary conversation at the court became more
elegant, the prose and poetry produced by courtiers also became
equally elegant and less natural. Minister Myawaddy still continued
to write, but he more and more sought solace in music; instead of
writing new court plays, he collected songs from all sources, Siamese, Burmese, Mon, and from all levels, songs sung at court, songs
sung by spirit-worshipers, songs sung at feasts, and folksongs. He
continued his experiments in blending the various musical traditions

of the country. Historical ballads, poems in praise of the king, epics, and martial poems went out of fashion, and most court poems dealt with the theme of love in a formal and conventional style. In the hands of the wife of a minister, the Lady Khin Sone, and the queen, Lady Myagalay, the court poem achieved artistry; saturated with emotion, it had a background of gentle melancholy. Lady Myagalay's *All My Love*, addressed to the king and written while she was in prison, possessed a special quality that carried it beyond the walls and moats of the palace to the ears of the common people.

The greatest achievement of the court, however, was in scholarship. The lords and ladies became interested in the countries and peoples beyond the seas, and their contact with English envoys and Christian missionaries roused their curiosity in Christian ritual, especially in the music and themes of the Christian hymns. Fearing that their kingdom was soon to pass, and wanting to put its checkered history on record, the courtier-scholars, with the assistance of some learned monks and under the patronage of Bagyidaw, met in committee regularly in the chamber of the glass throne in the palace and produced their monumental work in five volumes, *The Glass Palace Chronicle of the Kings of Burma*. Objective, restrained, but with a quiet dignity, it is without a doubt the finest historical work in southeast Asia before modern times. The scholars endeavored to be objective in writing the chronicle; knowing that they could not be so with the recent past, with whose sorrows their hearts were still laden, they stopped their narrative with the death of Bodawpaya and the coronation of Bagyidaw.

The court plays were first performed by the courtiers themselves, but, as time passed and the plays became popular with the lords and ladies, professional musicians and dancers were engaged to take part in the production of the plays. These professional musicians and dancers thus became professional actors, and they took the new drama to the people. But because the court plays were too artificial and far removed from the life of the common people, and audiences of common folk demanded to see swift action and hear easy dialogue, these professional players, traveling from village to village, began to improvise a new kind of play. Soon professional writers became interested in the new literary form. The greatest of these new dramatists was U Kyin U, who wrote his best work after the end of the first Anglo-Burmese war. In his plays he gave his audiences glimpses of happy Burmese village life, and at the same time he posed therein the problem of human conflict. The tragedy of life was not the struggle between good and evil, but between good and less good; therefore at some times in life the hero was the villain and at other times the villain was the hero. And he tried to show that often the struggle had no point to it: in one play the villain-hero fought an enemy who, unknown to him, was his own younger brother, in order to win a princess who, unknown to him, was his betrothed bride. His plays, to please his audience, contained great fighting scenes, but they were really anti-war plays, and an atmosphere of intense world-weariness always pervaded the final act of each play. Both U Kyin U and his audiences never recovered from the wounds that their mind and spirit suffered in the war of 1824–1826.

XI The British Conquest of Burma, 1885

Mindon was one of the ablest kings that Burma ever had, but right from the beginning of his reign he was doomed to meet disappointment and humiliation in his relations with the British. Like his great contemporary, King Mongkut of Siam, he possessed unusual qualities—he was idealistic yet practical, autocratic yet humble, nationalistic yet fully aware of the limitations and weaknesses of his own nation. Unlike Mongkut, however, in the end his reign proved not to be a glorious one; the fate of both these kings was entirely in the hands of the British, who in effect decreed that Mongkut should succeed while Mindon should fail.

Instead of spending his youth on chargers and war elephants, as his predecessors had, Mindon devoted himself to manuscripts of palm leaf and parchment in the shelter of a monastery. He was essentially a man of peace, and he led the rebellion against his elder brother Pagan Min not as a seeker after power but as a humanitarian yearning to end a purposeless war in which Burmese lives were being sacrificed in counterattacks against impregnable British positions. His rebellion was unique in that it was the only rising during the period of Alaungpaya's dynasty that was not followed by executions. Mindon re-appointed most of his brother's ministers to their former offices and treated Pagan with courtesy and consideration, assigning him a spacious mansion and permitting him even to hold audiences as if he were still king. Mindon placed a strong guard around the mansion, but he gave strict orders to the sentries that they should endeavor to be as unobtrusive as possible.

Mindon felt confident that the British would react to diplomacy and international goodwill and after due negotiation would give back Lower Burma to him. On returning to Amarapura as king, he freed all Europeans who had been kept under detention by Pagan Min and sent them to the British commander, bearing his official message that all Burmese troops had been given orders to break contact with the British forces and that a peace mission was on its way. The British commander referred the matter to Lord Dalhousie, who gave instructions that the British forces should remain in firm possession of all the territories they had seized, but he appointed at the same time Major Arthur Phayre, the commissioner of Arakan, as the new commissioner of Pegu, investing him with plenipotentiary powers to receive the embassy from the Burmese king. The Burmese mission duly arrived and requested the withdrawal of British forces from the province of Pegu as part of the peace settlement. Phayre replied that as the annexation of the province had already been proclaimed it was an accomplished fact and he had no power or authority to deal with the matter, except to fix the boundary between the kingdom of Burma and British-Burma. Accordingly, he offered to withdraw the British forces from Thayetmyo to Prome, provided the Burmese would sign a treaty recognizing that the territory up to and including Prome belonged to the British. Obviously Dalhousie himself realized that his seizure of Pegu did not quite conform to the requirements of international law and was attempting to procure some legal basis for it by blackmailing the Burmese king to sign what would have been in effect a treaty of cession. As Mindon naturally refused to agree to the suggested treaty, Dalhousie merely issued a declaration that the second Anglo-Burmese war was now at an end, thus retaining the territory to the north of Prome.

Dalhousie's action was a blow to Mindon's prestige, as well as a bitter disappointment to him and his followers, including his brother, the prince of Kanaung, who prepared to attack the British again, feeling convinced as Pagan Min had been that the British would never show mercy or consideration toward the Burmese. It was only Mindon's courage, wisdom, and personality that prevented the Burmese troops from returning to Lower Burma to continue the war. In Lower Burma itself not only the Burmese, but all racial groups, were angered both by Dalhousie's acquisitiveness and Mindon's patience. Furthermore, a famine resulting from the neglect of the rice fields during the war was intensifying the people's discontent. A Burmese leader, with the avowed purpose of setting up a Lower Burmese kingdom independent of control by Mindon or Dalhousie, gathered an army of a mere 4,000 guerrillas and made desperate but effective raids on the British forces. Similarly a Karen leader, claiming that he was destined to be the first Karen king of Lower Burma, roused his own racial group in the delta region to make guerrilla raids on all government outposts. When the Burmese guerrillas chose to come out in the open after the initial victories, they were defeated after a few pitched battles. In contrast, the Karens remained in ambush for some five years, inflicting substantial losses on both civilian and military personnel of the new British government. Mindon, however, realizing that such rebellions could result only in further loss of Burmese lives, restrained his followers from contacting and encouraging the rebels. In spite of the fact that those rebels were legally no longer his subjects, his heart still went out to them and he sent messengers to the rebel leaders advising them to abandon their vain endeavor for independence. As the famine continued unabated in Lower Burma, he bought all the surplus food grains in his kingdom and sold them at cost to the British authorities to feed the starving thousands. Doubtless he would have given them free had his kingdom not been impoverished by the loss of Pegu, or if the British had not possessed vast financial reserves.

In the absence of a peace treaty Dalhousie would not send a

representative to reside at the Burmese capital, but Mindon, realizing the importance of maintaining friendly relations with the British, appointed as his advisers a Scottish merchant, Thomas Spears, and two British officers, Major Allen and Captain Latter. He also appointed an Armenian merchant named Mackertich as the governor of the border town of Minhla on the Irrawaddy river, giving him special instructions to entertain regularly at his table British and Burmese frontier officials. Lord Dalhousie, even in the face of such friendliness and goodwill on the part of Mindon, remained unresponsive. In 1854, deciding to take the bull by the horns, the king sent his embassy to Calcutta, pleading for the return of the province of Pegu to him. But Dalhousie was adamant and, imperiously pointing with his forefinger at the sun, said, "As long as that sun shines, Pegu shall remain British." However, the Burmese envoys, who were not familiar with the imperialist boast that the sun never set on the British empire, thought that Dalhousie was pointing to the Union Jack flying on the flagpost in front of the governor-general's residence and understood his remarks to mean that as long as the British flag flew Pegu would remain British. The Burmese embassy misunderstood the details but did not miss the import of Dalhousie's words. Pegu would never be returned and their mission had failed.

Thus rebuffed by the British, Mindon resolved to develop the economy of his kingdom even without the resources that Pegu possessed. Although he had no formal training or experience in economic planning, his ideas were far in advance of his contemporaries'. His plan, to use a modern economic term, was to nationalize his country's international trade while maintaining free trade in the kingdom itself. His great dream was to administer the kingdom with profits from his control of international trade, exempting his people from all direct taxation. As a first step toward the realization of this ideal he ordered that the total amount of all duties and taxes payable by any person in one single year should not exceed 10 percent of his annual income. He substituted salaries of stated amounts for grants of revenue, thus gradually abolishing the old system of assigning villages or towns as fiefs to royal officials as rewards for special services already rendered or as stipends for services currently being performed. It should be noted that in Burmese usage the assignment of a village or town as a fief did not involve any feudal tenure or conferment of administrative rights and duties; it merely meant that the assignee received from the king the annual revenue collected from that particular locality.

King Mindon gradually established a coinage system to replace the existing system of barter and occasional use of gold or silver bullion as the medium of exchange; he also set up a royal mint, which issued the official Kyat with the insignia of a peacock embossed on it. He confirmed the uniform system of weights and measures approved by Bodawpaya and appointed royal inspectors, whose duty was to travel to market villages and towns to ensure that correct weights and measures were used in all transactions. Taking advantage of new roads and railways rapidly being built by the British in Lower Burma, he improved both road and riverine communications within his kingdom. The British government in Lower Burma established regular steamer and mail service between Calcutta, Penang, and Singapore through Rangoon. With the opening of the Suez Canal in 1871 Rangoon became even more important as a port. The British also established the Irrawaddy Flotilla Company, which set up regular steamer service between Thayetmyo and Rangoon, passing through Prome and the delta towns. Mindon took advantage of all these developments by buying a number of steamboats for use in his kingdom and encouraged and permitted the Irrawaddy Flotilla Company to run a tri-weekly service to Mandalay and a monthly service to Bhamo. He sent a number of young students on stipends to Rangoon and Calcutta to learn telegraphic engineering, and on their return he established with their assistance a system of telegraphic communications through his kingdom, linking it with the British system in Lower Burma and evolving at the same time the Morse code in the Burmese language.

Fully realizing the importance of industry to his small country,

Mindon obtained the services of European experts to survey and improve the existing native methods of mining minerals and cutting timber. Also with European help he established about fifty small factories of various kinds, such as textile mills, rice and wheat mills, and even sugar refineries. He appointed the prince of Mekkara, one of his ablest sons, who was more interested in Western technology than affairs of state, as minister for industries. At first the British merchants made fun of Mindon's factories in their clubs in Rangoon, but after a few years they became secretly concerned at the great strides Prince Mekkara's mills were making. The British merchants were also highly critical of Mindon's monopoly over the international trade of the kingdom and were especially annoyed when the king instructed his royal buyers to buy imports directly from Calcutta instead of buying them in Rangoon, where these British merchants themselves had raised the prices. In other words, they criticized Mindon's monopoly over the exports and at the same time wanted to establish their own monopoly over goods imported to the Burmese kingdom.

Arthur Phayre, who led the return embassy from Lord Dalhousie in 1855, tried to persuade Mindon to sign a commercial treaty but, although Mindon received him with great hospitality and regard, Phayre failed to obtain the agreement. In 1862, at the repeated request of the British merchants in Rangoon, Phayre went again to the Burmese capital and was able to negotiate a commercial treaty that contained the following three important stipulations: (1) The king and the British authorities in Lower Burma would reduce their custom duties on goods crossing the Anglo-Burmese frontier. (2) Merchants from both countries would be permitted to travel in each other's territory without restriction of any sort. (3) The British would send a resident envoy to the Burmese capital. Mindon had been especially keen to have a British representative resident at the capital, but he was still disappointed because the British would not permit him to send a Burmese resident representative to London. In other words, just as Tharrawaddy and Pagan Min had failed to secure agreement from the British authorities to open diplomatic relations directly with the British monarch in London, Mindon did not succeed in getting recognition from the British that he was equal in rank and status with Queen Victoria. Yet by this time Britain had established direct diplomatic relations with King Mongkut of Siam. British humiliation of King Mindon had now begun in earnest.

Sir Arthur Phayre and the British merchants expressed great disappointment at Mindon's refusal to give up his monopolies, but the commercial treaty of 1862 constituted a substantial victory for British interests. The stipulation granting freedom of passage to merchants was reciprocal only in theory, for Burmese merchants had no occasion to travel in British territory, and even if they did they could do no harm. In contrast, British army and civilian officers, calling themselves merchants, penetrated the remoter regions of the kingdom, and, although their interest was alleged to be the opening of new trade routes, they not only acted as spies, prying into the internal affairs of the kingdom, but also engaged in subversive activities. For example, British army officers who were ostensibly exploring the possibility of extending their commercial sphere along the Salween valley were really spreading propaganda against Burmese rule and inciting the Karenni chiefs to rebel. They also wandered into the Shan states and indulged in secret negotiations with some Sawbwas, promising them military assistance should they decide to rebel against King Mindon. Colonel Sladen, who took up residence at Mandalay as the British representative under the treaty, first won the confidence of the kindly king and then betrayed it by spying on him and, what was worse, by taking a more than academic interest in palace intrigues. Although he was the official envoy of the British government, he seemed to have been also in the pay of British merchants in Rangoon. The betrayal of Mindon by the British over the stipulations of the commercial treaty gave proof that Mindon's doubts regarding the wisdom of signing such a treaty were not groundless, and it was only his high personal regard for

Phayre that prompted him finally to agree to it. Mindon's tragedy was that he was too honest and trusting. When the British were facing disasters during the Crimean War and the Indian Mutiny, and he was presented with a chance to regain Lower Burma, he restrained the Kanaung prince, who was so eager to invade British territory, saying, "We must not stab a friend in the back." But the British never hesitated to stab him in the back many times over.

In spite of his later failures Mindon succeeded in restoring a sense of confidence among his subjects, as well as a sense of pride in the nation among all the Burmese, whether they lived in his kingdom or under British rule. Before the Burmese people had recovered from the shock of the first Anglo-Burmese war, the second war came, and reeling under the fresh blow they felt lost and ashamed. They feared that their centuries-old way of life and their ancient faith of Theravada Buddhism would swiftly disappear under alien rule. Their fears increased when the British government refused to grant patronage to Buddhism and approval to the monastic schools, which served as the keystone of the Burmese education system. In place of the monastic schools, government schools and Christian missionary schools appeared like mushrooms; in the government schools Burmese kings were belittled, and in the mission schools Burmese religious beliefs were openly ridiculed. Many monks felt that they could not hope to survive in such conditions and migrated to Upper Burma, still under the rule of a Burmese king and as such the official patron of Buddhism. Those few monks who remained in Lower Burma were neither pious nor learned, and without a central authority to maintain discipline they reverted to loose and immoral living, bringing further discredit to the national religion.

The Burmese were in real danger of losing their national heritage, and it was King Mindon who saved them on the brink of disaster. He first obtained the assistance of learned and pious monks in Upper Burma; taking drastic disciplinary measures, he purified the Buddhist Order in his own kingdom. He introduced a system of public examinations in religious learning, for which he awarded honors and stipends. The examinations were divided into grades, the highest being opened to monks and the lowest to children still in their teens. The result was a great revival of interest in studying the scriptures. He set up five thousand stone pillars on which were inscribed the entire volumes of the scriptures, including the commentaries. He encouraged devout monks to migrate to Lower Burma, or at least to visit regularly Lower Burmese villages, many of which were now without monasteries. Although the Christian missions were openly hostile to Buddhism, Mindon had no prejudice against them and granted plots of land to the Reverend Dr. Mark, head of the English Society for the Propagation of the Gospel, and to Bishop Bigandet, head of the French Roman Catholic Mission, to enable them to build their churches and schools. He even sent his sons to study English under Dr. Mark. As the old capitals of Ava and Amarapura were associated with the inglorious and tragic defeats of 1824–26 and 1852, he built a new capital, the golden city of Mandalay. Started in 1857, the city was completed in 1861, but he moved his court in 1858, after only the palace had been built.

Since he could not make Mandalay the political center of mainland southeast Asia as in the days of Anawrahta, Bayinnaung, and Alaungpaya, he was determined to make it the cultural and religious center of the region. The people of Burma found it difficult to forget that Siam had collaborated with the British in the wars of 1824 and 1852, but Mindon wanted to ignore the unhappy past and end the long years of conflict between the two countries. He would have liked to send an embassy to the king of Siam but was afraid lest he should be rebuffed both by Siam itself and by Britain as its ally. Accordingly, he sent a mission of monks bearing offerings and messages of goodwill to the primate, the head of the Buddhist clergy in Siam. King Mongkut was impressed with this friendly gesture and immediately sent his own mission of monks to the Burmese primate at Mandalay. Mindon arranged for some of the great monks who acted as his advisers in religious matters to visit Buddha Gaya and was disappointed when the British authorities in Ceylon refused to allow the same monks to visit Ceylon, on the obviously false excuse that an epidemic of cholera was raging at that time on the island. He then started to make preparations to hold the Fifth Great Synod of Buddhism at Mandalay.

This was no easy task that Mindon set for himself, for only powerful Buddhist monarchs, whose authority was recognized throughout the entire Buddhist world, had been able to hold these great assemblies of Buddhist monks from various countries. The First Great Synod was held immediately after the Buddha's passing away, the Second, some one hundred years later, and the Third in the third century B.C. under the patronage of the Emperor Asoka himself. All these assemblies were held in India. A few years before the beginning of the Christian era, a synod was held in Ceylon, which was recognized as the Fourth only by the Theravada school of Buddhism, and another was held in India in A.D. 78, which was recognized as the Fourth only by the Mahayana school. During the intervening centuries no monarch had felt himself qualified to hold another synod. Although King Mindon belonged to the Theravada school, he invited monks from all countries to participate in the assembly, and the high esteem all Buddhist countries had for Mindon and Burma was acknowledged by the fact that the entire Buddhist world sent representatives to the synod. At its conclusion Mindon proudly assumed the title of "Convener of the Fifth Great Synod of Buddhism."

Mindon desired to demonstrate that there was still only one Burmese nation, notwithstanding the existence of the political frontier above Thayetmyo; that all Burmese living in various parts of the country shared in the glorious traditions of the past; and that the many new shrines that he had built at Mandalay belonged to the whole nation, and the Shwedagon pagoda at Rangoon was the pride not only of the Burmese of Lower Burma, but of the Burmese of his kingdom also. He sought permission from the British authorities to come down to Rangoon and put a new golden spire studded with precious stones on the Shwedagon pagoda but the British, consistently following a policy of humiliating the king, refused. The Burmese in Lower Burma, who respected and loved Mindon, protested and finally the British authorities reluctantly granted permission for the king to send an embassy with the sole purpose of re-crowning Shwedagon pagoda on his behalf. Thus Mindon's embassy duly arrived in Rangoon, bringing with them the golden spire, and amidst scenes of ancient pageantry and mass enthusiasm the king's pious gift of beauty and splendor was placed on the top of the great shrine.

Mindon's reign had dawned with the Burmese sky overcast by the storm clouds of disaster and despair, and in spite of the sunshine of its noon it was now to close in darkness and gloom. Just as the British had betrayed him, a few of his sons and some of his courtiers were plotting treachery against him. He had appointed his brother Kanaung as the crown prince, and by character, experience, and ability he was the most fitting to succeed Mindon on the throne. A fiery soldier, he had mellowed with experience and learning. He had in recent years assiduously studied international affairs and law, and he had swiftly become a noted jurist, regularly presiding over the High Court of Hluttaw. As the commander-in-chief, he had improved the equipment and training of the army and, sharing his brother's interest in industry, he had set up a factory to manufacture guns and ammunition. He was bitter against the British over their humiliation of his brother, but at the same time he fully realized that the Burmese army would never be able to challenge the British because the disparity in arms remained as great as ever. The prince and Colonel Sladen never liked each other from the very beginning, and he disapproved of the special favors shown to the British resident by the king. The king's son, Prince Myingun, unlike Prince Mekkara, the minister for industries, was politically ambitious, arrogant, and aggressive, and he naturally resented his uncle's appointment as crown prince. Mindon knew of this resentment, but he never expected Myingun to rebel because the prince was married to his cousin, the daughter of the crown prince. In 1866, however, Prince Myingun and his brother Prince Myingondaing entered the Hluttaw as it was sitting in full session and assassinated the crown prince and the other judges.

Mindon at that time was not in the palace but at a summer camp outside the city. As the two princes were attacking the Hluttaw, they sent an assassin to the summer camp; when he entered the king's presence with a drawn sword, however, Mindon ordered him to drop the weapon. The assassin obeyed and Mindon escaped on horseback and entered the palace a few moments before Myingun's followers attacked the palace. The two princes rushed from the Hluttaw to the summer camp and were surprised to learn that the king had fled. Then they went back to join the attack on the palace but their followers, not knowing that the king was back in the palace, thought that he was in the city organizing a counterattack. Accordingly they withdrew to the river bank, where they were caught and routed by loyalist forces. Myingun and Myingondaing escaped in an Irrawaddy Flotilla Company boat into British territory. Both were interned by the British authorities in Rangoon, but soon afterwards Myingun appeared in the Karenni states and raised his standard there. Mindon had to send a powerful army to suppress the rebellion, and finally Myingun returned to Rangoon. Both brothers were now sent by the British to Calcutta, where the younger prince died; Myingun was then taken to Banares and interned there.

Myingun's rebellion threatened to cause a rupture in Anglo-Burmese relations because Mandalay market gossip alleged that the British were involved, and some of Mindon's ministers openly accused Colonel Sladen of at least knowing about the conspiracy before it broke out in open rebellion. They could offer no substantial proof, but they pointed to certain mysterious occurrences before and after the attack on the palace. Colonel Sladen, who had standing permission to visit the palace at any time he chose, had entered the palace gates immediately before the attack on the Hluttaw was launched and remained in the palace until the rebels had withdrawn. It was true that the British captain of the Irrawaddy boat had been threatened at sword point by the rebel prince, but many Burmese believed that it was merely for show, for they asked, why did the captain not make some attempt to resist when the rebels approached? After Myingun had been interned in Rangoon, he could not have departed for Karenni without cooperation from the British authorities, and Karenni after all had been the scene of anti-Burmese subversive activities by British officers. Until the final fall of the kingdom in 1885, the Burmese court remained convinced that Myingun was a protégé of Colonel Sladen. But Mindon still had confidence in Colonel Sladen and the British authorities at Rangoon and refused to believe the gossip and the accusations.

The Myingun rebellion was a national catastrophe of the highest magnitude; it was in many ways almost as disastrous as the two Anglo-Burmese wars, and it hastened the fall of the kingdom. The massacre at the Hluttaw deprived the king and the country of the ablest group of officials, who were in the full bloom of maturity and experience. Those officials had grown up in the shadow of defeat at the hands of the British and, in contrast to those who served Bodawpaya and Bagyidaw, they were not arrogant nor did they ever struggle or conspire for power. As the next generation of officers was still too young and inexperienced, Mindon had no choice but to recall to royal service older courtiers from their retirement. For some time, the High Court of Hluttaw consisted of only four officials, all old and decrepit. A famous abbot, who was respected not only for his great learning and piety, but also for his biting satirical wit, wrote the following lampoon and posted it on the doors of the judges' chambers:

> Pakhangyi has too much wind,
> Laungshay has a sword wound;
> Khanbat has no ear at all,
> Can one oil lamp light the kingdom?

The lampoon referred to the fact that of the four judges who also acted as privy councilors, three were physically unfit for their duties; the lord of Pakhangyi suffered from colic, the lord of Laung-shay had never fully recovered from a sword wound suffered while fighting for the king in the recent rebellion, and the lord of Khanbat had become deaf through old age. The "oil lamp" referred to the only physically fit member of the court, the lord of Yenangyaung; Yenangyaung was the chief town of the oil field region of Burma.

The rebellion brought in its wake a spate of lawlessness and disorder all over the kingdom, and as time passed it became obvious that Myingun, although exiled in India, still had supporters and sympathizers both outside and inside the court. Adding to the general lawlessness, some regiments who were loyal to the dead crown prince mutinied to show their dissatisfaction with the king's delay in declaring Kanaung's son as the new crown prince; many of the soldiers dispersed into the countryside with their arms and ammunition. Mindon felt the need of re-building and re-equipping the army so as to restore law and order. In 1866, before Myingun's rebellion, Phayre had gone again to Mandalay and attempted to gain a second commercial treaty even more favorable to the British than the first. Mindon had refused to consider the matter. Now, hoping for British assistance in the procurement of desperately needed arms, Mindon had to eat humble pie, and he himself invited the governor-general to send an embassy to discuss the signing of the second commercial treaty. The governor-general seized the opportunity to flog a dead horse; he instructed the new commissioner of Pegu, Albert Fytch, to make the terms as favorable to the British as possible and to include in the treaty the stipulation that the king should surrender the control of his country's foreign relations to the British. In other words, without fighting another war the governor-general hoped to turn the kingdom of Burma into a mere protectorate and to reduce the status of Mindon to that of a maharajah in British India.

Fytch showed respect and friendliness to Mindon, but he did not hesitate to drive a bargain as hard as that of the Treaty of Yandabo. Beggars could not be choosers, and Mindon had to give way, but even at that desperate hour he would not sell the sovereign independence of the kingdom; at the last moment Fytch decided not to press for the surrender of control of Burma's foreign relations. The treaty was finally signed in 1867, containing the following stipulations: (1) Both signatories would reduce the existing rates of custom duties payable at the frontier and would fix the new rate at 5 per cent of the total value of each consignment of goods. (2) Both signatories would agree to permit without restrictions the import or export of gold and silver bullion. (3) The king would agree to assist the British authorities to open trade relations with China across Burmese territory. (4) The king would receive a deputy British representative to reside at Bhamo. (5) The king would abolish all his monopolies except in timber, petroleum, and precious stones. (6) The king could procure arms and ammunition in or through British territory, subject to prior approval of the British commissioner of Lower Burma. There were two other provisions in the treaty, one relating to the extradition of criminals and the other relating to the revision of the treaty. The latter stipulation was vaguely worded and was to become a subject of dispute during the reign of King Mindon's successor, King Theebaw.

From the point of view of the British mercantile interests, the commercial treaty was a victory for British aims, as the back door to China was now open to them. With indecent haste, Colonel Sladen, with his expenses paid by British firms in Rangoon, proceeded at once to Bhamo and then to Yunnan. On the way, as usual, he occupied himself in subversive activities against the king, and when local Burmese officials reported the matter to Mindon he ordered them to continue to give assistance to Sladen as all terms of the treaty would have to be honored. Sladen's expedition reached Yunnan at a most inopportune time, for the state was then in the throes of a rebellion. Sladen, however, continued his journey until one of the members of the expedition was murdered by rebels. On returning to Burma he appointed one of his subordinates, Captain Strover, as deputy representative at Bhamo and doubtless instructed him to continue subversive activities against Burmese interests. Strover promptly attempted to persuade Kachin chieftains to rebel against the Burmese king and regularly sent consignments of rifles and bullets to them as presents from the great white queen.

Mindon had slowly learned to be less trusting of British promises, and at the time of the treaty he asked for and received an official note from Albert Fytch stating that the required approval from the British commissioner for procurement of arms through British territory would ordinarily be given as a matter of course. The British, unlike the Burmese king, had no scruples about breaking promises made in the treaty, and when Mindon attempted to buy arms in British India the governor-general prohibited British merchants from selling weapons to the king. When the king bought military equipment from Italy and France, the British commissioner in Lower Burma promptly refused to allow the military materials to pass through British territory. As Lord Ripon, who became governor-general after the death of Mindon, later pointed out, the British were guilty of a breach of faith in refusing to sell arms to the Burmese king and in denying transit over British territory of arms bought by him elsewhere.

At long last Mindon realized that the governor-general in India and the British commissioner in Lower Burma had merely been playing with him as a cat plays with a mouse it catches. He was emboldened however by the receipt of a message of goodwill from Queen Victoria herself through the governor-general, and in 1872 he sent an embassy headed by the rising star in his court, the minister Kinwun Mingyi, who had been a close associate and subordinate of the dead crown prince. Kinwun Mingyi, an erudite jurist and a scholar, was gradually winning the respect and regard of the nation. The main purpose of this first Burmese diplomatic mission to Europe was to gain acceptance of the Burmese kingdom as a truly sovereign state by the international world, especially by England. On the way to England the embassy passed through Italy and France and was accorded high honors by the governments of the two countries. In England, also, the embassy was well received and taken to such

aristocratic social occasions as the Eton and Harrow cricket match
and the Ascot races. The various chambers of commerce presented
welcome addresses, but Kinwun Mingyi was never given an opportunity to announce the real purpose of his visit, namely to establish
direct diplomatic relations with the British sovereign's Court of St.
James's. Whenever he broached the subject to the British protocol
officer or to the British secretaries and escorts attached to the embassy, all shook their heads.

When at long last Kinwun Mingyi was informed that Queen
Victoria would grant the embassy an audience, his blood quickened
with excitement because he felt that success was now within his
grasp. When the great day dawned, however, the British protocol
officer whispered in his ear that it would be a breach of protocol
to discuss the matter of the Burmese representation at the Court of
St. James's directly with the queen; it must be done through the
secretary of state for foreign affairs. Kinwun Mingyi was not yet discouraged, for surely he would be able to see the secretary of state
for foreign affairs at Windsor Castle just before entering the presence
of the queen, as he would be waiting there to present the embassy
to the queen. When he and the other members of the embassy arrived
at Windsor Castle, to their chagrin they found the secretary of state
for India waiting to present them. It was a further humiliation for
King Mindon, for the absence of the secretary of state for foreign
affairs and the presence of the secretary of state for India proclaimed
that at the Court of St. James's the proud kingdom of Burma was
ranked below the kingdom of Siam and was considered to be already a minor state within British India. Queen Victoria was gracious, but in their disappointment the Burmese ambassador and his
entourage were almost silent. The shrewd American ambassador to
the Court of St. James's, who was a guest at the glittering reception
given by the queen in honor of the Burmese embassy, noted in his
report to his government that the presentation of the Burmese embassy to the queen by the secretary of state for India and not by the

secretary of state for foreign affairs clearly indicated the British attitude toward the kingdom of Burma—they regarded it no longer as a sovereign state but as a conquered colony.

Kinwun Mingyi tried to save the honor of his king by obtaining treaties of commerce and friendship with France and Italy. The treaty with Italy merely contained expressions of goodwill and friendship, suggesting the establishment of closer commercial relations between Italy and Burma at a later date. The treaty with France contained definite commercial arrangements, including a grant to a French company of a concession to work the ruby mines. The two treaties constituted a poor recompense for the embassy's long voyage to Europe, but Kinwun Mingyi felt that the treaties at least demonstrated the sovereignty of the Burmese kingdom. Mindon ratified the treaty with Italy but rejected the one with France on the ground that the ruby mines, like royal regalia, were personal to the king and could never be leased or given away.

The cup of sorrow for King Mindon was not yet full to the brim; he was to suffer still further humiliations. Throughout his reign the British had been interfering in the affairs of the Karenni states. The subversive activities of the British military and civil officers in the region now showed success, and some of the Karenni chiefs rose against Mindon, receiving military assistance and advice from the British. How bold and brazen the British had become in their dealings with the Burmese king is clear from the following incident. When a Karenni chieftain, in spite of British promises to assist and reward him if he should rebel, came in person to the king to take the ceremonial oath of allegiance, Colonel Sladen, who was present at the ceremony, sought and obtained permission to see the chief; during the interview Sladen attempted to win the chief over to the British side. The chief indignantly reported Sladen's treachery to Mindon, who became angry but made no protest to the British authorities, knowing full well that his protest would be in vain. The position in the Karenni states worsened, and there was a real danger of conflict between the Burmese forces who were fighting the rebels

and the British troops assisting them. Although Mindon felt humiliated over the British intervention in the Karenni states, he selflessly
resolved to avoid war at all cost, for it would bring only death and
disaster to the Burmese people. Accordingly, when the governor-
general sought his consent to send an embassy headed by Sir Douglas
Forsyth to discuss Karenni affairs, Mindon welcomed the proposal.

In 1875 the embassy arrived and Forsyth proved to be as unsympathetic an ambassador as Cox and Crawfurd had been. He did
not negotiate but merely presented the demand that Mindon should
recognize the independence and the neutrality of the Karenni
states. Even Kinwun Mingyi felt that the kingdom should go to war
in spite of the certainty of defeat, but Mindon swallowed the bitter
pill and signed away the territory of Karenni states, which had been
held by Burmese kings since the days of Anawrahta. Forsyth's victory was complete, but he brooded over the fact that he had to remove his shoes on entering Mindon's audience chamber, in accord
with Burmese court etiquette. Cox and Crawfurd had also noted in
their reports their objection to this custom, which they considered
to be barbaric and shameful to an Englishman. Forsyth had suffered
no physical discomfort by having to walk in his socks because the
passage was clean and polished and heavily carpeted. However, he
registered a strong protest with the governor-general, who welcomed
yet another opportunity to humiliate Mindon; he gave instructions
to the British resident at Mandalay that he should not enter the
king's audience chamber unless he was permitted to keep his shoes
on and to wear his sword. The governor-general also informed
Mindon of his new instructions to the British resident. Mindon was
saddened by the governor-general's decision to revive this "shoe
question," but he could not do anything about it except to stop inviting the British representative to come to the palace for formal
and informal discussions. His ministers and his people were already
highly critical of his acceptance of the British demands over the
Karenni states, and he could not afford to lower his prestige any
further by permitting the British representative to stride into the

audience chamber looking like a conqueror, wearing heavy leather boots and a sword. Mindon's heart was broken; although he lived on for three more years, a despondent and sick man, he took no further interest in the affairs of his kingdom.

During those three remaining years Mindon was reluctant to name any of his sons as the crown prince for fear that he would be in effect singling him out for assassination. The prince of Nyaungyan was the obvious choice but, although popular with the people, he was too friendly with Colonel Sladen. The minister for industries, the prince of Mekkara, would have been a happy choice but he had no aspirations for the throne and, moreover, he was stern and aloof with the courtiers. The prince of Thonze was another possibility, but he was almost unknown to the people. In 1878 as Mindon lay dying, the chief queen, the minister Taingdar Mingyi, her favorite, and Kinwun Mingyi plotted to seize power by placing an unknown Prince Theebaw on the throne. Theebaw at the time was a monk who had been studying the scriptures for a number of years in the monastery. Theebaw was persuaded to leave the Buddhist Order and to marry the queen's daughter, his half sister, who was lively, gay, headstrong, and ambitious. This practice of keeping the dynasty pure by marrying a king's son by one queen to a daughter by another queen was common in Oriental countries, but not in Burma until the later periods of Alaungpaya's dynasty. Under Burmese customary law, marriage between a half brother and a half sister was deemed incestuous and was prohibited, and the fact that the later kings of Alaungpaya's dynasty thought it necessary to keep their blood pure by breaking a rule of customary law was a further illustration of the arrogance and artificiality of their courts. The conspirators were certain that Theebaw would be entirely dependent on them, for he was an absolute nonentity, without influence or support from any quarter.

In the king's name, all the other sons and cousins who had any claim to the throne, together with their families, were arrested. Nyaungyan and his brother, the prince of Nyaung-ok, escaped in disguise and sought asylum in the British residency; they were at once sent to Rangoon in the British resident's special armed steamboat. Some of the more loyal courtiers reported the arrest of the princes to Mindon, who ordered their release and appointed a regency council consisting of Nyaungyan, Mekkara, and Thonze. Nyaungyan was included, for it was believed that he was still in the British residency. As the princes and their families were leaving prison, however, they were re-arrested by the conspirators, who had been informed by the court physicians that the king could not live for more than a few hours. As the physicians had diagnosed and predicted, the king died on the following day, and the Hluttaw immediately proclaimed Theebaw as king. At the same time the conspirators ordered the immediate execution of the princes and their families who were under arrest. The prime responsibility for the manipulation of the election by the Hluttaw must be placed on Kinwun Mingyi, for it was his prestige and personality that swayed the privy councilors to Theebaw's side. For the massacre of the royal kinsmen, also, Kinwun must bear the blame, for he could have stopped the orders for the executions passed by the queen and the other conspirators because they had no legal authority. In fact, the kinsmen were executed not by public executioners but by some of the queen's bodyguards, who were appointed executioners for the occasion. As Kinwun Mingyi was a liberal statesman and a learned judge, it is difficult to conjecture for what motive he joined the conspiracy. His critics said that in spite of his great learning he was a mere seeker after power, while his admirers explained that he wanted a weak king on the throne so that he could take necessary measures to transform the kingdom into a constitutional monarchy. In any case, just as Mindon was betrayed in his lifetime by Colonel Sladen, whom he trusted, he was betrayed in death by Kinwun Mingyi, in whom he had the greatest confidence.

For a few years during his reign Mindon was able to make the court reach out to the people and thus modify the artificiality of court life. This had a happy effect on Burmese literature. Lady

Hlaing, who was the consort of the assassinated crown prince, inherited the lyrical and musical gifts of her mother, the Lady Myagalay. She introduced a new kind of song and a new type of tune, in which the words and music together gave an effect of dignity and stateliness tinged with a gentle melancholy. She wrote a long court play in which princes and princesses fell in and out of love; although the story was romantic and unreal, the dialogue was lively and vigorous. U Pon Nya, who was later executed for his involvement in the Myingun rebellion, produced a number of great plays in which the court drama and the popular drama were fused in such a way that his plays were performed both inside and outside the palace walls. During Mindon's reign *The Glass Palace Chronicle* was brought up to date by a committee of scholars; their account of the two Anglo-Burmese wars was written with the objectivity of the true historian, and the great national defeats were described faithfully in detail. In addition to many works of prose and poetry, monks and laymen alike wrote extensively on the scriptures. The introduction of cheap printing presses from India and the improvement in communications encouraged literary activity, and it was considered the hallmark of a citizen of Mandalay to be able to compose at least a few epistles and one or two lyrics. The difficulties and the uncertainties of the closing years of Mindon's reign discouraged writers and poets, however, and the court again divorced itself from the people, taking refuge again in an atmosphere of artificiality and makebelieve. The people no longer cared what was happening inside the palace and the courtiers no longer knew what was happening to the people.

The British merchants at Rangoon, who wanted the kingdom to fall so that they could share in its riches, shed crocodile tears over the massacre of the royal kinsmen and spread fearful rumors that the new king and his supporters were plotting to kill Mr. Shaw, the British resident. Shaw was critical of the massacre, but at the same time he did not think that the British had any cause for alarm. Unfortunately he suddenly died of fever and his successor was inept and nervous. When across the sub-continent of India the British resident in Afghanistan was murdered by a mob, the governor-general, fearing for the safety of the personnel of the residency, recalled the entire staff and closed down the residency. Theebaw and his advisers were alarmed, and the king immediately sent an embassy to the governor-general as a gesture of friendliness and regard for the British. The British authorities in Lower Burma detained the embassy at Thayetmyo and refused to permit it to proceed any farther, on the ground that the embassy had no plenipotentiary powers. To overcome this empty objection of the British, Theebaw conferred full plenipotentiary powers on the embassy. As the embassy waited at Thayetmyo, Lower Burma was full of rumors of Burmese provocations and Burmese plans to invade British territory, and the British merchants sent request after request both to the governor-general in India and to the British government at London for the annexation of Upper Burma.

The third Anglo-Burmese war seemed imminent, and both Nyaungyan and Nyaung-ok princes were permitted to return to Rangoon, as the British planned to place Nyaungyan on the throne in place of Theebaw and turn Upper Burma into a British protectorate. The Burmese embassy, after waiting for months at Thayetmyo, was finally informed by the British commissioner that he could not allow them to proceed and they should immediately return to Burmese territory. But war did not come, for two reasons: the British were busy subduing Afghanistan and the Zulus in Africa, and the British civilian officials in Rangoon discounted the wild rumors spread by the merchants. In 1880 the crisis passed, and the two princes were instructed by the British government to return to internment in Calcutta. As they waited for passage the younger brother Nyaung-ok and a group of Burmese followers, equipped with arms supplied or sold by the British merchants, invaded Upper Burma from Thayetmyo. He was driven back and returned to Calcutta. The Burmese king held the British authorities in Rangoon responsible and demanded full compensation for the loss of Burmese life and property resulting from the attack by Nyaung-ok. The demand was ignored, but there were no more frontier incidents. Throughout the rest of Theebaw's reign, however, the threat of British invasion hung like a sword over his head, and he had no opportunity to do anything else but to remain constantly on the alert.

With the king and his ministers focusing all their attention on the threat of another British invasion, lawless elements in the kingdom were encouraged to resort to robbery and banditry, and spies and secret supporters of Prince Myingun harassed the kingdom. In spite of this unrest, the trade of the kingdom was rapidly expanding. The effects of the Suez Canal's opening were now seen in the fivefold increase in the volume of trade between Britain and Burma, and the wise measures taken by King Mindon to improve communications continued to facilitate the smooth flow of trade. However, the rising profits made the British merchants at Rangoon hunger for more, and they made loud clamors that Theebaw was standing between them and access to China. Similarly, Theebaw and his advisers wanted to re-nationalize imports and exports and restore the royal monopoly. The commercial treaty which Fytch obtained from Mindon in 1866 contained a vague statement that there could be a revision after ten years, but it was not made clear whether this meant the revision of the entire treaty or merely the revision of the particular stipulation relating to the rates of custom duties payable at the frontier. The Burmese took the attitude that the treaty was no longer valid as the British had already broken it by refusing the transit of arms through their territory; in any case, because the stipulated ten years had passed, the treaty was due for revision. As was to be expected, the British merchants in Rangoon raised their usual hue and cry about "Burmese aggression." The tension was eased by the appointment of Lord Ripon as the new governor-general on the retirement of the old, and he was a liberal statesman who was sympathetic toward the Burmese interpretation of the treaty. On his invitation, Theebaw sent an embassy to him in 1881 but the negotiations broke down on the usual Burmese request for direct diplomatic relations with the Court of St. James's.

The failure of negotiations with the British ended the influence of Kinwun Mingyi at the Burmese court, which had already been waning. Kinwun Mingyi's plan of making Theebaw a puppet was found unworkable because of the firm control exercised over the weak king by his Queen Supayalat. She was ambitious and had the confidence of youth, and she soon began to brush aside the advice of her mother and Kinwun Mingyi. The only person who had some influence over her was the Taingdar Mingyi, and there soon developed a bitter rivalry between Kinwun Mingyi and Taingdar Mingyi. Kinwun Mingyi's belief that the British would relent and agree to the revision of the treaty if properly approached had been criticized by Taingdar, and, now that Kinwun had been proved wrong, Taingdar's proposal that an embassy be sent to Italy, Germany, and France was considered by the queen. Myingun's secret supporters decided that a bold bid should now be made for the throne and they prepared to rebel, but their plot was discovered in time. Coming in the wake of the failure of negotiations with Lord Ripon, their plot convinced the queen that British secret agents were working for Myingun so that a king more favorable to the British should replace Theebaw. This seemed to clinch the matter, and in 1883 a Burmese embassy prepared to depart for Europe.

The British were suspicious of the intentions of the Burmese and, furthermore, feared that the French would encroach on their Burmese preserves because the French, having lost out to the British in other parts of the world, were pursuing an aggressive and ambitious policy in southeast Asia. The British had repeatedly informed France and other European powers that they had a special interest in Burma but felt they had to be careful with the able but reckless French foreign minister, M. Jules Ferry. At this juncture Prince Myingun disappeared from his internment in Banares and suddenly re-appeared in the French Indian possession of Chandernagore. The Burmese court was convinced that the prince could not really have escaped and made his long journey to the French possession without the permission and help of the British and that therefore his appear-

ance on French territory was engineered by the British authorities
to embarrass the French government and to prevent the embassy
from going to France. The queen, however, decided that the mission
should leave but instructed the envoys not to touch on any political
matter while negotiating for treaties of friendship and commerce
with various European powers.

On arrival in Paris the embassy started negotiations for a convention that would serve as a supplement to the treaty of commerce
negotiated by Kinwun Mingyi in 1873, and the envoys remained in
France for some months, which increased the suspicion of the
British. The delay was due to the great caution exercised by the
Burmese mission to reject any proposal that would affect in any way
the sovereign independence of the kingdom. For example, the
envoys rejected the repeated requests of the French government
that the French consul in Burma should have jurisdiction over
French nationals resident in the kingdom. The British ambassador
in Paris watched all movements of the Burmese mission with disapproval and bluntly informed the French foreign minister that
the British government would protest if the proposed supplement to
the treaty should contain any stipulation that was not purely commercial in character. The convention was finally signed in January
1885 and all twenty articles contained therein were purely commercial in character except those relating to the extradition of
criminals. The mission then proceeded to the Netherlands but failed
to obtain any treaty there. In Germany the negotiations were successful and a treaty of commerce, peace, and friendship was signed.
The British merchants in Rangoon spread rumors of secret military
clauses in the treaty with France, but even they were silenced when
Ferry was forced to resign his post and the convention negotiated
by the Burmese mission was left unratified by the French government. The Burmese mission returned to Mandalay with a sense of
failure for its only significant achievement was the establishment
of a permanent Burmese embassy at Paris.

In August 1885 a sudden flood of rumors was begun by British merchants at Rangoon who insisted that under secret clauses of the convention France had gained four important concessions. The ruby mines were to be leased to a French company, the Burmese post and telegraph system would be placed under a French supervisor, a railway was to be constructed across the Shan states, linking French Indo-China with Mandalay, and a French flotilla company would be established on the upper Irrawaddy. The rumors were absolutely false, because the ruby mines were a royal monopoly that Theebaw could not give up without further loss of prestige with the people, the post and telegraph system was doing so well that it was the pride of the nation, it was physically impossible because of the terrain to construct a railway linking the kingdom of Burma with French Indo-China, and no French steamboat could ever hope to get past the rigid British control of the lower Irrawaddy. The British merchants at Rangoon sent frantic cables to the various chambers of commerce in the British Isles, requesting that they should agitate to pull down Theebaw from his throne. But the British officials in Lower Burma, including the commissioner himself, were skeptical of the rumors. One Chevalier Adreino proved to be the arbiter of Burma's destiny.

This worthy gentleman held three separate appointments; he was the Italian consul to the Burmese court, he was the agent in the Burmese kingdom of the Bombay Burma Trading Corporation, and he was the head of the British spy ring at Mandalay. He now produced a document purporting to be a copy of a letter written by the French foreign minister, Ferry, at the time the Burmese mission was visiting Paris to negotiate the convention. In the letter Ferry promised to supply arms to the Burmese king from Tongkin. The British merchants in Rangoon made shrill cries of protest at this treachery of the Burmese king. Even in London the British government was annoyed and played with the idea of making Myingun their candidate for the Burmese throne although he was on French Indian territory. But by that time the French had taken Myingun to Saigon, planning to help him invade Burmese territory from French

Indo-China, or even from Siam with the latter's consent. The British government called upon the French envoy in London to explain Ferry's letter; after hearing him they became convinced that France had no hold on Theebaw and the rumors of the concessions and the secret clauses were not true. It is difficult to understand why the British were so concerned over the alleged copy of Ferry's letter, dated some seven months before, since Ferry had already fallen and, even if the document was genuine, it was already politically outdated.

In the midst of all this excitement the Hluttaw delivered its judgment on the long-standing case involving the Bombay Burma Trading Corporation, which had a virtual monopoly of the export of Burmese timber. It worked not only the forests of British Burma but also some forests across the frontier in Upper Burma under a series of contracts with the king. The suit that came before the Hluttaw was initiated not by the Burmese king but by some foresters who claimed payment from the corporation of the balance of the total sum due to them for logs supplied. The court found that the lists submitted by the contending parties were conflicting and obtained copies of records from the corporation's own forest office at Toungoo. The copies were obtained officially from the forest office with the permission of the British commissioner of Lower Burma, and with the consent of both parties. Relying on those records, the court found that the sum of 33,333 pounds was due by the corporation to the foresters, as the previous payments were made on incorrect lists. The court also found that, as the corporation had used the same incorrect lists in calculating the revenue due to the king, there had been a short payment of revenue, leaving an unpaid balance of 36,666½ pounds. Under Burmese law, a short payment of revenue could be settled only by a double payment and the Hluttaw ordered the corporation to pay to the royal treasury the sum of 73,333 pounds.

According to Burmese law and procedure the judgment contained no flaw. The British commissioner of Lower Burma gave the opinion that the finding of the court was justified, although the fine was excessive. By implication, he did not question the correctness of the sum found due to the foresters, and by "the fine" he was obviously referring to double payment of the balance of revenue. But the British merchants at Rangoon saw in the judgment an opportunity to agitate again for turning Burma into a protectorate. Chevalier Adreino, who as agent was named along with the two managers of the corporation as defendants in the case, had played his cards well. Through a palace spy he had obtained a copy of the judgment awaiting formal delivery; determining to save his company from having to pay the sum as ordered by the court, he thought out a plan to rouse British public opinion against the king. He kept the copy of the judgment aside and forged the alleged copy of Ferry's letter for submission to the British authorities in Rangoon. Lord Dufferin, the new governor-general of India, hoping to add the kingdom of Burma to his British Indian empire, demanded that the Burmese king submit the matter of the corporation's fine to arbitration and added the astounding proviso that there should be a sole arbitrator, to be appointed by Dufferin himself. As the Burmese king paused to consider this ridiculous proposal, the British merchants at Rangoon were already celebrating their victory, openly saying that Lord Dufferin would put Prince Nyaungyan on the throne. In spite of the opinion of the British officials at Rangoon that the matter could still be settled by negotiation, both the British government in London and the governor-general decided to present an ultimatum to King Theebaw.

The ultimatum contained the following demands: (1) The king should receive a special envoy from the governor-general to settle the dispute over the fine ordered to be paid by the corporation without submitting him to any humiliating ceremony. (2) The decree against the corporation should be kept suspended until this special envoy had settled the dispute. (3) The king should receive again a representative of the governor-general to reside at Mandalay and should permit him to have a British guard of honor consisting of

1,000 soldiers and a fully armed steamer. (4) The king must provide proper facilities for the British to open commercial relations with China through Burmese territory. (5) The king should conduct his foreign relations only under the supervision and control of the governor-general. In other words, the ultimatum required the king to accept the status of an Indian maharajah. Theebaw had no choice but to reject the ultimatum, for whether he accepted or rejected it Burma would lose her sovereignty; at this crisis in his life, he acted with dignity and restraint. He and his advisers hoped that the international community of free nations would give some moral support to the Burmese kingdom and help it to survive.

Accordingly, the king sent back a reply containing the following points: (1) No special envoy was necessary to discuss the judgment of the Hluttaw, as the case against the corporation was decided according to the principles of Burmese law, justice, and equity. (2) A petition for review of the judgment still lay, and while the king awaited its presentation by the corporation the judgment would remain suspended as in all such cases. (3) A permanent British resident at Mandalay would be welcomed. (4) The king was always willing to assist Britain to build up a trade with China through Burmese territory. (5) According to the understanding of the king, the external and internal affairs of a sovereign state were regulated and controlled by that state only. Therefore, the king would suggest that the British proposal to supervise the external relations of the kingdom be submitted for consideration to France, Germany, and Italy, with whom both Burma and Britain maintained diplomatic relations.

The governor-general never expected that the king would accept his harsh demands and had ordered that a British expeditionary force be assembled immediately at Thayetmyo. The ultimatum was to expire at midnight on November 10, but a full six days before the appointed date Dufferin received the Burmese reply. However the expeditionary force still stood at Thayetmyo, and at the prow of one of its ships a prince in full regalia was seen surrounded by people dressed as ministers and courtiers. The rumor went up and down the

Irrawaddy river that Prince Nyaungyan was with the expeditionary force, ready to ascend the throne. To all the commanders of Burmese forts along the river there came secret orders, purporting to be from Kinwun Mingyi and instructing them not to resist the British forces, as they had come in support of Nyaungyan. November 10 arrived, and passed, and still the expeditionary force remained at Thayetmyo, as if it were waiting for Kinwun Mingyi's orders to reach all the river garrisons. In actual fact, Nyaungyan had died at Calcutta a few weeks before, but the British kept the news hidden from the public. On November 17 the expeditionary force finally left Thayetmyo for the frontier, but in the meantime a Burmese official had accidentally discovered that the young man on the prow was not a prince at all but a clerk in the British commissioner's office who had been dressed to look like Prince Nyaungyan. The Burmese official now doubted the authenticity of the orders not to resist the British. He sent messages up the river informing the commanders of his discovery, but his information arrived too late.

He himself made a desperate effort from Minhla fort to stop the British advance, but after a fierce battle he was killed and the fort destroyed. The British met with no resistance at all until they reached Ava. A peace mission arrived from Theebaw asking for an armistice, but the British commander demanded an unconditional surrender, to which the king then agreed. However, the commander of the Ava fort was training his guns on the approaching British expeditionary force. Theebaw sent an urgent message asking him to refrain, but the commander requested written instructions, insisting that he had been receiving conflicting orders thoughout the day. Theebaw sent his orders in writing, and the British ships sailed past Ava to Mandalay, where the troops disembarked and surrounded the golden palace. It was now November 28. The British had won an inglorious victory, and the war had lasted just eleven days.

The following morning the king and the queen held their last audience in the lacquer and gold pavilion in the palace garden, awaiting the arrival of the British commander, General Prendergast.

Soon, Prendergast and Colonel Sladen strode in noisily, wearing their scarlet uniforms. In the ensuing silence the courtiers could not help noticing the change in Colonel Sladen's demeanor. The former ingratiating manner had been replaced by a look of triumph, and Theebaw gave a sigh, realizing that he could expect no mercy from the conquerors. The British general was courteous but firm, and gave the fallen monarch and his queen exactly forty-five minutes to start on their journey to exile on the western coast of India. As the royal chamberlain hastily packed a few clothes and some jewels, the king requested permission from the British general to leave his city in state, riding on an elephant or a palanquin. But Prendergast obviously wanted to humiliate Theebaw; he placed him and his queen in a common box carriage drawn by two bullocks.

The streets were lined with people, many of whom had never seen Theebaw before, because throughout his reign, knowing that he was out of touch and unpopular with the people, he had seldom ventured out into the city. Suddenly the crowd realized that they were losing their national independence and Theebaw was being taken into exile. The sight of the tiny, dignified figure, helpless, humiliated, and pale, riding on a common cart surrounded by hundreds of red-coated and bearded giants, won for Theebaw the hearts of his people, which he had never known before. As many women threw themselves into the dust, lamented, and wailed, the men left the city carrying with them all the arms they could find. Outside the city a loyal Sawbwa with a handful of personally chosen men waited to rescue his sovereign from the hands of the British, but the double ring of British soldiers around the king made it impossible for him to work out his plan. Some youths threw stones at the soldiers, but the British general, wanting to avoid a riot, hurried the royal party on until it reached the troop ships at sundown. The king and his small entourage were swiftly put on one of the ships and sent down the river and then across the ocean to exile on the Bombay coast of India, where the king was to die in 1916.

Except for a few sonnet-like poems of melancholy regret, Theebaw's reign was devoid of any important literary development. However, in Lower Burma under alien rule, there developed two new literary forms, the decadent drama and the monk's tale. The sentimental regret on the part of the people at the certain passing of the Burmese kingdom resulted in the appearance of a number of new plays. No playwright of the caliber of U Kyin U or U Pon Nya ever came forth, but the new playwrights were more prolific, and their plays, in addition to being performed, were quickly printed on cheap paper and sold to an admiring public. Every play had a long scene in which the king held audience with his ministers, which reflected the sentimental attitude the audience had toward the doomed king and his court. The atmosphere of those plays was similar to the atmosphere of darkness and doom that pervaded Jacobean drama in seventeenth-century England.

In contrast, the monk's tale had a gay and optimistic tone. The inventor of this new literary form was Thingazar Sayadaw, one of King Mindon's great monks, who came down to Lower Burma just before Mindon died with the purpose of preparing the Burmese people to receive the shock of the inevitable loss of the Burmese kingdom and most of its institutions. Since the re-crowning of the Shwedagon pagoda by King Mindon's embassy, the people of Lower Burma had learned to look to the king at Mandalay for the preservation of their religion and their way of life, but now Mindon was dying and, no matter who might be chosen as his successor, the days of the monarchy were known to be numbered. Thingazar Sayadaw's merry tales emphasized that the final passing of the Burmese kingdom should not necessarily mean that the Buddhist religion and the Burmese traditions of the past would disappear, provided the people themselves strove toward their preservation. The tales gave vivid cameos of Burmese social life on the eve of the British conquest and restored courage and confidence to a stricken people.

XII   The Regaining of Independence, 1886–1948

After the removal of Theebaw, Lord Dufferin at first played with the idea of placing his own nominee on the vacant throne and making the kingdom a British protectorate. Finally however he decided to annex the territory altogether and, with a view to further humiliate the Burmese people, declared the whole country to be a mere province of the Indian empire. He probably hoped that the Burmese would lose their separate racial identity under a flood of Indian immigrants. But the Burmese, refusing to accept the British victory as final, resorted to guerrilla warfare against the British occupation army. There were spontaneous uprisings all over the country, led by officers of various grades of the disbanded royal armies, village headmen, former officials in the service of the king, princes of the blood, and even Buddhist monks. The British authorities refused to recognize them as patriots and declared them to be bandits, who should be killed or executed at sight. For the next four years, although no martial law was proclaimed, it was the provost marshal who meted out justice. There were mass executions of those patriots, and sometimes whole villages including women and children were massacred. Unacquainted with the Burmese language, Burmese attitudes and aspirations, British troops were angered by the ferocity of the guerrilla attacks and the sympathy shown to them by villagers. The British had to maintain a force of some 30,000 regular soldiers and another 30,000 military police to quell the uprisings.

As the guerrillas fought on, in 1887 Sir Charles Crosthwaite became chief commissioner for the whole of Burma and served until 1890. He was a ruthless administrator and introduced carefully planned measures to frighten the villagers into submission. Villages suspected of being in sympathy with the guerrillas were burned and re-building was prohibited. Families who had supplied the headmen of villages for several generations were singled out for persecution. New villages were established so that their new headmen would not have any links with the past. Finally, any person found carrying any weapon was hanged on the nearest tree and his head cut off to be taken to the district police headquarters for purposes of identification. Thousands were killed in battle or executed on capture during a period of four years immediately following the annexation of the country, but the British authorities later admitted that not one of them showed fear. Finally the uprisings were suppressed, but the people still refused to accept that the British had come to stay. By the year 1890 Crosthwaite could sing a paean of triumph, which he later expanded into a book entitled *The Pacification of Burma*, but the Burmese villagers quietly built little pagodas on the sites of the executions and kept alive the spirit of nationalism so nobly demonstrated by the guerrillas. The following poem, written by a British army captain who later served as a police officer, shows that at least a few Englishmen felt ashamed of the British atrocities.

> Under a spreading mango tree
> A Burmese Chieftain stands,
> His hour has come: a captive he
> Within the conqueror's hands;
> And they fasten around his sturdy neck
> A noose of hempen strands.
>
> Under a spreading mango tree
> A lifeless body swings.
> Though bound its limbs, a soul is free

And spreads on joyful wings
To solve the perplexing myst'ries of
Ten thousand hidden things.

Under a spreading mango tree
A Buddhist chapel stands,
Where children pray on bended knee,
Amidst the shimmering sands,
That the seeds of Western culture may
Take root in Eastern lands!

The period of 1890 to 1920 was a period of peace for the country. The people were dazzled by the new economic development and by the restoration of law and order by the British. Outwardly, also, British rule did not seem to affect the general structure of Burmese society. Buddhism continued to prevail. The British officials of this period also showed sympathy toward the people, and unlike in India and Ceylon they did not expose the Burmese nor their religion to social persecution. In other words, no social barrier was created between the ruler and the ruled. The British officials were so few in number that, except in Rangoon, they could not set up exclusive social clubs and had to mix freely with junior Burmese officials. The European trouser and coat did not replace the native sarong and jacket, and dress never became a political issue as it did in other Asian countries. However, the foundations of Burmese society were being slowly shaken by British rule.

One fundamental change was in the educational system. The monastery, which had served the people as the center of secular and religious education, suddenly lost its social importance. The government schools and the Christian missionary schools offered the type of education that would lead a student toward clerical service in the government. Before the British conquest, education was free, and under the British government, the fees charged were still nominal. But the new schools were established only in towns and cities and, as a result, educational opportunities were denied to villagers. Monastic education now became a badge of inferiority because obviously only those children whose parents could not afford to send them to the new schools in towns studied at monasteries. The initiation ceremony became merely a social occasion because boys studying in the new schools could take the lower Ordination only during their vacations, and they learned nothing of monastic discipline nor were they introduced to scriptural studies. In fact, the Burmese boys and girls who went to the Christian schools knew more about the Ten Commandments than the Five Precepts. However, they had not become Christians, but merely misfits in Burmese society. The centuries-old custom of the pupil showing respect to the teacher and the happy teacher-pupil relationship disappeared from Burmese society. The Christian missionaries who served as teachers in mission schools did not realize the social value of this relationship until it was too late, and their show of favoritism to a handful of Christians in their classes resulted in resentment against the teachers on the part of non-Christian pupils. In the government schools the teachers were salaried civil servants, and as mere civil servants they could not gain the love and respect of their pupils. This was later to result in strikes and boycotts in schools and the university.

There was also a dearth of national leaders. The Burmese never had a hereditary nobility, and able princes and princesses had long ago lost their lives in the Myingun rebellion and in Theebaw's massacre of his kinsmen and kinswomen. Nyaungyan and Myingun, in spite of their patriotism, had gained an evil reputation for all princes as mere stooges of the British or the French. A few other princes who escaped the massacre and also retained some personal prestige had been shot or hanged as leaders of guerrillas. Sir Charles Crosthwaite had destroyed the natural leaders among villagers, namely the families of village headmen, and, as he had intended, the new headmen were mere officials at the bottom of the service scale and had neither the influence nor the power to act as leaders of their villages. The Burmese officials who were appointed by the British government could not become leaders because they held only subordinate positions, although because of their comparatively good salaries they could prepare their sons for leadership by sending them not only to the best schools in Rangoon or to the University of Calcutta, but even to the Inns of Court in London. As a result, government service gradually began to loom large in the structure of Burmese society, and the most talented among Burmese youth sought appointments to the civil service.

These Burmese officials came to form the foundation of a middle class because the English officials were socially above them, and, as the economic conditions for the Burmese villager deteriorated, a social gap began to appear between the Burmese officials and the villagers. Yet the first rumblings of discontent and criticism of the British government came from those Burmese officials themselves. After a few years, the Burmese who had been appointed to the junior grades of the civil service came to realize that, although they had to perform similar duties, there was a great disparity in salary scales and other privileges. One of the consequences of this discontent was seen in the growing popularity of the legal profession. The sons of Burmese officials, on returning from England as barristers, were able to assert themselves as social equals of the British officials simply because they were outside government service.

After the first Anglo-Burmese war the British introduced the Indian rupee into the Burmese maritime provinces they had acquired, and after the second Anglo-Burmese war they opened British banks at Rangoon, Akyab, and Moulmein. King Mindon himself felt the necessity of introducing a similar money economy in his kingdom. In 1883 the British established a paper currency office in Rangoon. The opening of the Suez Canal in 1871 and the resulting increase in trade hastened the pace of substitution of a money economy for the old barter system, and by the year 1890 the new money economy extended to the whole of Burma. The average Burmese villager was not yet psychologically prepared, and because he was still untrained and inexperienced in the use of cash he was bewildered by the capitalization of his main agricultural produce and staple food, rice.

Before the first Anglo-Burmese war, the exporting of rice was controlled and restricted by the kings because they considered that an adequate supply of rice was the foundation on which the prosperity and power of their kingdom was built. The second Anglo-Burmese war coincided with a rapid growth of population in the neighboring British territories of India and the Malay peninsula, and the British began to develop the delta of the Irrawaddy as the rice bowl of their Indian empire. After the rebellions had been suppressed and the fields again cultivated in Lower Burma in 1857, it was found that the price of rice had increased by some 25 per cent, and by 1890 the price had become more than double the 1857 price. After that, the price of rice continued to increase until the depression that followed the first world war. The Burmese farmers gained nothing from this development in the cultivation and sale of rice.

The Burmese as a people had never held capital accumulations and, with the increase in the price of rice, land holdings were extended by cutting down the mangrove forests and by draining the swamps. The money needed for these operations had to be borrowed from the Indian moneylenders at the exorbitant interest rate of 120 per cent, because the British banks would not grant loans on mortgage of rice lands and the British government did not consider it necessary to open land mortgage banks or agricultural loan agencies. In line with its policy of laissez faire the government did not attempt in any way to control the usurious rates of interest. After all, to the British government, Burmese were also Indians because Burma had become a province of India, and so it seemed perfectly logical to them that they should not interfere in the business transactions of Indians with Indians. The Burmese farmer also failed to get any profit from the development of trade in rice. A handful of British firms entirely controlled the wholesale trade in rice and Indian and Chinese merchants controlled the retail trade. The British firms agreed among themselves not to buy any rice until the harvesting season was long past and the new planting season was approaching. The average Burmese farmer could not afford to wait, for his Indian moneylender was threatening to fore-close the mortgage unless the interest was paid in full. In other words, the British firms forced a seller's market to become a buyer's market. In effect the British firms exercised a double monopoly, and they were thus able to lower the price in the internal market and raise it to an artificial level in the international market at their own will and pleasure.

If bare statistics alone were to be considered, it would appear that the Burmese economy rapidly developed within a few years of the British conquest. The British government had opened a rail-way between Rangoon and Prome in 1887 and within four years of the fall of the kingdom they completed the construction of a railway between Rangoon and Mandalay. In 1898 they extended it up to Myitkyina; by 1907 the British government had constructed three branch lines, to Lashio in the northern Shan states, to Bassein, and to Moulmein. The Irrawaddy Flotilla Company increased and extended its services until it had a fleet of nearly 1,000 boats. The British government also constructed a number of roads all over the country. However, in improving the communications the British took into consideration the military value of roads and railways, for troops could be rushed to any part of the country where a rebellion might break out. A British company was given a concession of work-ing the ruby mines, which soon became exhausted, however. A small British company that regularly bought the produce of the oil wells which mostly belonged to the king was quickly re-organized in 1886 to become the Burma Oil Company, which rapidly developed the petroleum industry in the country. In 1891 a British company, the Burma Corporation, obtained a virtual monopoly of extracting silver, lead, and other minerals in the northern Shan states, and tin and tungsten in Tenasserim. The extraction of timber remained un-der the monopolistic control of the Bombay Burma Corporation, whose disapproval had caused Theebaw to lose his throne. The figures of imports and exports throughout the period of British rule showed on paper a balance of trade well in favor of Burma. For example, for the financial year 1899–1900 the value of exports was approximately 160 millon rupees and the imports 100 million; in 1913–1914, on the eve of the first world war, the value of exports was 390 million, and imports 250 million; and in 1926–1927 the value of exports was 660 million and imports 390 million.

However, as the profits of trade accrued not to the Burmese but to the British companies, and as there was no control of foreign exchange and remittances, all the profits left the country in the form of remittances, of which no statistics were ever compiled. In addition, the salaries of the British and Indian troops, of the British officials, and of the Indian personnel in the clerical services of the government were also remitted to England or to India. The wages of Indian laborers were also sent back to their relations in India. In other words, the Burmese candle was being burned at both ends. Her minerals and her timber were extracted but the money obtained in exchange for her products went out of the country. Thus the economic development of Burma was in reality economic exploitation of the country. In the meantime, the Burmese farmer continued in his downward course. Within two decades of the conquest the majority of the Burmese farmers had lost their lands to the Indian moneylenders, but, even as paid laborers working on the very land they used to own, they had to compete with Indian laborers, who came in thousands. Because of their low standard of living the Indian laborers were able to undercut their Burmese counterparts by accepting lower wages. The desperate position of the Burmese farmer was seen in the occurrence of small peasant rebellions all over the country from time to time. With only swords and spears, the peasants were ready to follow any charlatan who would promise them invulnerability against British bullets.

The obvious measure the British government should have taken was to restrict the immigration of Indian laborers, but again it refused to recognize the separate identity of the Burmese; as Burma was merely an Indian province, it seemed only right that Indians should come and go at will. In other words, just as the British government would not interfere with the exploitive practices of the Indian moneylender, it would not stop the Indian laborer from coming to Burma or prevent him from sending back to India 90 per cent of his wages. Under the kings, the Burmese farmer had worked without respite for nine months of the year; for the remaining three months, which coincided with the hot, dry season, when the ground was parched, the vegetation died, and many trees shed their leaves, he took his vacation. Pooling his surplus wealth with those of his neighbors, he would hold initiation and ear-piercing ceremonies for his sons and daughters, offer ceremonial alms to the monks, and arrange for strolling players to give their performances at the village square. It was the time also of the annual festival at many pagodas nearby, and in his gaily decorated cart he would take his family on a pilgrimage to the pagodas and also to visit friends and relations. The rhythm of his life was broken when he was forced to become a farm laborer, for during the three months of the hot season he would be without any employment and without funds.

A few of the more fortunate among his fellow villagers continued to hold such ceremonies and festivals. The displaced farmer looked back with longing to his past and looked forward with despair to his future; he joined hands with other unfortunates like himself to form a rowdy gang, which created disturbances and fought the police, often turning the joyous social occasion into a crisis of riot and lawlessness. As for the Indian laborer, he blithely went back to his home in South India to find temporary work there, for steamer tickets to India were cheap because the steamship companies were subsidized by the government of India, or he went to the docks, to factories, or to oil fields to obtain employment easily. The Burmese laborer was experienced only in farm work, and with his higher standard of living he could not stay in the congested workmen's quarters of the factories and the oil fields. Within a few years the Burmese villager came to acquire a reputation of being

lazy, violent, and not amenable to discipline, which gave the excuse
to the Indian moneylenders and to the British commercial interests
to bring in more laborers from India.

The British government, looking at the consequence and not
at the cause, introduced laws giving power to the police to arrest a
villager who had no "ostensible means of livelihood" or who was
suspected of being a habitual delinquent and bring him to trial
before a magistrate, who could sentence him to a term of im-
prisonment. Once imprisoned, the unfortunate villager was considered a criminal, and embittered and emboldened by his prison
experiences he actually became a thief or a robber. What the displaced farmer needed was social legislation. But to introduce social
welfare programs would have cost the government money, and the
British government of Burma was always short of funds. The customs duties, personal taxes, and royalties on minerals, oil, and timber
extracted were substantial, but the British government of Burma
worked on a deficit budget because it had to pay back to the British
government of India in annual installments the cost of the third
Anglo-Burmese war and the operations against the guerrillas, provide for the cost of maintaining the British and Indian garrisons in
the country, and also pay high salaries to the British civil servants.
The unsympathetic attitude of the British government of India toward the Burmese is summed up in an amusing but bitter poem by
the same British official who wrote the verses regarding the executions of the patriots. The poem is supposed to be a letter written
by the viceroy of India; two verses are given here:

> For example, your Burmans unjustly complain
> Of the tax we've imposed upon paddy and grain;
> But they seem to forget that they pocket our price
> When we purchase their precious consignments of rice.

> When poor Oorya coolies to Burma migrate,
> They endure all the torments of racial hate;
> Yet they visit your shores, lazy Burmans to aid.
> Was ingratitude ever more coarsely displayed?

By about the year 1910 a number of Burmese who had been called to the bar in London were in active practice both at Rangoon and Mandalay, where the British government opened the highest courts in the country. While in England they had lived and studied with the sons of wealthy English families and of the English nobility, for in those days the Inns of Court were the exclusive domain of British aristocracy; therefore on their return to Burma they were neither impressed nor overawed by the British civil servants or the British judges. The British, who had protested vehemently against the "barbarous and humiliating" practice of having to remove one's shoes on entering the audience chamber of the king, did not feel too conscience-stricken to insist that all Burmese, including the junior civil servants, remove their shoes on entering the office room of a British official. But, although gritting their teeth in anger, British judges and senior officials could not protest while young Burmese barristers walked into their chambers with their shoes on. No wonder an irate British official bitterly coined the phrase "the Burmese barristocracy."

The Burmese barristers could not yet do anything for their country, however, except to watch with bated breath the Boers of South Africa attempting, and nearly succeeding, to topple the British giant. Two or three Burmese newspapers had started to circulate throughout the country by then, but the editors were yet too inexperienced and too timid of British laws regarding sedition, so they wrote no editorials but gave detailed news of the defeats the Boers were inflicting on the British. In the villages, the villagers basked in the reflected glory of a fellow fighter against British imperialism, the Boer General Botha, and some even claimed with a twinkle in their eyes that Botha was none other than a Burmese guerrilla leader, Po Tha, who managed to escape from the country by obtaining employment on a Dutch cargo ship. The Burmese as a nation felt again the pangs of a national disaster when the Boers, in spite of their great gallantry, finally were defeated. But soon they were heartened once more by the victories of the Japanese against the Russians.

Just as in other countries of Asia, the emergence of Japan as a great world power was hailed in Burma as the dawn of a new era in which Asians would at last become social and political equals of the domineering Europeans. About this time also, the first cinemas were opened in Burma and the films shown were those of the Boer War and the Russo-Japanese War, and the audiences groaned when they saw on the screen pictures of the relief of Mafeking and cheered when they saw pictures of Japanese soldiers falling upon a trainload of Russian troops. There was of course no censorship of films in those days and, moreover, the British officials thought there could be no harm in showing films depicting their victories over the Boers or depicting the victories over the Russians by the Japanese, who after all were the allies of the British.

As was usual in Burmese history, nationalist fervor was again to be roused by Buddhism. In spite of the merry tales of Thingazar Sayadaw, it seemed at first that Buddhism was being overwhelmed by alien ideas and by the unsympathetic attitude of the new government. But by about 1910 Thingazar Sayadaw's work was bearing rich fruit, and in spite of their economic and social troubles the Burmese were still finding Buddhism as their rallying point. At this juncture two great monks appeared, U Thila and Ledi Sayadaw. U Thila won the admiration and respect of the whole nation by his extremely austere way of life. He slept in caves and under trees and wore as his robes shrouds discarded at the cemeteries. He would not give any sermon, and like a medieval European friar observing a vow of silence he spoke but few words. He wandered from village to village, and the saint-like qualities of his personality caused the villagers to be awed by his mere presence. He readily accepted gifts of alms, food, and robes offered by villagers, but once the gifts had been made he promptly distributed them among the old and the poor of the village. He became so popular with the people that the

British government sent police officers and detectives to follow him around the country and keep him under strict surveillance. But after a time the police had to admit that the monk was neither a charlatan nor a seditionist.

He was followed by the learned scholar Ledi Sayadaw, who realized that only monks and antiquarians knew Pali, which was necessary in order to read the scriptures in their original; he there-fore made the scriptures accessible to the people by re-telling the stories from the life of the Buddha in simple but effective verses, which little children could easily learn to recite. In addition Ledi Sayadaw wrote a number of works, some for the erudite Burmese Buddhist scholars and others for the average layman. He encour-aged villagers to form small religious groups to go around the village reciting his verses or simpler texts from the scriptures and discussing some of the main teachings of Buddhism. His more learned works reached across the ocean to the monks of Ceylon, who praised him as the greatest Buddhist scholar of his age. The monks of Ceylon and Burma were reminded of their close association before the ad-vent of colonial rule and, taking advantage now of the fact that travel across the Bay of Bengal had been made easy by the British, monk scholars and pilgrims from Ceylon again came to visit Burma; the compliment was returned by the Burmese, who visited Ceylon to worship at the Temple of the Sacred Tooth.

The renewed contact between Burma and Ceylon resulted in the Burmese barristers becoming interested in the Young Men's Buddhist Association of Ceylon. In Ceylon, Buddhism was officially persecuted under the Portuguese, as well as under the Dutch, al-though less violently. Under the British, religious freedom prevailed, in theory, but Buddhism was socially persecuted in that in schools and colleges Buddhist boys were jeered at until they came to regard the national religion as a badge of shame. Buddhism as the Sinhalese national religion was revived in the closing years of the nineteenth century through the efforts of a Sinhalese monk who was a past master in debate and argument before the public, and through the efforts of an American scholar and philanthropist, Colonel Olcott. Under Colonel Olcott's guidance, a Young Men's Buddhist Association, modeled on the Young Men's Christian Association of the West, was set up, and a number of Buddhist schools were established under its control. In Burma students of the Rangoon College and government high school at Rangoon had already established a Young Men's Temperance League to combat the growing practice among educated youth of cigarette smoking and whisky drinking, and in the course of a few months it came to have branches all over the country.

The young barristers, who were being rapidly recognized as emerging national leaders, used the Temperance League as the foundation stone of the new Young Men's Buddhist Association movement. Because of the absence of any political aim and because of its emphasis on Buddhism and moral character, the British government did not consider the movement to be dangerous. When the newly established Y.M.B.A. founded a number of Buddhist schools all over the country and applied for educational grants to cover 50 per cent of the expenses, as the other 50 per cent was covered by public donations, the British government was not pleased but could not refuse the grants because it had been giving the same educational grants to the Christian mission schools. The new Y.M.B.A. schools were required to use the same curriculum as the government and mission schools, and, just as the mission schools were permitted to give daily lessons in the Christian Bible, the Buddhist schools had to be permitted to give daily lessons in the Buddhist scriptures. The establishment of the Buddhist schools coincided with the rapid growth of the nationalist movement for freedom in India, and the government of India rather foolishly exiled some of the Indian political leaders to Burma, thus making it possible for the more enthusiastic members of the Y.M.B.A. to make contact with those Indian politicians. The Burmese civil servants were also growing vociferous and forming service associations; they were "respectfully demanding" from the government promotion to the senior civil service, namely to the ranks of "heaven-borns," in other words, those English officials recruited in England. The inevitable clash between nationalism and imperialism was postponed for a time because of the outbreak of World War I in 1914.

Since 1885 the British had carefully followed a policy of divide and rule; they deliberately separated the hill peoples from the Burmese. This policy had the full support of the Christian missions, who had looked upon the Burmese as their opponents since 1826 and who regarded the British victories as their own. Finding it almost impossible to convert the Burmese Buddhists to Christianity, they turned their attention to the hill peoples, with whom they had some success since those peoples were still primitive animists. Only a minority of those peoples accepted Christianity, however, and those who accepted retained much of their primitive beliefs. The missionaries, in preaching Christianity, attempted also to build up a psychological barrier against the Burmese by giving false accounts of Buddhism and inventing stories detrimental to the Burmese. For example, among the Chins they spread the stories that the Chin girls tattooed their faces to look ugly so that the Burmese marauders would not be tempted to snatch them away. In actual fact, the practice of tattooing faces was not confined to the Chins but was widespread all over the world, and it was considered as an enhancement of beauty. The missionaries singled out the Karen myth of the flood and tried to prove that the Karens were one of the lost tribes of Israel, ignoring the fact that similar myths existed among the Chins and the Kachins.

The British government kept the racial groups further apart by denying military training to the Shans and the Burmese and giving that privilege only to the Chins, Kachins, and Karens. It was not a mere question of meek acceptance of British rule, for after the second Anglo-Burmese war the Karens of Lower Burma harassed the British, and after the third Anglo-Burmese war the Chins remained on the war path against the British for a number of years. Although there were Chin, Kachin, and Karen regiments, no one

among the hill peoples was considered good enough to be conferred what was known as the king's commission, for otherwise
some hillmen would have become members of the elite officers'
corps. The outbreak of the world war made it necessary for the
British government to have the support of the Indians and the Burmese, and a Burmese labor corps was raised for service in Meso-
potamia. The people were enthusiastic but murmured their dissatisfaction at the fact that the commanders were all British. Across the
Bay of Bengal the Indian people were also making the same demand
that full commissions be given to Indians, as Indians had been fighting in British regiments since the days of the East India Company.
It may be noted in passing that the Burmese had always regretted
that in the Anglo-Burmese wars, and in the campaigns against the
guerrillas, Indian troops fought side by side with the British in their
regiments.

In 1917, when the British armies were facing disaster in Europe,
the British government of India as a gesture of good will gave a
number of commissions to selected Indians and Burmese, and four
young Burmese, one a graduate of Cambridge and Dublin Universities and the others graduates of Rangoon College, were given
commissions. There was great satisfaction in Burma, but after the
war the most senior, U Tin Tut, entered the Indian civil service
and the others were gradually edged out of the army by their
fellow British officers. There was renewed agitation for military
training, and the British government set up the Burma Territorial
Army, consisting of four regiments, but only two regiments were
actually recruited. One was for the Shans and the other was for the
Burmese. But the government meant it to be a gesture and nothing
more, and admission to this new army was restricted to clerks and
junior civil servants, and the actual training was not only elementary
but given during a period of two weeks at the annual camp. In
addition, those junior civil servants could not aspire to gain a king's
commission, as it was made a requirement that applicants for such
commissions should possess previous military training. As a result,

the officers of the Territorial Army were British officers who had been given a leave of absence from their regular regiments and who therefore had no understanding or sympathy with the Burmese privates whom they commanded.

The British government in London, needing the continued support of Indians, promised to grant them a certain measure of self-government, but the Burmese were excluded from the promise on the ground that the Burmese were quite contented with British rule and were not ready for any degree of self-government. It was a most surprising conclusion on the part of the British, in view of the fact that as recently as 1910 British rule in Chindwin and Monywa districts had been paralyzed by a rebellion led by a simple villager of princely appearance, and in view of the fact that the Burmese had been agitating for military training. Either the British were dense and stupid, or they were merely finding an excuse to keep Burma under direct British rule. In 1917, when a British parliamentary delegation toured India to report what reforms in the structure of government should be introduced, it did not include Burma in its itinerary. The Y.M.B.A. therefore sent a delegation consisting mainly of barristers to travel to India and appear before the commission. Their endeavors proved fruitless, for when the commission submitted its report to the parliament in London it was found that Burma was not included in the proposed program of reforms to be granted to India. In 1919 another delegation of Y.M.B.A. leaders was sent to appear before the British parliament. However, when the Government of India Act was finally passed in the same year by the British parliament, it was found that Burma again had been left out.

This was the signal for a nation-wide protest, and the Burmese leaders felt that they must close ranks, agitate, and organize to be granted the same measure of self-government as the Indians had been given. They also decided that the struggle was no longer social and religious but political, and religion and nationalism must now be separated. They wanted the Y.M.B.A. movement to become more political in character and in aim, and at the same time they feared lest their religion should become merely a tool of politics. Accordingly, at a national convention they merged the Y.M.B.A. with various patriotic organizations, which had appeared like mushrooms in a matter of a few weeks, and named the new organization the General Council of Burmese Associations. This action was most opportune, because as part of the protest against the exclusion of Burma from the reforms a nationalist movement called the Wuntharnu movement had suddenly appeared and instigated a boycott of British goods. The movement was quite successful but, as usual, there were a few who still bought British goods. Wuntharnu associations sprang up with the self-imposed task of enforcing the boycott, and some monks roamed the markets with small canes to discourage those who would insist on buying British goods. The very name "General Council of Burmese Associations" emphasized the fact that the national movement for freedom was a political movement and not a religious one. Another delegation was sent to London representing the G.C.B.A., and, when a crowd of 100,000 Burmese lined the fore shore at Rangoon to greet the delegates on their return from London, the British feared that a nation-wide rebellion might break out. In addition, the Wuntharnu movement was hurting their commercial interests. Defeat had fallen upon the British government. To humiliate the Burmese they had made Burma an Indian province and now it could not be kept apart from the Indian reforms.

In the wake of the Wuntharnu movement came the great university strike of December 1920, which was nationalism's first open challenge to the authority of the British government. Rangoon College was established in 1880 as an affiliate college of the University of Calcutta, with British professors who were also made civil servants. When the Indian universities of Calcutta, Bombay, and Madras were established in the middle of the nineteenth century, liberalism was very much in the air, and university autonomy and academic freedom were catchwords. They were state institutions, but administrative control was in the hands of various university bodies. By 1920, however, the University of Calcutta especially had become a hotbed of political agitation, and the British government therefore was determined that when the new University of Rangoon was established by expanding and enlarging Rangoon College the control should remain in British hands. Thus, under the University of Rangoon Act, the administrative control was vested in a council whose members were government nominees, and academic control was vested in a senate consisting of members of the senior grade of the university civil service; but as no Burmese as yet had been appointed to that senior grade the senate consisted entirely of British professors. The University of Rangoon officially came into being on December 20, 1920, but a few minutes after the classes had assembled the students walked out in protest against what they considered to be an anti-national University Act. The strike soon spread to the schools, and although the government hastily suspended classes, using the approaching Christmas and New Year holidays as an excuse, the students refused to return to their homes but stayed on in the monasteries and pagoda platforms where they had taken shelter.

All monks and pilgrims shared their alms food with them and soon the strike changed its original character and became a nationwide movement of protest against British rule in general. People now vied with each other to provide food for the students and to organize "parallel classes" so that the students should not miss their lessons. At first the British government tried to subdue the nationalists by publishing list after list of students expelled from the university and from schools for taking part in the strike, and also by giving written notices to those fathers who were government servants that they would be dismissed from service unless they called back their sons from the strike camps. As the strike dragged on the nationalist leaders organized the Council of National Education, and all the Y.M.B.A. schools voluntarily came under its jurisdiction, calling themselves "National Schools." The government, realizing that the situation was becoming worse for them, canceled the expulsion lists and appointed a committee, some of whose members were from the ranks of the nationalist leaders, to amend the University Act. The students called off the strike, but many of the strikers never returned to the government schools but joined the new national schools. It was a great victory for the people, and the strike was to have repercussions right up to the re-gaining of independence in 1948.

In 1923 the British government decided to grant to the Burmese the same dyarchy, or dual government, which had been given to India. But many Burmese felt that it was too little and too late. In India itself the dyarchy was bitterly criticized by many leaders of the freedom movement, and during the short period of two years after its introduction its many defects had become apparent. In Burma the people had become militant and had also learned to be suspicious of British intentions. The British themselves were now considering the desirability of separating Burma from India because they believed that Indians would make more and more demands for self-government, whereas the Burmese would remain quiet after the dyarchy reforms. This made some of the Burmese leaders even more suspicious of the sincerity of the British in granting the reforms. Moreover, the British government placed more emphasis on its policy of dividing the Burmese from the hill peoples.

The British had forced King Mindon to recognize the independence of the Karenni states, which had always been part of Burma, but after the fall of the Burmese kingdom they promptly turned the Karenni states into British territory but kept them entirely separate from Burma. Now they were separating the hill regions of the Chins and the Kachins, and the plateau of the Shans entirely from the rest of Burma, on the excuse that the people in those regions were politically not advanced and must be kept under the direct control of the British governor of Burma, and they declared that the affairs of those regions were not discussable by the legislature that was to be established under the dyarchy reforms.

In addition, they divided the people in the plains into racial groups, namely Burmese, Indians, Anglo-Indians, and Karens, on the excuse that racial minorities were entitled to special protection by the British government. Anglo-Indians included Anglo-Burmese, whose number was small because intermarriage between the British and the Burmese was not common. The total population of the Anglo-Indians themselves was small and the majority of them had come from India; except that they wore trousers and coats and had English names, they were really Indians and could have been classified as such. As to the Karens, in spite of exaggerated claims by the Christian missionaries, at least 85 per cent were non-Christians, and thus for the sake of a small Christian minority the idea of racial division was introduced.

Under the dyarchy system, certain branches of government were reserved for the governor; nonetheless, the portfolios of education, public health, agriculture, and forests, which were placed under the people's elected representatives, were vital ones for a nation whose economy and society were disintegrating under the impact of the West through British rule. As all suitable measures to be taken by the new legislature would have benefited the whole nation, there was no need at all to divide the people into various racial groups. After all, the vital subjects of government, such as foreign affairs, defense, internal security, immigration, commerce, and general financial control, were still directly under the British governor, and the governor possessed the right of veto even in those subjects transferred to popular control, and he could have protected the minorities by withholding consent to any measure he considered unjust to the minorities.

By itself the dyarchy scheme was workable, and much could have been done to evolve a system of parliamentary government adapted to suit Burmese society and prevailing local conditions. The legislature consisted of 103 members, of which 79 were to be elected and 24 were to be appointed by the governor. Of those 24, 14 were senior British civil servants in charge of various branches of the

secretariat. Among them there could be no Burmese, of course, because only a handful of Burmese were in the senior civil service,
and even the most senior among them, U Tin Tut, was not senior
enough for appointment as head of a department. If the government
had been wise enough not to continue its divide-and-rule policy,
the elected members would have been in the majority, and any
abuse or misuse by the elected members of their majority could at
once be nullified by the governor's veto. But as the racial element
was introduced, 21 of the elected seats were divided among the
minorities and a parliamentary convention was rapidly established
—the 21 representatives of the minority groups and the 24 nominees
of the governor would always oppose the 58 elected Burmese members. With 58 seats balanced against 45, it would become a scramble
for office, with the more influential members forming small groups
of their own. Among the Burmese elected members themselves there
would arise personal jealousies and maneuvering for leadership. The
criticism against the reforms grew and the G.C.B.A. split into two
groups, those who would take part in the elections and work the
new system, and those who would express their disapproval by boy-
cotting the elections. The split in the ranks of the G.C.B.A. bewildered the people who had given it their full support, and as a
result they became apathetic toward the new reforms. The British
government thus lost again a chance of regaining the loyalty of the
people and laying the foundation for the evolution of a genuine
parliamentary system.

In the elections that followed, only 12 per cent of the electorate cast their votes, but it would still have been possible to save
the reforms if there had been more unity among the Burmese leaders
themselves. The group from the G.C.B.A. headed by U Ba Pe won
twenty-eight seats. U Ba Pe was an experienced and able leader,
having served as a member of all the Y.M.B.A. delegations sent to
India and England, but he labored under a number of disadvantages.
His group, consisting of twenty-one members, could not use the
magic name of G.C.B.A. because they were in the minority and

were out-voted when the resolution to boycott the elections was carried. In his haste to stand for elections he chose the name "Twenty-one Party," which was not only unimpressive as a name but reminded the country that they were going against the majority decision of the G.C.B.A. In addition, he was not a barrister but a professional journalist, who after taking a degree at the University of Calcutta had started the first Burmese daily newspaper, *The Sun*, and he was more radical than the barristers in his group. On the other hand, he was not so extreme as U Chit Hlaing, who, although a barrister, sided with those who were suspicious of the British intentions in introducing the reforms. In other words, U Ba Pe fell between two stools.

Realizing the insecure position of U Ba Pe among his own followers, British senior civil servants and British merchants encouraged a right-wing moderate party to emerge. Calling themselves the "Golden Valley Party," they had the support of some elected members not belonging to the Twenty-one Party and eight members nominated by the governor; they were under the leadership of J. A. Maung Gyi (later "Sir"), a barrister, who had been away in the civil service of the Siamese king for some years and was therefore not connected with the Y.M.B.A. movement. U Ba Pe found himself without the necessary majority to form a cabinet and refused to agree to a coalition with the Golden Valley Party, accusing it of being in the pocket of the British. But some members of his own Twenty-one Party were not so reluctant, and the following cabinet came into being: (1) the governor, (2) member for home affairs, U Khin (later Sir Maung Khin), (3) member for financial affairs, a British official of the Indian civil service, (4) minister for education and public health, U Maung Gyi (later "Sir" and usually referred to as M. A. Maung Gyi, as he held the Master of Arts degree from Calcutta University, to distinguish him from J. A. Maung Gyi), and (5) minister for agriculture and forests, J. A. Maung Gyi.

The members for home and financial affairs were nominated

by the governor and in India they were usually from the Indian civil service. U Khin was a barrister who after long practice had been appointed a judge of the High Court, and the fact that he was chosen above the heads of British civil servants clearly showed that the British government desired to appease Burmese public opinion. M. A. Maung Gyi had been a founding member of the Y.M.B.A. and was the president of the Council of National Education, and he used the power and influence of his new office to increase the privileges and financial support of the national schools. Sir J. A. Maung Gyi resigned from the cabinet on accepting his appointment as a High Court judge, and U Pu, a barrister and a member of the Y.M.B.A. delegations, was appointed minister for forests and agriculture. The most powerful member of the cabinet was, of course, the member for home affairs, and Sir Maung Khin succeeded in persuading the British government to throw open the senior grades of the civil service to some selected Burmese. In the meetings of the cabinet he usually supported the proposals of the two Burmese ministers so that, whatever the intentions of the governor were, the cabinet became a nationalist one.

But Sir Maung Khin died suddenly in 1924. The governor, again seeking to win support from the people, appointed U May Oung to succeed Sir Maung Khin. U May Oung was also a barrister and after a period of practice had been appointed a High Court judge and was a founding member of the Y.M.B.A. But he did not approve of extreme nationalistic aspirations of the G.C.B.A. even before the split, and he came to identify himself more and more with the British. Accordingly, the character of the cabinet changed and people gradually came to regard it as hostile to national interests, with a pro-British majority. In the legislature itself the Golden Valley Party, fretting because it was not represented on the cabinet after J. A. Maung Gyi's resignation, was drawn closer to the pro-British members. When new elections were held, the public proved apathetic as before and only 17 per cent of the electorate cast their votes. U Ba Pe, whose party was now known as

"The People's Party," won the elections, but as before it lost in the maneuverings that followed and both the ministers were appointed from the Golden Valley Party. In the third elections, held in 1928, the G.C.B.A. again broke into two factions over the question of participation in the elections, and this time U Chit Hlaing decided to stand for election. Again only 20 per cent of the electorate voted; U Ba Pe and his party won a substantial number of seats, but it was the Golden Valley Party that supplied the two ministers. However, the people had ceased to care and were now firmly convinced that the British government was merely playing a game of pretense.

In 1930 the world economic depression reached Burma, and the price of rice fell to the level of the 1860s. The Burmese cultivator and the Burmese laborer, without savings of any sort, found themselves unable to cope with this situation and came to the conclusion that the British government was responsible for it all. A great earthquake nearly destroyed the town of Pegu, and the Burmese masses, in deep despair at the callous way the British government and the Burmese politicians had handled the dyarchy reforms, looked upon this earthquake as a sign and portent of a change of government. A native physician, Saya San, who had been a monk for some years and who had often made astrological predictions, became convinced that, just as a great earthquake had heralded the victory of the British in 1824, the recent earthquake foretold the close of British rule. He traveled to the Shan states but could not interest the Shans in his scheme of rebellion. He went to Upper Burma but could not make the villagers believe that he was born to be king.

When he reached Lower Burma, however, he found that the villagers of the Tharrawaddy district were on the verge of rebellion. The stocks of rice remained unsold, and although there was plenty of food there was nothing else. Many had lost their lands to the Indian moneylenders long before and, with the price of rice touching rock bottom, the Indian landlords would not engage labor to cultivate their fields. Those who still owned lands just sat on their stocks of rice, unable to find the cash to re-pay the interest on their debts. Their clothes had been worn out during the year, but without the cash to buy new supplies the men went about half naked and the women sat behind closed doors. Such dire poverty they had not even heard of before. To add to their troubles, the annual taxes were overdue. Saya San, in spite of his superstitious beliefs, was a genuine patriot, and, poverty stricken himself, he felt that the only way for the people of Tharrawaddy to end their misery was to rise in rebellion against the British. The villagers, like a drowning man clutching at a straw, were ready to follow him. They only half believed his promises of invulnerability, but in their despair they remembered again the tales of amulets and runes that made their possessors immune from bullets and bayonets, tales which had been gradually discarded after the defeat of the guerrillas. Even those who did not believe in the supernatural were ready to make a try for freedom. Was not death preferable to this misery of poverty under an alien rule? The elders of the villages, however, were a little cautious because they realized that they did not possess the arms necessary to defeat the British. They appealed to Saya San and his enthusiastic followers to give them a chance to negotiate with the British government for the cancellation or at least postponement of the annual taxes. Saya San consented and they went to the district headquarters and pleaded for mercy, but their plea was summarily rejected. With gloomy faces they returned to their villages to report the failure of their mission.

Within a few days Saya San declared himself the new king and his followers attacked government outposts over a wide area. The British officials laughed at the superstitions of the rebels, but they soon had to call in two battalions of British troops, for the rebels, armed only with swords and sticks, fought on and refused to surrender, although all hope of victory was abandoned after the first skirmishes. Remembering the tactics successfully used by Sir Charles Crosthwaite, the British troops resorted to mass executions of rebels and burning of villages. The national leaders and the people of Rangoon were sympathetic but could not assist the rebels in any way. The British, perhaps because they were callous or perhaps because they wanted to show a bold front, held dances and receptions at their exclusive clubs in Rangoon every night to which the British officials and army officials would come after the day's work of massacre and arson, for Tharrawaddy was only some two hours away by automobile.

Saya San was soon captured, but the rebellion continued unabated in the Tharrawaddy district and rapidly spread to all the delta districts, then to Central Burma, then to Upper Burma, and finally to the Shan states. New guerrilla leaders appeared, such as Saya Nyan, a school teacher in Kama in Thayetmyo district, and the hermit Bandaka in the Shwebo district. The rebellion was finally suppressed in 1932 by which time 10,000 rebels had been killed, 9,000 had been captured and given prison terms, and 128, including Saya San, Saya Nyan, and hermit Bandaka, had been hanged. The rebellion of 1930–32 was perhaps the nearest Asian counterpart of the peasants' rebellion in medieval England, and it was a rebellion born of sheer desperation. However, the British officials and the British merchants saw only the amulets and the charms on the bodies of the dead rebels and marveled at the superstition of the Burmese, not sensing their utter desperation and bitter hatred of the British rule, which had caused the tragic rebellion.

The British parliament had meant the dyarchy system of government in both India and Burma to be a constitutional experiment for a period of ten years only, and so in 1931 they appointed the Simon Commission to report on the working of the system and to make recommendations for further reforms. The British government of Burma now openly suggested to the Burmese leaders that in their opinion Burma should now be separated from the Indian empire so that it could work out its own political destiny independent of Indian politics. The British mercantile interests gave their full support to the proposal for separation. U Ba Pe was enthusiastic but U Chit Hlaing was not. In the legislature an open quarrel broke out between the two and soon the whole country

became divided into two factions, those who wanted the separation
and those who did not. The British government believed that, coming at the height of anti-Indian feeling, its separation proposal would
be unanimously approved by the masses, but it forgot that the people
looked upon the government with suspicion after its cruel suppression of the rebellion, and the very fact that the proposal was supported by both the British government and the British merchants
was taken as clear evidence that the British wanted to slow down
the pace of political reforms in Burma so that it would lag far behind India. Some of the Burmese leaders reminded the people that
at the time the dyarchy reforms were first discussed the British had
proposed to leave out Burma.

This controversy embittered Burmese politics, for both factions
waged an abusive, acrimonious, and personal campaign against each
other, with the result that all the older political leaders lost their
prestige and their hold on the masses. Two new and younger leaders
emerged, both barristers, U Kyaw Myint and Dr. Ba Maw. U Kyaw
Myint was an elected member of the Imperial Legislative Assembly
at New Delhi, representing Burma, and he was a follower and a
friend of the Indian leaders Mahatma Gandhi and Pandit Nehru. In
a series of brilliant speeches he proved to be a fierce critic of the
proposed separation. Dr. Ba Maw was a younger member of the
G.C.B.A. group led by U Chit Hlaing, who, with his personal
reputation tarnished by vehement attacks from U Ba Pe, decided
to step down from the leadership of the anti-separation faction. U
Kyaw Myint and U Ba Maw then founded the Anti-separationist
League to fight the 1932 elections on the issue. The strategy agreed
upon was for Dr. Ba Maw to stand for election and, when successful, to oppose the British proposal in the Burma Legislative Council
while U Kyaw Myint was to retain his seat in the Imperial Legislative Assembly and to continue his fight there.

U Kyaw Myint and Dr. Ba Maw toured the country and the
masses flocked to the polling booths to vote for the Anti-separationist
League. U Ba Pe's separationists were soundly beaten although the

leader himself managed to retain his seat. But even as the crowds were celebrating their victory U Ba Pe won Dr. Ba Maw over to his side. Together they formed a coalition and declared their support of the separation proposal in spite of U Kyaw Myint's protests and appeals. Many of those who had been elected as anti-separationists followed Dr. Ba Maw to the side of the separation. U Kyaw Myint resigned his seat in the Imperial Legislative Assembly and, still in his thirties, he retired from politics. The country was shocked at the betrayal of its mandate by the politicians it had elected, and finally it lost faith both in the British government and the Burmese politicians.

The peasants' rebellion of 1930–1932 and the mishandling of the issue of separation from India by the elder politicians created a vacuum in leadership, into which stepped some young patriots from the University of Rangoon. Like the masses, these young men were definitely of the opinion that only a revolution could bring freedom back to their nation. They had entered the university from national schools, where they had especially studied Burmese history and literature, and they found the university too pro-British. All the senior administrative and academic positions were held by Englishmen, who, as civil servants, assumed an attitude of superiority over the students. All the wardens of the dormitories were English, and the sight of professors and their guests dining and dancing on the campus irked the students. In history classes the English professors belittled the achievements of the Burmese kings and tried to impress upon the students their view that the Burmese were indeed fortunate to be under British rule. The young revolutionaries expressed their disapproval of the university by coming to classes in their shirt sleeves and walking noisily along the corridors in wooden slippers. Dressed untidily in homespun clothes, they deliberately assumed an uncouth, obstinate, and stupid appearance.

All the time, however, they were reading the latest English publications on politics, economics, and socialism, and they were training themselves to be skillful orators and writers. They composed a militant national song, in which they demanded both economic and political freedom, and they sang it regularly at busy corners of the campus, to the amusement of their fellow students. The English professors, not realizing that a militant nationalist movement was taking shape within the very walls of their university, merely sighed and regretted the new rowdyism that was disturbing their guests at their dinner table. Yet this was the song that was to rouse the people to revolutionary action, and, with some toning down of the fierce language, it was the song that eventually would be adopted as the national anthem of independent Burma in 1948. The leaders of this group were "Thakins" Ba Sein, Ba Thoung, Lay Maung, and Thein Pe Myint. They had made the prefix Thakin part of their names as an open challenge to the British officials and British merchants. Since 1886 all Englishmen had referred to themselves as Thakins, meaning "masters," and even in the British regiments the Karens, the Kachins, and the Chins had to refer to their British officers as Thakins.

At first this group of angry young revolutionaries was small in number and could not win over the general body of students to their side, but after graduating from the university they toured the villages, making a tremendous impression on the imagination of the masses. At first they had no definite political aim but, finding themselves winning the confidence of the people, in 1935 they organized a political party under the name of Do-Bama Asi-ayon, meaning "We, the Burmese Confederation."

In 1936 a students' strike again shook the university. The founders of the Thakin movement had left the university, leaving no specific followers behind, but other students continued the cold war against the English professors. At the beginning the strike had no political undertones; the students merely wanted the university to be run like an educational institution and not as a mere department of government, and they wanted the professors to behave as teachers rather than as senior civil servants. However, the older politicians welcomed the strike as an opportunity to attract the youth of the country to their side. The legislative council elected in 1932 was in its last few months, and new elections under the new constitution, which would make Burma a separate unit of the British empire on April 1, 1937, were soon to be held. The political leaders in the legislature wanted to prevent a general upheaval of students from occurring, whereas political leaders outside the legislative council wanted the upheaval to take place so as to embarrass the legislators. Both sides wooed the student leaders, who became distressed at the lack of genuine sympathy for them on the part of the politicians.

The strike was led by Maung Nu and Maung Aung San. Maung Nu had left the university in 1929 on graduation, and after serving as a principal of a national school had returned to the university to take his law degree. Maung Aung San was in the final year of his university studies and was full of nationalist fervor because he had been at a national school and because his grandfather was one of the guerrilla leaders executed in 1886. His sincerity, his character, and his personality had given him a maturity unusual for so young a man and the students, although his age, looked up to him for leadership. Maung Nu was much older, and his obvious sincerity and the fact that he had been the principal of a national school greatly impressed the students. These two had as their lieutenants a number of able young men, for example, Maung Ba Swe, Maung Kyaw Nyein, Maung Hla Pe, M. A. Raschid, Maung Kyaw Myint, Maung Tun Win, and Maung Khin Maung Gale, all of whom later helped in the establishment of the independence and became cabinet ministers. Maung Nu and Maung Aung San, fearing that students all over the country would become mere pawns in the game of politics that was soon to be played during the elections, quickly called off the strike. They also felt that their services were needed by their nation beyond the narrow confines of the university and joined the Thakins in recognition of their sincerity. The Thakin movement was greatly strengthened by the participation of the two student leaders.

In the legislative council, the members had been maneuvering for power and position with an eye to the elections. In spite of the coalition between U Ba Pe and Dr. Ba Maw, which led to the acceptance of the separation proposal, it was the Golden Valley Party again which gained the two portfolios of forests and education. Some months before the university strike took place, U Ba Pe and Dr. Ba Maw, by a superhuman effort, managed to topple the Golden Valley Party and at last became ministers. However, in the 1937 elections they parted company and Dr. Ba Maw founded a party of his own, calling it the Sinyethar Party or the "Poor Man's Party." As the Thakins boycotted the elections on the ground that the new constitution was as much a sham as dyarchy was, U Ba Pe and Dr. Ba Maw became the main contestants in the election.

Under the new constitution, the House of Representatives was to consist of 132 members, all to be elected. The Upper House was to consist of 36 members of which 18 were to be appointed by the governor and the other 18 were to be elected by the House of Representatives. The reforms introduced under the new constitution were quite substantial except that the British perpetuated their divide-and-rule policy by declaring the hill regions as frontier areas to be administered directly by the governor and by retaining the racial groupings of the electorate. There was to be a fully responsible cabinet consisting of a prime minister and nine ministers, and it was to exercise full control over the finances of the country. In the elections U Ba Pe was re-elected, together with 45 members of his party. Dr. Ba Maw was also returned, with only 15 members of his party. Yet because of petty jealousies among his own followers, U Ba Pe was unable to form a government and Dr. Ba Maw became prime minister with a coalition cabinet. For the next two years Dr. Ba Maw had a difficult time, especially with a nation-wide racial riot between Burmese and Indians, a religious riot between Burmese and Indian Muslims, a labor strike, and a students' strike. In February 1939 Dr. Ba Maw fell from power, and the People's

Party formed a cabinet with U Pu as prime minister and leaving U Ba Pe out. Within a few weeks there was more dissension in the People's Party itself and one of the ministers, U Saw, broke away and formed a new party, calling it Myochit Party or "Patriots' Party." As most of the members of the People's Party followed him, U Saw became the new prime minister.

The second world war broke out in Europe and rumors of an open rebellion against the British started to circulate; the Thakins and Dr. Ba Maw began to collect private armies of their own, although they could be armed only with sticks. U Saw also collected a private army, but since he was the prime minister it was not clear whether he was going to fight against or for the British. Finally he declared that he would side with the British if Britain would give a definite promise that Burma would be granted dominion status immediately after the war was over. There followed a wholesale arrest of political leaders from all parties, including the People's Party. Dr. Ba Maw himself was arrested, together with many Thakins. Dr. Ba Maw had been making overtures to the Thakins, suggesting they join forces with him against both U Saw and the British, and the arrests of Dr. Ba Maw and many Thakins created a sense of comradeship between the Thakins and members of Dr. Ba Maw's party. As the subject of defense was still under the direct control of the governor, it is obvious that some of the arrests at least were ordered by the governor and not by U Saw.

Thakin Aung San was no longer in the country. Knowing that a warrant of arrest was out against him, he took passage in disguise on a Chinese cargo boat and reached the port of Amoy. He had no definite plans but attempted to make contact with some Chinese left-wing groups. As he waited, the Thakins in Burma had contacted some Japanese secret agents and received a promise of Japanese assistance if they should decide to rebel against the British. One Colonel Suzuki, who had spent some time in Rangoon as a secret agent while professing to be a Japanese journalist, contacted Thakin Aung San at Amoy and took him to Tokyo. In March 1941

Thakin Aung San returned to Rangoon in a Japanese cargo boat and, together with Maung Ba Swe and Maung Kyaw Nyein, selected twenty-nine young men. Among those selected were Thakin Hla Pe, who was to become in 1948 the minister for defense under the name of Boh Let Yar, and Thakin Shu Maung, who had left the university in 1931 and who was to become the commander-in-chief of the armed forces of the Union of Burma in 1949 under the name of Boh Ne Win. Together with the young patriots, Thakin Aung San left Rangoon in the same Japanese ship. Later known as the "Thirty Comrades," these dedicated young men placed their lives in the service of their country, for had they been arrested they would have been hanged for treason. They assumed new names chosen from the pages of Burmese history, hiding their identities to prevent the British from giving trouble to their relatives left behind in Burma. Taken to the Japanese territory of Formosa, they received intensive military training.

In the meantime U Saw still hoped that dominion status could be obtained by negotiation; taking U Tin Tut as his adviser, he flew to London to see Winston Churchill. Mr. Churchill assumed an uncompromising attitude toward U Saw and his aspirations and bluntly said that he would not grant dominion status to Burma. Disappointed, U Saw hurried home, but the airplane carrying him and U Tin Tut touched down at Lisbon on receipt of the news of the Japanese attack on Pearl Harbor. As the aircraft remained grounded for some days while the pilot waited for further instructions from London, U Saw slipped out of his hotel without the knowledge of U Tin Tut and interviewed the Japanese ambassador to Portugal. Lisbon at that time was full of spies and within minutes the British learned of the interview. U Saw and U Tin Tut were arrested for treason. U Tin Tut was later released and re-instated in his rank in the Indian civil service, but U Saw was taken to Kenya and interned. The arrest of U Tin Tut, the most senior Burmese civil servant and a popular and respected figure, was greatly resented by the Burmese public.

Japan was interested in Burma because of the recently constructed Burma road to China. At the time of the construction by the British government a few years before, there were protests by many Burmese leaders and they pointed out that Burma would become involved in international politics because Japan would certainly attempt by every means at its disposal to capture that road. As they had feared, Japan found it necessary to make plans to invade Burma, and as part of those plans they had contacted the Thakins. Aung San and his group genuinely believed that the Japanese would declare Burma to be an independent sovereign state the moment war broke out between Japan and the allies. However, the Japanese authorities postponed making the declaration, but formed the Burma Independence Army when they occupied Thailand. Together with the Japanese troops, the Thirty Comrades and their Burma Independence Army entered Lower Burma at various points and their ranks were swelled by enthusiastic Burmese recruits. There were no pitched battles except at three or four places, because after the fall of Singapore the strategy of the British military command was to withdraw into India with its armies intact. The Burmese people were surprised not at the British defeat itself but at its rapidity. The Burmese populace did not make guerrilla attacks on the retreating British forces and even showed sympathy for them.

The Japanese air force then gained control of the skies and rained death and destruction on Burmese towns. Aung San and his comrades were growing suspicious of Japanese intentions, for Lower Burma was occupied and then Rangoon fell and yet there was no declaration of independence. Finally, Upper Burma fell and the Japanese authorities disbanded the Burmese Independence Army, which was a clear indication that Japan wanted to forget its earlier promise to grant independence to Burma. The Japanese authorities established a new Burmese army under the name "Burma Defense Army," and although they made General Aung San its commander it was actually under the control of Japanese officers attached to it as advisers. The Japanese authorities then set up a military government and treated

Burma as if it were an occupied enemy territory. At the same time, they appointed Dr. Ba Maw as head of a civilian government but it had no power, as it was under the control of the Japanese military government. Aung San was furious and soon after the fall of Mandalay in May 1942 he secretly sent Thakin Thein Pe Myint overland to India to contact the British authorities so that an underground movement for freedom against the Japanese could be started. This action on Aung San's part has been misunderstood and misrepresented by commentators. Aung San's only goal was to gain independence for his country and his conscience was perfectly clear when he made the offer to join hands with British forces against the Japanese, for he took the view that the Japanese were no longer entitled to his loyalty as they had treacherously broken their promise of independence for Burma.

The period of Japanese military rule lasted only three years, but to the Burmese people it was more irksome than some sixty years of British rule. In addition to the widespread feeling that the Japanese had maliciously broken their promise of granting independence, the Burmese people were angry at being subjected to acts of tyranny and barbarous treatment. The introduction of a Gestapo type of military police resulted in tortures of persons suspected of crimes and merciless beatings of witnesses to elucidate information. The general public were subjected to humiliating treatment. For example, when a person riding on a bicycle was a little slow in putting on his brakes at the signal from a Japanese military policeman, he was certain to have his face slapped, and, if a girl was slow in showing her certificate of inoculation against cholera, the Japanese military police would simply pull up her skirt in full view of the public to see whether there were inoculation marks on her buttocks. The health measures of the Japanese military were not in any way due to their concern for the people, but due to their fear that an epidemic would decimate their troops. In short, the Japanese imposed a reign of terror.

As the fortunes of war slowly changed and their invasion of

India continued to fail, the Japanese tried to lure the Burmese, and all other Asian nations they had subjugated for the time being, by dangling their conception of a co-prosperity sphere, in which there would be a commonwealth of Asian nations with Japan as the leader. Promising full independence except the control of external relations, the military government instructed Dr. Ba Maw and other Burmese leaders to draw up a constitution. Neither the leaders nor the masses were impressed, for they remembered the British ultimatum of 1885, in which the British demanded the same control of Burma's foreign relations. However, fearing arrest or execution, Dr. Ba Maw duly drew up the constitution, making himself the chancellor of the country with a nominated cabinet. The Japanese, approving the proposed constitution, declared Burma a fully sovereign state effective from August 1, 1943. Dr. Ba Maw appointed members of his own Sinyethar Party and the Thakin Party to his cabinet. But it was merely a piece of propaganda and a game of make-believe, and General Aung San and his group prepared for a mutiny against the Japanese without sharing the secret with Dr. Ba Maw and his followers. At the beginning of the Japanese occupation there was an unfortunate incident in which a former Karen minister in U Saw's cabinet and his followers were killed by a contingent of the Burma Independence Army, but both Burmese and Karen leaders joined together and restored harmonious relations between Karens and the Burmese. General Aung San shared his secret with the Karen leaders and the Karen contingents of the Burmese Army. In March 1945 General Aung San received the long-awaited signal from the British commander-in-chief, Lord Louis Mountbatten, and he and his army mutinied. There were simultaneous uprisings by civilians all over the country.

By May 1945 the British had liberated the whole of Burma, and the Burmese leaders and the Burmese people welcomed them as friends and colleagues in the great fight for human freedom. For the past three years Burma had been continuously a battlefront and exposed to bombings first by the Japanese and then by the allies;

all her cities and large towns were reduced to rubble, and there was not a single small town left that did not have some scars of war. Through lack of drugs and medicine thousands died, and uncounted numbers of Burmese youth perished in the forced labor camps, working shoulder to shoulder with British and Dutch prisoners of war in the construction of the "death railway" between Burma and Thailand. The country's economy was entirely destroyed. In their retreat the British had pursued a scorched-earth policy, and the oil wells, silver and tungsten mines, harbor installations, and rolling stock were blown up.

The British banks, on closing their business at the approach of the Japanese, required all Burmese depositors to draw out their deposits in the form of British currency notes. As it was death by torture at the hands of the Japanese military police to be found in possession of British currency notes after a certain date, the Burmese were forced to exchange them for Japanese military notes. During the next three years trade with the outside world was at a standstill, and although the people had plenty of food there was a great shortage of clothing. As the Japanese occupation forces issued their military notes without restraint, prices of commodities increased over a hundred times. The first action of the British military administration on liberation was to declare all Japanese currency notes invalid, so at once every Burmese became penniless. During the Japanese period the civil service lost all its previous luster. Those who worked as civil servants during these years did so either because they feared that the Japanese military police would harass them as former civil servants of the British government, or because their services had been requisitioned. In addition the civil servants under the Japanese had no power or authority. As the Japanese approached the Burmese frontier in 1942, not only the British but the Indians and Chinese left the country. Thus, in spite of the many troubles and tribulations, the classless nature of Burmese society was emphasized and restored by the war.

Lord Louis Mountbatten's commanders and troops behaved as

true liberators and treated the Burmese with sympathy and consideration. General Aung San and his Burmese troops were even absorbed into the British forces. As the military administration headed by a former British member of the civil service was producing a jarring note by threatening to arrest Aung San, Mountbatten strengthened it by replacing the vengeful civil servant with a real soldier, Major General Hubert Rance. The Burmese were just beginning to look into the future with some optimism when the British parliament published its plan of suspending even the 1937 constitution and placing the whole country under the direct rule of the governor as soon as the hostilities ceased. The Burmese people were aghast and could only hope that the war would not end as yet. General Aung San now made public his secret Anti-Fascist League and, expanding it into the Anti-Fascist People's Freedom League, he invited all parties to join and turn it into a national congress. He received the full support of the country. General Rance promptly appointed some representatives of the new A.F.P.F.L. to his advisory council. At this point Aung San and the people were still aiming at dominion status rather than full independence.

However, before Rance and his military administration had time to gain the confidence of the Burmese, the war with Japan suddenly ended, and in October 1945 Sir Reginald Dorman Smith, the former governor, returned and restored the civilian government. The governor offered some places in his cabinet to the A.F.P.F.L., but instead of leaving the choice of the members to its president, General Aung San, he proposed to make the choice himself. This was correctly interpreted by General Aung San as an attempt to undermine his authority over his own league and he refused to agree. The governor then proceeded to form his cabinet without any member from the A.F.P.F.L. The new government at once showed itself to be reactionary. U Tin Tut, because of his nationalistic aspirations, was forced to resign from the Indian civil service. The government then planned to arrest General Aung San on a charge of murder, on the ground that he was the president of a court-martial that had sentenced a man to death during the Japanese period. The people protested and began to collect arms and ammunition. The British parliament in London realized the seriousness of the situation and swiftly appointed Sir Hubert Rance as governor, for by this time Rance had left the army and become a civilian. Rance was able to save the country from rebellion but could not save it for the British empire, for the attitude of the Burmese had hardened and they now wanted full independence.

It was now September 1946 and Sir Hubert Rance immediately on arrival in Rangoon opened discussions with all the political parties in the hope of setting up a national cabinet. Finally he formed his cabinet with himself as chairman and nine other members, of which six were from the A.F.P.F.L., nominated by Aung San himself. Aung San was given the important portfolios of defense and external affairs and was also made deputy chairman. Among Aung San's nominees were Thakin Mya, the chairman of the newly founded Socialist party, U Ba Pe, and Thakin Thein Pe Myint from the newly founded Communist party. These parties were of course within the A.F.P.F.L. The governor nominated the three other ministers, U Saw, U Tin Tut, and Thakin Ba Sein, one of the founders of the Thakin party who broke with Aung San during the Japanese period and was exiled by the Japanese authorities. U Tin Tut at that time had no political affiliations, but his appointment to the cabinet was acclaimed by Aung San and the general public.

Rance's effort to restore friendship between the Burmese and the British was a noble one, but the time for friendship was now passed and dissension was the order of the day. The Communist party broke into two factions and Thakin Soe led one section away from the A.F.P.F.L. Thakin Than Tun and his faction, although remaining within the organization, were openly showing hostility to Aung San and to the Socialist party. In the following December the British prime minister, Clement Attlee, invited a delegation of Burmese leaders to come to London and discuss the future of Burma. By that time the extremists among the people were calling Aung

San a "moderate" and the moderates were calling him "extremist." Aung San left for London taking with him Thakin Mya, U Ba Pe, U Tin Tut, U Saw, and Thakin Ba Sein. The discussions were cordial but Aung San and his colleagues were already committed to ask for independence outside the empire, and the change of conception of the British empire as British commonwealth of nations did not make any difference, for the Burmese people would not be satisfied with anything less than independence.

Prime Minister Attlee accepted all the requests and suggestions of the delegation, and on January 27, 1947, an agreement was signed between the British government in London and the Burmese delegation. The concessions given to the Burmese by the agreement were substantial. (1) Elections for a constituent assembly were to be held within four months and the British would accept the decision of the assembly as to the future status of Burma. (2) The British would recognize immediately Aung San's cabinet as an interim government with the rank and powers of a dominion cabinet. (3) The British would sponsor Burma's application for membership in the United Nations and its specialized agencies. (4) A delegation from the British parliament and a delegation from the Burmese cabinet would meet representatives of Chins, Kachins, Shans, and Karennis in a conference to discuss the future of the frontier areas. (5) The British government in London would assist in the reconstruction and rehabilitation of Burma by financial grants and loans.

Aung San's many critics were not satisfied, however. U Saw and Thakin Ba Sein disassociated themselves from the agreement and, resigning from the cabinet, they joined Dr. Ba Maw to organize a party opposed to the A.F.P.F.L. Thakin Than Tun was not satisfied that the Communist party had only one member in Aung San's cabinet, namely Thakin Thein Pe Myint, and on his instructions Thakin Thein Pe Myint resigned. The breech between Aung San and Than Tun widened. Finally Thakin Than Tun and the Communist party were expelled from the A.F.P.F.L., but he and his followers did not at once go underground. As they had a substantial following in the countryside, many people were persuaded to believe that Aung San had betrayed them. In the midst of these criticisms a conference of hill peoples was held, and, to the disappointment of some local British officials and Aung San's critics, the leaders of the hill peoples unanimously agreed to support Aung San and unite with the Burmese. In the elections for the constituent assembly, out of a total of over 200 seats, A.F.P.F.L. lost only 10. In the following June, the constituent assembly approved the London agreement and also resolved to leave the British commonwealth. Prime Minister Attlee was obviously disappointed, but in a show of magnanimity that impressed the entire Burmese nation he accepted the decision of the constituent assembly that Burma would sever its ties with the British. U Tin Tut, who had been holding the important portfolio of finance and had played a leading part in the negotiations for independence and in the negotiations with hill peoples, was sent by Aung San to London to arrange the transfer of power to the new Burmese republic.

U Saw was greatly disappointed. He probably felt that General Aung San's triumph should have been his, and he labored under a sense of injustice because sometime before accompanying Aung San's delegation to London he had been seriously wounded by a would-be assassin, and without any justification he held Aung San and the A.F.P.F.L. responsible. He decided to seize power by force before independence was actually granted, and gathering arms and followers he directed the assassination of Aung San on July 19. Aung San and his entire cabinet were mowed down by three gunmen in the conference room of the cabinet. As the nation reeled under this grievous blow, the British could have taken advantage of the situation by withdrawing the promise of independence and by appointing a cabinet of carefully selected persons who would not hesitate to introduce reactionary measures on the ground that law and order had to be preserved. But Rance and Attlee were above any thought of revenge and within a few hours of the assassinations the governor invited Thakin Nu, the president of the constituent assembly, to form a new cabinet. By this noble action all the misdeeds committed by the British in the past were atoned.

Thakin Nu was a most reluctant politician after the war. He had been in prison at the outbreak of the war in the east and was appointed foreign minister by Dr. Ba Maw when the so-called independence was granted by the Japanese to Burma in 1943. But the events of the war had tired and disillusioned him and, when he accepted General Aung San's invitation to stand for election to the constituent assembly, the understanding was that he would be allowed to retire from politics after independence was achieved. But he took up the burden of the prime ministership, hoping to restore peace and harmony to the nation. He extended the hand of friendship to the communists, inviting them to rejoin the A.F.P.F.L. and share in the glory of the achievement of independence. But the communists rejected his overtures for reunion and continued to agitate against the London agreement.

U Ba Pe had resigned on the eve of the elections to the constituent assembly and General Aung San and Thakin Mya had been assassinated; U Tin Tut was thus the only one of the four signatories of the agreement who was still in office. He was therefore made the scapegoat for all the alleged shortcomings of the agreement, and unfair criticism and even abuse were heaped upon his head. He too was to die at the hands of an assassin within a few months. In the face of such bitter criticism from the extremists, Thakin Nu wisely refused to reconsider the question of accepting membership in the British commonwealth, and, making no changes in the agreement approved by General Aung San, he signed the formal treaty of independence together with Mr. Attlee on October 17, 1947. As a sign and token that the fight for independence was over, Thakin Nu dropped the prefix and became U Nu again. On January 4, 1948, as dawn broke over Rangoon and the Shwedagon pagoda glimmered in the faint light, Burma left the British commonwealth and became a sovereign independent republic.

Postscript   Burma after 1948
A Dialogue between the Editor and the Author

EDITOR: You have told the story of your country in a unique way, as well as from the point of view of a Burmese nationalist. But why have you stopped at the point when Burma regains her independence on January 4, 1948?

AUTHOR: It is but twenty years since that day, and in spite of the general acceleration of history in southeast Asian countries since World War II, twenty years is a short period of time in the long history of the Burmese people. Moreover, the events are too recent and my three elder brothers and I have been too much involved in them for me to have the correct perspective.

E: Is it because you are disappointed or the Burmese people are disappointed with the independence? What happened to the dreams and plans of the makers of the independence about which you have written so well? Were they ever realized? In telling of the Burmese scholars who compiled the first volumes of *The Glass Palace Chronicles* in 1826, you said that they stopped their narrative at 1819 because they did not want to write of the "recent past," as their hearts were laden with sorrow and despair. Can it be that you will not write on the "recent past" for the same reason?

A: No; admittedly there have been sorrows and disappointments, but they were not of the same nature or intensity as those of 1826. In the post-independence period there were occasions when it seemed to outside observers that the federated republic, the Union of Burma, was on the verge of a terrible disaster, but the Burmese never felt a sense of impending doom nor did they despair, as they did in 1826.

E: If your book, for whatever reason, contained no reference to the events that followed the independence of 1948, it surely would have a serious deficiency. I will again stress the fact that you have written the book from the Burmese point of view, or more correctly from the point of view of a nationalist. That is no great drawback, and it even adds to the value of the work in many ways. As a result, throughout the book, although under the surface, there is the argument that the movement of Burmese history, notwithstanding the vicissitudes of national fortunes, is always toward freedom and independence. Yet you stop your story at its climax, the independence of 1948, and leave your reader hanging in the air, as it were.

A: To answer you I would like to use a method of narration used on the Burmese stage. The presentation of a Burmese classical play takes place at night, and, because the audience demands interludes of dancing and clowning between the acts, at dawn it is usually found that there is still one whole act left to be performed. Then the leader of the troupe of strolling players comes out and gives a synopsis of the final act; afterwards he answers questions put by the more interested members of the audience. I will first give the synopsis and then will attempt to answer your questions afterwards.

E: Please proceed.

A: Many Western writers have dubbed the post-independence period of all Afro-Asian nations as "The Morning After," "The Rude Awakening," "Great Expectations Unrealized," or "A Desperate Search for Identity." None of these epithets really fits the Burmese case. Even as drums were being beaten and trumpets were being blown on January 4, 1948, the Burmese as a nation were fully aware of the trials, tribulations, and dangers that were awaiting them only around the corner. The communists had already gone underground and it was only a matter of time before another group of insurgents would decide to take up arms against the newly established republic. In addition, the Karens were growing restive. Therefore, the task that the first prime minister of independent Burma, U Nu, set upon himself was the preservation of the Union. During the period 1948–1950 the danger was from insurrections. During the period 1951–1956 the danger was from a deteriorating economy. In the period 1957–1958 the danger was from political fission. U Nu was the central figure in the first decade after the independence, and the epoch ended with his fall in March, 1962. This is my synopsis of the period 1948–1962.

E: Was not U Nu searching for a new identity for the Burmese nation? After all, Burma became a republic in 1948 for the first time in her history.

A: No. The territorial entity that became the Union of Burma in 1948 was identical with the traditional, old Burmese kingdom, which served as the core of successive Burmese empires. Even the Karenni states, which the British conquered and kept separated from British Burma, voluntarily returned to the Burmese fold. Both U Nu and the Burmese people were determined that Burmese society, which had begun to show some signs of decay and disintegration under the British and the Japanese, and the strain and stress of war and revolution, should be preserved at all cost. The conception of a republic was not alien to the Burmese mind. The monarchy was not revived but many of the symbols and other trappings of the Burmese monarch were retained by the elected president of the Union of Burma. The president did not sit on a throne, but King Theebaw's throne in all its golden splendor stood in the president's reception hall, a reminder to the people that the new republic evolved out of the ancient Burmese kingdom and empire. Although the idea of a republic was not new, the idea of a federal union was, because it was a federation of states based on ethnic grouping. The very conception of a Shan state, a Kayah state,[1] a Kachin state, or a Chin special division had unfortunate political and colonial undertones, a heritage of the divide-and-rule policy of the British overlord.

E: But surely parliamentary democracy was something new?

A: That was so. The Burmese have a centuries-old tradition of democracy themselves, but U Nu and the makers of the independence felt certain that the Western-oriented parliamentary democracy should at least be given a trial. It was true that the rudiments of parliamentary democracy introduced into the country under the dyarchy reforms and the reforms of 1937, when Burma was separated from India, failed dismally to win the confidence and the trust of the people. But U Nu, holding that the fault was not with the reforms themselves but with the way the reforms were worked out and distorted, felt that parliamentary democracy was still the best form of government.

E: Were the insurgents against parliamentary democracy?

A: Not exactly. Only the communists in their ideological beliefs were against parliamentary democracy, but as practical politicians they were more concerned with the treaty of independence. So the target of their criticism was the Nu-Attlee Treaty. The second group of insurgents were the People's Volunteer Organization (P.V.O.), consisting of General Aung San's veterans who could not be absorbed first in Mountbatten's army and later in the Burmese army. They remained organized as a private army behind General Aung San, ready to take up arms and fight the British if independence were not obtained. The British acceptance of the general's demand for independence, followed by his assassination, left the P.V.O. leaderless and uncertain of its future role. They had no objection to parliamentary democracy as such. But they broke into two groups, the Yellow Band P.V.O., supporting the treaty, and the White Band P.V.O., rejecting it and accepting the communists'

[1] Karenni states after 1948 became Kayah state, and Shan states became Shan state.

contention that the independence obtained was not real since Burma was still inside the British sphere of influence, still within the sterling bloc, and still dependent on the British for arms and aid. The Karens, who later rose in rebellion against the Burmese government, were against the treaty because they held that they had been let down by the British. The civil strife in Burma that followed the independence of 1948 was in many ways similar to the civil strife in Ireland that followed the establishment of the Irish Free State in 1922, for in both cases the issue between the government and the insurgents was the treaty of settlement with the British.

E: Surely you could not group the Karen insurgents together with the communists and the P.V.O.s. Wasn't the Karen rebellion an indication that the tribal peoples were against the new republic?

A: I'm afraid the Karen rebellion has been misunderstood or deliberately misrepresented by outside observers. The animosity between the Burmese and some Karen groups started only after the first Anglo-Burmese war and the advent of the Christian missionaries. If there was any racial conflict between the Karens of Lower Burma and the Burmese, it was merely a consequence of the racial conflict between the Mons and the Burmese that disfigured Burmese history, especially in the eighteenth century. Some Karens were culturally akin to the Burmese while others were culturally akin to the Mons. The terms "Sgaw-Karen" and "Po-Karen" were nineteenth-century terms brought into prominence by the missionaries. Before that the terms were "Burmese-Karen" and "Mon-Karen."

E: The explanation that the problem of the minorities in Burma is merely the result of the divide-and-rule policy of the British and the missionaries may sound too anti-colonial to be generally accepted. Isn't it possible that the animosity between the Burmese and the Karens went back many centuries before 1826?

A: No one can deny that both the British government and the Christian missions deliberately followed a policy of divide and rule; and if any latent spark of hatred existed between the Burmese and the Karens, it was fanned into a terrific flame by this policy. The dyarchy and the 1937 reforms emphasized it by introducing the idea of communal representation in the legislature. As the Chins, Kachins, Shans, and Karennis were under the direct administration of the British governor and were not represented in the legislature, communal representation envisaged only the Karens among all the indigenous races as constituting a rival community to the Burmese.

E: There was of course the difference in religion, as the Karens were Christians.

A: That is not correct. Only a minority among the Karens became Christians. There were of course Buddhist Karens also, but they were in the minority. At least 75 per cent of the Karens remained loyal to their ancient tribal religion, a form of animism. However, the Christian Karens, benefiting from the mission schools, became the educated elite and assumed leadership of the Karen people. This Karen elite as a group was naturally conscious of the fact that the Karens were a minority, surrounded by a sea of Burmese.

E: Did the Karens ever take part in the national movement for freedom?

A: Not in the 1920s, although a few Karen students from the American Baptist mission college did take part in the university strike of 1920. It was during this period that the term "the loyal Karens of Burma" came into general use in British official circles, and it served as the title of a book written by the Karen leader, Sir San C. Po, who was a devout Baptist, had received the M.D. degree from an American university, and was later honored with a knighthood by the British government. In the 1930s, however, the ranks of the educated Karens split between those who wished to remain loyal to the British government, remembering the old animosity, and those who wanted to forget the past and work shoulder to shoulder with the Burmese toward independence. In the 1936 university strike, Karen students from the Baptist Christian college fully participated, and some of them later became political colleagues of the Burmese students who led the strike.

The second world war unfortunately did not bring the Karens

and the Burmese together, and there were clashes between the Karens of the delta region and less responsible local units of the Burma Independence Army. The Burmese must bear the blame for those ill-starred incidents. General Aung San rushed to the scene of those clashes and, with the assistance of Sir San C. Po, was successful in restoring harmony between the two ethnic groups. A Karen battalion was raised as a unit of the Burma Defense Army, and, later on when General Aung San rose against the Japanese, this regiment under the command of a Karen colonel, Saw Kyar Doe, won glory for itself in fighting the Japanese and in maintaining order and security in the delta region. When Aung San and his colleagues set up the A.F.P.F.L. the Karens joined it. Sir San C. Po himself was convinced that the Karens must throw in their lot with the Burmese.

E: Was that the opinion of the rank and file?

A: At the time, yes. But Sir San C. Po suddenly died in 1946. At the Panlaung Conference held by the British government in 1947 the tribal minorities were given the right to choose their political future; although the other tribal groups voted to go along with the Burmese (to the surprise of some British officials), a small minority among the Karens was a little hesitant. But the majority trusted General Aung San, U Nu, and U Tin Tut, and so the Karens also chose to join the proposed federal Union of Burma. But the minority group was still unsatisfied and sent a delegation of its own to London when General Aung San was negotiating the independence. The delegation's proposal was that the Karen state, when established, should not be included in the Union of Burma but should be a separate British colony or protectorate. When Prime Minister Attlee refused to consider its proposal, the delegation expressed bewilderment at the "emptiness" of British "promises."

The Burmese leaders, however, with the cooperation of the Karen majority groups, went on with the task of defining the frontiers of the Karen state, for a careful definition was necessary in view of the fact that, unlike other tribal peoples, the Karens did not live in a separate and distinct geographical area. The assassination of General Aung San removed from the scene one of the three Burmese leaders the Karens trusted, and they began to doubt whether the remaining Burmese leaders could protect their interests. To allay such fears U Nu appointed a Karen, General Smith Dun, as the commander-in-chief of the Burmese armed forces. But this wise measure was counteracted by the communists and the P.V.O.s, who went underground; on the plea of security, the Karens formed a private army of their own, the Karen National Defense Organization (K.N.D.O.). The assassination of U Tin Tut in September 1948 made the situation worse. U Nu, in a gesture of goodwill, offered to grant official recognition to the K.N.D.O. In fact, U Nu attempted to accommodate the Karens so much that some Burmese newspapers commented that Thakin Nu had become Karen Nu. But his efforts were in vain. The K.N.D.O.s rose in rebellion in January 1949. It was by no means a popular movement, for many Karens remained loyal to the Burmese government. The Po family continued to cooperate with the Burmese leaders, and Sir San C. Po's daughter, Mrs. Ba Maung Chain, became the first woman minister in U Nu's second cabinet. The K.N.D.O. insurrection was neither anti-Buddhist nor was it a "right-of-center" movement. Many prominent Baptist families continued to support the Burmese government, and one of the most fiery leaders of the K.N.D.O., U Hla Pe, was a Buddhist. A Karen battalion in the Burmese army mutinied and joined the K.N.D.O. Most of the officers, however, remained loyal, but they resigned their commissions out of embarrassment. General Smith Dun himself resigned and General Ne Win was appointed in his place. In the following February the government troops had to withdraw inside the city of Rangoon itself, and the campus of the University of Rangoon became a no man's land between the K.N.D.O. and the government forces. In the following March the K.N.D.O. joined hands with the Communist insurgents, captured Mandalay, and set up a joint administration.

E: Yet the insurrection failed?

A: To begin with, as I said before, the K.N.D.O. rebellion did

not have the support of many of the Karens themselves, who chose
to remain either against or at least aloof from the movement. Then
the other tribal groups remained steadfast in their loyalty to the
Burmese government, and the Chins and Kachin members of the
armed forces did not waver but fought the Karen rebels, who only
recently were their companions-in-arms. Another factor, of course,
was the strength and sincerity of U Nu and his political colleagues
and General Ne Win and his troops, who placed the preservation of
the Union above all other considerations. Finally, there were dis-
sensions and open quarrels among the K.N.D.O. leaders and units
themselves. Many of the rebels, who had been encouraged to believe
that they would receive weapons and other aids from overseas,
were now disillusioned.

E: Did the insurrections end in 1950?

A: They should have, but they did not because of a new factor,
the entry of Nationalist Chinese troops into Burma. By 1950 the
Burmese government had re-taken the territory lost to the Karens
and the communists, and to the P.V.O., who did not join hands
with the Karens. The government offered a generous amnesty, and
many insurgents took advantage of it. But the hard core of the
K.N.D.O., made up of extremists and other die-hard insurgents,
were able to take advantage of the Burmese government's preoccupation with the Nationalist Chinese troops, and, what was more
important, they were able to buy arms and ammunition from those
troops. Thus small bands of insurgents roamed the remoter regions
of the country, bent more on banditry than on rebellion.

E: Why did the Nationalist Chinese troops intervene in the
insurrections?

A: They didn't intervene, nor were they interested in any in-
surgent group. They originally were remnants of a Nationalist Chinese (K.M.T.) army defeated by Chinese Communist forces, and
when they first entered the Shan state from Yunnan early in 1950
they numbered only 2,000. They brought their families along with
them, and under the circumstances the Burmese government was

ready to regard them as refugees and intern them. But their commander, General Li Mi, who flew back and forth between Taiwan and Burma, decided to build up a new army with a view toward invading Yunnan from Burma. In no time, fresh and well-armed troops were flown in from Taiwan. These Chinese troops proceeded to occupy a large stretch of Burmese territory and held it against attacks by units of the Burmese army. Then they began to live off the land, and some became quite rich by smuggling opium and arms from across the Thai frontier and selling them to the K.N.D.O. and other insurgents.

As supplies of United States origin were regularly air-dropped from airplanes with U.S. markings, the Burmese government approached the U.S. government to use its good offices to effect the evacuation of the Nationalist Chinese troops from Burmese territory. On receiving no response, and as the build-up of the Nationalist Chinese troops continued, the Burmese became alarmed. They realized that this was yet another consequence of Burma's being the back door to China, and they remembered the ravages caused by the troops who accompanied the last Ming emperor's flight into Burmese territory, and the new Manchu emperor's pursuit. They were reminded of the claim made by Imperial China to Upper Burma at the time of the British conquest in 1886, which was repeated and re-affirmed by Nationalist China at the time of the allied liberation of the country in 1945. They feared that the armies of the new Communist Chinese government might come in pursuit. So the Burmese government took the matter before the General Assembly of the United Nations, and when the member states would not declare the Nationalist Chinese troops to be "aggressors" the Burmese felt that their trust in the world body had been betrayed.

This intrusion by the Nationalist Chinese troops had a serious effect on Burma's economy and foreign policy. Although the constitution of 1948 envisaged a neutralist foreign policy, up until the K.M.T. intrusion the Burmese were inclined toward the West. Prime Minister Attlee and his socialist British government were immensely

popular with the Burmese, and American economic aid was welcome. When the Chinese troops persisted in remaining on Burmese
territory, and their supplies of U.S. origin continued to be dropped
by U.S. airplanes, Prime Minister U Nu informed the U.S. government that Burma could not continue to accept American economic
aid. Some years were to pass before Burma again accepted U.S. aid,
but by that time a policy of strict and just neutrality had been
evolved, and aid was accepted only to a limited extent, and that
after very careful appraisal. The rebuff by the United Nations convinced the Burmese that they should not get involved with either
side of the cold war and must "go it alone" to preserve their independence. Burma, however, continued to participate in the United
Nations, and its impartiality and good faith were made so clear in
the voting record of the world body that a Burmese came to be
unanimously elected to the office of Secretary-General.

E: With all this preoccupation with the insurgency and the
presence of foreign troops, did U Nu find time to look after the
economy of the country?

A: Until the tide turned in favor of the government, U Nu and
his colleagues were hard put to find the money needed to administer
the country and to buy the necessary arms to suppress the insurrections. In the dark days of 1949 the government was virtually bank-
rupt and no foreign bank would make loans. The position of the
government was indeed desperate until an Indian bank took the risk
and advanced the money. By 1950, however, the position had improved, as the government was able to make some sales of rice. By
1951, U Nu had turned his attention toward the creation of a welfare
state, Pyidawthar, or "the country of peace and prosperity."

U Nu was not a member of the official Socialist party, which
dominated the A.F.P.F.L., after the communists had left it. However,
he was a left-of-center politician, as most Burmese politicians were
after 1948. Before 1886 Burmese law and social custom did not encourage the accumulation of capital. After 1886 the average Burmese
had no chance of even acquiring capital, and the peasants lost their

lands. What little capital some Burmese were able to acquire and accumulate was lost during the Japanese occupation. The second world war completely devastated the country, and the insurgency continued the devastation. In such circumstances the only agency that could obtain the capital needed to rehabilitate and reconstruct the shattered economy was the government. Therefore, any Prime Minister after 1948 would have had to be a socialist, both in theory and in practice.

E: What was the land policy of U Nu's government?

A: Even before the actual attaining of independence, General Aung San repeatedly declared the A.F.P.F.L.'s intention of abolishing landlordism. When the constitution was being drawn up, General Aung San saw to it that the right of the government to introduce land reforms was specifically expressed. The Two-Year Plan that was drawn up under his guidance dealt mainly with the project of land nationalization. It was followed by the Land Nationalization Act of 1948. The act was an exploratory and experimental measure, and amendments were later made, but by 1953 nationalization of arable lands was complete. The government paid compensation to the landlords and then re-distributed the lands among working farmers. Each cultivator received about ten acres, and these re-distributed lands could not be sold or transferred except under special prescribed rules of procedure. But as long as a cultivator worked it, the land was his own private property and would be inherited by his heirs under the general law of inheritance. He paid an annual revenue direct to the government and could receive assistance from the government in the form of loans at reasonable rates of interest and advice from experts regarding improvements to his land. In other words, the Burmese became again a nation of small, land-owning farmers as in pre-British days. Thus the land reforms had both economic and social implications.

E: Were there other instances of economic and social planning besides the Two-Year Plan that you mentioned?

A: The Two-Year Plan was drawn up before the actual attainment of independence, and naturally it was not adequate to the needs of the country. Then the insurrections interfered with its implementation. The Pyidawthar Plan, mentioned earlier, was a full-dress affair. Approved by a national conference held at Rangoon in 1952, it was an Eight-Year Plan, envisaging a completion of all its projects by 1960. Although it contained plans for a welfare state and dealt in detail with the problems of housing, education, health, and democratization of local administration, the main aim of the Pyidawthar was to raise the gross national product from the prewar level by one-third. To achieve this goal, although agriculture was not to be neglected, a program of industrialization was stressed.

E: Was the Pyidawthar Plan successful?

A: Not in its entirety. One problem was the lack of funds. Following a policy of strict neutrality, the Burmese government had to scrutinize every offer of a loan or economic aid to ensure that it had no political bias. Thus the only aid that could be accepted without fear of any involvement in the cold war was the Colombo Plan Aid, which unfortunately was usually available only in the form of technical assistance. The second problem was the program of industrialization. Rice remained the main source of foreign exchange, and more and more attention had to be paid to the modernization of methods of cultivation. The procurement of fertilizers, farm equipment, and machines took a sizable portion of the capital funds available. Some projected industries had to be scrapped. All this was to be expected, but it resulted in a dispute between those cabinet ministers who favored substantial industrialization and those who would play safe and concentrate on agriculture.

In spite of these difficulties, and surprising in retrospect, many of the projects of the Pyidawthar Plan were successfully implemented. There was very little corruption or wastage, and Burma's population increased at a conservative rate, unlike in neighboring countries. In addition, many of the welfare schemes were realized. Many more schools were built, and the University of Rangoon, under one rector from 1946 to 1958, expanded and was able to transform itself from an alien institution into a national one. Under its wing colleges were established at Mandalay and other important towns. Buddhism was revived. Under government patronage the Sixth Great Synod of Buddhism was held in Rangoon in 1953, marking the two-thousand-five-hundreth anniversary of Buddha's passing away. Buddhism has always been a cementing force in Burmese society and politics, and there is no doubt that the international prestige of the country was enhanced by the holding of the Great Synod. The Burmese need not be ashamed of their Pyidawthar Plan.

E: When did the political "retrogression" start?

A: It came suddenly, like a summer storm. In February 1958 Burma had just completed ten years as an independent republic. U Nu and his A.F.P.F.L. Party had won resounding victories in the general elections of 1952 and 1956, and it was a foregone conclusion that they would repeat their victory in 1960, when the next general elections were due. The Pyidawthar Plan was working quite well. Benefiting from one whole decade of administrative experience, the government was streamlining itself for greater efficiency. U Nu had become a colorful international personality and was one of the accepted leaders of the neutralist group of nations. His dashing young socialist colleagues were now ten years older and had become more mature and tolerant. Delegates from all over the country had just returned to their towns and villages after attending a nation-wide A.F.P.F.L. convention. Even die-hard insurgents were surrendering in batches, taking advantage of the general amnesty declared by the government. Like a bolt from the blue came the official announcement that the A.F.P.F.L. Party had split into two sections, one headed by Prime Minister U Nu, and the minister for agriculture, Thakin Tin, and the other headed by Deputy Prime Minister U Ba Swe and the minister for industries, U Kyaw Nyein. Thakin Tin was older than even U Nu, and as an elder Thakin was well respected and influential. U Nu, U Ba Swe, and U Kyaw Nyein had been close associates of General Aung San

and comrades since the university strike of 1936. They formed the
ruling triumvirate of the A.F.P.F.L., and thus the split was right at
the very top. The rank and file members, flabbergasted and desperate, simply put themselves at random in one section or the other,
and the split was now complete.

E: What was the cause of the split?

A: At the time, many stories purported to give the true story
behind it. Many said it was over the appointment of the secretary-
general of the party. Some said it was really a continuation of the
cabinet debate on "agriculture versus industry," others explained
that the split occurred because of corruption in high places, and a
few even went so far to say that it was really a quarrel of the wives
of the leaders. As time passed, however, it became clear that there
was no story to tell. The disagreement over the secretary-general-
ship was not a serious one, and the triumvirate had always been
able to come to some compromise even with more serious disagree-
ments. The debate over "agriculture versus industry" had ended
with some amendments to the Pyidawthar Plan. The Burmese leaders
had no numbered Swiss bank accounts, no shares in business con-
cerns, no monopoly of any business venture, and were without any
monetary reserves in the form of savings. No one among the leaders
was found to have lined his nest. Some would make the wives of
the leaders the scapegoats simply because there was no other explanation. The split was the result of overstrain on the part of the
triumvirate. U Nu never wanted to hold office, as his interests
were religion and writing. He would have preferred to be either a
monk or a dramatist. U Ba Swe and U Kyaw Nyein considered
themselves too young and too immature to take office, but the death
of their Socialist party leader, Thakin Mya, had left them no choice.
Thus the assassinations of General Aung San and the older leaders
had forced the second line to come to the forefront. It may be noted
in passing that the assassinations robbed the minorities of their experienced and trusted leaders, the Karen leader Mahn Ba Khaing,
the Shan leader Sawbwa of Mongpong, and the Burmese Muslim

leader and educationist Sayagyi Razak, and thus the later unrest among the minorities also had its roots in the assassinations of 1947. U Nu in the cabinet of 1948 was only forty years of age, U Ba Swe and U Kyaw Nyein were still in their middle thirties, U Tin Tut, considered a gray-beard elder statesman, was fifty-two. As they themselves had composed the second line, U Nu, U Ba Swe, and U Kyaw Nyein were without any second-line leaders to relieve them of some of their burdens. They were the vanguard in the battles for freedom waged in the decade immediately before independence, but for them the achievement of their goal brought no rest. The turbulent and fateful decade that followed the independence had exhausted the strength of these three leaders. The split had no villains, only heroes.

E: Was it not due to the failure of the parliamentary democracy?

A: I hold that the failure of parliamentary democracy was not the cause of the split, but its tragic result. During the decade under consideration, parliamentary democracy was indeed too successful in that the people elected to the legislature the party that believed in parliamentary democracy, namely the A.F.P.F.L. The general elections held in 1952 and 1956 were really free and fair elections, and the results fully expressed the will of the people. The consequence was a one-party government without an opposition. Many of the debates made in the cabinet should have been properly made in the legislature, between the government and the opposition, if an opposition had existed. Thus, the Burmese electorate could in no way be blamed for the failure of parliamentary democracy in the country.

The monster that really killed the parliamentary democracy was the bitter acrimony that discolored the struggle for power between the two factions of the broken A.F.P.F.L. U Ba Swe and U Kyaw Nyein resigned from the cabinet and with their followers formed the opposition. Again, theirs was not a real opposition, for they were in full agreement with all the measures before the legislature for consideration, as they themselves had approved of these measures as members of the cabinet. All that they wanted was to topple U Nu's cabinet with a vote of no confidence, so that the general elections due in 1960 would have to be held at once. U Nu's purpose was to continue to hold the reins of government so that the date of the elections would not have to be advanced. It now became a battle for votes in the legislature itself, so as to defeat the motion of no confidence. It was a furious battle, and as no doctrinal or policy difference existed between the two factions the criticism leveled against each other became attacks on the character and integrity of the opponents. The no-confidence motion was defeated only by a majority of six votes. U Nu himself, realizing that his slender majority could disappear at the next voting, began to consider the advisability of dissolving the legislature and calling a general election.

With this prospect of an early election, the combatants took the fight to the electorate, and another campaign of personal abuse and recrimination resulted. The political leaders were now being discredited, in the same way as the political leaders of the dyarchy days were discredited, by their own vicious personal attacks against each other. The Buddhist monks, encouraged by U Nu and his patronage of Buddhism, had stayed aloof from politics, as required by the rules of their Order, but they now took sides. The ethnic groups were also drawn into the fray. There were rumors of secession, mutinies, and rebellions. The insurgents became braver, and there was a sudden deterioration of law and order. There were widespread fears that no fair and free elections could be held in this atmosphere of hatred, fission, and gloomy forebodings. There were reports of an impending coup d'état, but General Ne Win, with a firm hand, kept his troops away from the political turmoil. In the following November, U Nu, beginning to weary of his burden of office, called upon General Ne Win to take his place as caretaker prime minister. The opposition fully approved and the legislature formally requested General Ne Win to take over. As his assigned task was merely to restore law and order and oversee the holding of the general elections, he reluctantly agreed and appointed a cabinet of non-politician civilians, mostly members or former members of the civil service.

E: It was not a coup d'état, then?

A: Not at all. General Ne Win held the constitution in high respect and everything he did as caretaker prime minister was always constitutionally correct.

The general elections were held some eighteen months later, in May 1960. The electorate, making a supreme effort to save parliamentary democracy from oblivion, returned U Nu with a staggering majority. As a result, again there was no opposition in the legislature. Unfortunately, quarrels developed within U Nu's followers themselves, and the position became worse when U Nu announced his impending retirement from politics in the following year. U Nu's followers again split into two groups, each smearing the other, and U Nu watched as if he were the audience and his followers players enacting a tragi-comedy. Gloom and disgust seized the people, but they still looked to U Nu to reassert his leadership.

There were of course many controversial issues that divided the country. There was the question of a separate state for the Arakanese, and another for the Mons. The Arakanese had their own geographical unit, and an Arakanese state would not have broken up the Union. Nobody really believed that the Mons would have a separate state. For one thing, they lived scattered among the Burmese; for another, many of the so-called Mons now had Burmese blood in them. There was also the controversy over Buddhism's being made a state religion by U Nu. Actually, to a country where 85 per cent of the people were Buddhists, it did not greatly matter whether it was officially a Buddhist state or otherwise. The real danger was in the possibility of fragmentation of the country. The ethnic groups feared for the safety of their own states if law and order should break down at the center when U Nu left office; after all, the second Burmese empire under Nandabayin broke into pieces in similar circumstances. U Nu could have reasserted his authority and leadership to preserve the Union, had he wished. Perhaps he felt that, on the record made, he was entitled to release and retirement, and to leave the burdens of the Union on other shoulders. Perhaps he felt that he should now practice the Buddhist "rule of training" of detachment. Perhaps he was just bone-weary after some twenty years of high endeavor. It is difficult to say. But he did nothing to allay the fear and anxiety of his people and merely stood

> Like a bold seer in a trance,
> Seeing all his own mischance,
> With a glassy countenance.

Although without romantic overtones, the fall of U Nu was as tragic as the fall of the Irish leader Charles Stewart Parnell.

On March 2, 1962, at early dawn, units of the Burma army marched into Rangoon and seized control of the government. Suspending the constitution, General Ne Win appointed a revolutionary council of senior military officers, except for one civilian, to act as the supreme administrative and legislative body. As chairman of the revolutionary council he came to exercise the functions of president and prime minister. He abolished the Supreme Court. He took into protective custody the President, the members of the Regency Council, which acted when the President was "incapable," U Nu, and members of his cabinet. General Ne Win took these measures because he sincerely believed that they were necessary to preserve the Union. The civil service was left intact, and the courts continued to exercise their jurisdictions. Although the revolutionary council assumed all powers of the legislature, very few new laws were actually passed. Under General Ne Win, Buddhism ceased to be the state religion, but it continued to enjoy a special position under the patronage of the revolutionary government. Following the trend in the last years of U Nu's government, General Ne Win gave more and more emphasis to agriculture. The neutralist foreign policy remained unchanged.

General Ne Win was by no means a Johnny-come-lately who suddenly seized power. Dedicating himself to the cause of national freedom, he had left the university in 1930 and joined the Thakin movement. He was one of the Thirty Comrades who escaped along with Aung San to Japan to receive military training there. Throughout the war he was at General Aung San's side, and at its end he did not return to politics but chose instead to become a professional soldier. In the troubled months of 1949 he reluctantly accepted U Nu's invitation to join the cabinet as Deputy Prime Minister and Defense Minister, but possessing no political ambition he returned to active military life the moment the tide of battle turned in favor of the government. In 1959 he accepted the caretaker prime ministership on the distinct understanding that he would return to active military duty the moment the elections had been held and a prime minister chosen. Knowing the Burmese chronicles almost by rote, he looked to the Burmese past to create the Burmese future. Holding that the Union could be preserved only by the maintenance of traditional values, General Ne Win's aim was to define and follow the "Burmese way" in all aspects of life, in social affairs, in economics, in politics, and even in socialism. He had been a man of the world, gay, friendly, and fond of company, but overnight, to set an example to his officers and to the people, he became an austere recluse, whose only form of recreation was to play a round of golf by himself on a lonely course.

Appendix I Chronological Table

B.C. 500	Mons enter Lower Burma from the east.
	Mon and Burmese tradition asserts the original Shwedagon pagoda was built during the lifetime of the Buddha.
	Tibeto-Burmese tribes, with the Pyus as spearhead, entered Burma from the extreme north.
B.C. 300	Emperor Asoka's mission of Buddhist monks convert the Mon kingdom of Thaton to Buddhism.
Circa A.D. 0000	Pyu kingdom of Prome (*Sri Ksetra*) is founded.
	Sakra Era (beginning A.D. 78) is introduced to Prome from India.
	Overland trade routes from India to China through Upper Burma.
	Portage routes connecting the sea lanes of the Bay of Bengal with those of the Gulf of Siam, through southern Burma, controlled by the Mons.
400	Growing power of the Pyus over the Mons.
600	The Pyus withdraw to Upper Burma.
	Emergence of the Burmese.
	Mons approach zenith of their power.
638	The Burmese evolve a new Era of their own.

800   Nan-Chao raids.
Fall of Pyu kingdom.

849   Building of the fortified city of Pagan. (Dates become more definite at this point.)

1044   Anawrahta becomes king of Pagan.

1056   Anawrahta conquers Thaton, acting as patron of Theravada Buddhism.

1083   Revolt of the Mons.

1084   Kyansittha becomes king of Pagan.

1112   Alaungsithu succeeds his grandfather, Kyansittha.

1161   Dispute with Ceylon.

1173   Narapatisithu becomes king.

1210   Ascension of Nadoungmya, last of the temple-building kings.

1234   Ascension of Kyaswa and the beginning of the decline of Pagan.

1254   Ascension of Narathihapati, the last of the Pagan kings.

1277   War with Kublai Khan.

1287   Fall of Pagan.
Mons become independent.

1303   The Tatars withdraw from Burma.

1312   Kingdom of Pinya is founded.

1315   Kingdom of Sagaing is founded.

1364   End of Pinya and Sagaing.
Ava is founded.

1368   Swasawkè, king of Ava.

1385   Razadarit, king of Pegu.
War between Ava and Pegu.

1401   Minkhaung, king of Ava.

1404   Arakan becomes independent and powerful under the Mrohaung dynasty.

1422   Death of Minkhaung.

1423 Death of Razadarit.

1427 Burmese dynasty at Ava is established by Mohnyin-thado.

1453 Shin Saw Bu, queen of Pegu.

1459 Arakan acquires Chittagong.

1472 Dhammazedi, king of Pegu.

1531 Tabinshwehti becomes king of Toungoo.
Second Burmese empire.

1547 Tabinshwehti forces a treaty from Siam.

1551 Death of Tabinshwehti.
Breakup of the empire.
Mons revolt.
Bayinnaung becomes king.

1562 Bayinnaung conquers Siam.

1565 Bayinnaung re-conquers Siam.

1587 Siam regains independence.

1594 Siamese army invades Pegu but is repulsed.

1599 Arakanese and Toungoo armies sack Pegu.
Siamese army invades Burma.

1600 De Brito becomes king of Syriam.

1605 Anaukpetlun becomes king of Ava.

1613 Anaukpetlun defeats de Brito and partially restores the empire.

1635 Tharlun moves the capital from Pegu to Ava.

1650 The last Ming emperor of China, fleeing from the Manchu armies, enters Burmese territory.

1658 The fallen Chinese emperor is taken back to Yunnan and executed.

1666 Decline of Arakan, following loss of Chittagong.

1709 English open a dockyard at Syriam.

1729 French open a dockyard at Syriam.

1738   Manipuri horsemen start their raids on Ava.

1740   Rebellion in Lower Burma.

1747   The rebellion becomes a Mon rebellion.

1750   Mon embassy to the French viceroy Dupleix in India.
French ambassador de Bruno arrives in Syriam.
English embassy arrives in Pegu but is received coldly by the Mons.

1752   The Mons conquer Upper Burma.
Alaungpaya rises in rebellion against the Mons.

1753   The English, failing to get permission from the Mons to establish a settlement at Negrais, seize it.

1756   Alaungpaya conquers Syriam and executes de Bruno.

1757   Alaungpaya captures Pegu, completing his conquest of Burma.

1758   Alaungpaya conquers Manipur.

1759   Suspecting the English of treachery, Alaungpaya destroys their settlement at Negrais.

1760   Alaungpaya invades Siam.
Alaungpaya suddenly dies and the Burmese army retreats.

1763   Ascension of Hsinbyushin.

1766   Burmese invasion of Siam.

1767   The Burmese capture Ayuthia.

1766
to   } Four separate Chinese invasions of Burma.
1769

1769   The Burmese finally repulse the Chinese and sign a peace treaty.

1770   Manipur revolts but is subdued by the Burmese.

1776   Burmese invade Siam to suppress insurrections.
Hsinbyushin dies, the Burmese armies withdraw, and Siam becomes independent.

1782 Intrigues and struggles for the throne at Ava.
      Ascension of Bodawpaya.
      Conquest of Arakan.

1785 Burmese invade Siam and are repulsed.

1794 Insurrections in Arakan.

1795 Symes's first embassy to the court of Ava.

1802 Symes's second embassy to the court of Ava.

1811 Chinbyan, an Arakanese refugee in British territory, invades Arakan.

1813 The Burmese re-assert their authority over Manipur.

1817 The Burmese place their nominee on the throne of Assam.

1819 Ascension of Bagyidaw.

1824 The first Anglo-Burmese war.

1826 The Treaty of Yandabo and loss of the maritime provinces.

1830 Henry Burney, the first British resident at Ava.

1852 Second Anglo-Burmese war and loss of the province of Pegu.

1853 Ascension of King Mindon.

1866 Myingun rebellion.

1870 First Burmese embassy to England and Europe.

1872 Fifth Great Synod of Buddhism is held at Mandalay.

1875 The British authorities instruct their resident at Mandalay not to remove his shoes when entering the Burmese king's presence.

1878 Ascension of King Theebaw.

1883 Burmese embassy to France.

1885 (August) The Hluttaw passes judgment in the Bombay Burma Trading Corporation case.
      (November) Third Anglo-Burmese war.

1886 (January) Burma is declared a British colony.

(February) Burma is proclaimed a province of India.

1886
to } The Burmese wage a guerrilla war against the British.
1900

1920 The first Rangoon University strike.

1921 The dyarchy reforms.

1930
to } The peasants' rebellion.
1932

1933 Controversy over the British proposal to separate Burma from India.

1934 The Thakin movement gathers momentum.

1936 The second Rangoon University strike.

1937 Burma becomes separated from India.

1942
to } Burma under Japanese occupation.
1945

1947 Assassination of General Aung San.

1948 Burma regains independence and leaves the British commonwealth.

Appendix II Lists of Kings, 1044–1885

Pagan Dynasty, 1044–1287[1]

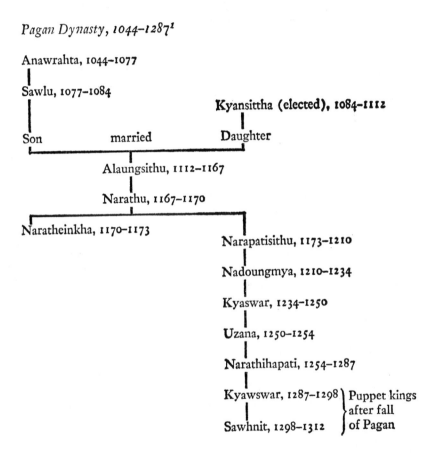

Anawrahta, 1044–1077

Sawlu, 1077–1084

Kyansittha (elected), 1084–1112

Son — married — Daughter

Alaungsithu, 1112–1167

Narathu, 1167–1170

Naratheinkha, 1170–1173

Narapatisithu, 1173–1210

Nadoungmya, 1210–1234

Kyaswar, 1234–1250

Uzana, 1250–1254

Narathihapati, 1254–1287

Kyawswar, 1287–1298 ⎫
⎬ Puppet kings after fall of Pagan
Sawhnit, 1298–1312 ⎭

---

[1] For lists of kings of Mon kingdoms, Prome, Arakan, and Pagan before A.D. 1044, see *The Glass Palace Chronicle*; Phayre, *A History of Burma*, pp. 289 ff.; and Harvey, *A History of Burma*, pp. 396 ff.

Kings of Pinya, 1312–1364

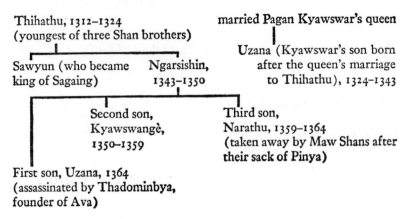

Thihathu; 1312–1324   married Pagan Kyawswar's queen
(youngest of three Shan brothers)
                                        Uzana (Kyawswar's son born
                                           after the queen's marriage
Sawyun (who became   Ngarsishin,   to Thihathu), 1324–1343
king of Sagaing)   1343–1350

          Second son,   Third son,
          Kyawswangè,   Narathu, 1359–1364
          1350–1359   (taken away by Maw Shans after
                                  their sack of Pinya)

First son, Uzana, 1364
(assassinated by Thadominbya,
founder of Ava)

Kings of Sagaing, 1315–1364

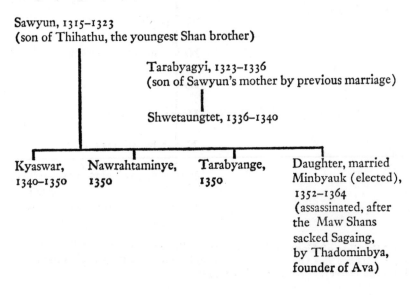

Sawyun, 1315–1323
(son of Thihathu, the youngest Shan brother)

          Tarabyagyi, 1323–1336
          (son of Sawyun's mother by previous marriage)

          Shwetaungtet, 1336–1340

Kyaswar,   Nawrahtaminye,   Tarabyange,   Daughter, married
1340–1350   1350   1350   Minbyauk (elected),
                                             1352–1364
                                             (assassinated, after
                                             the Maw Shans
                                             sacked Sagaing,
                                             by Thadominbya,
                                             founder of Ava)

Kings of Ava, 1364-1555

SHAN-BURMESE DYNASTY

Thadominbya,
1364-1368

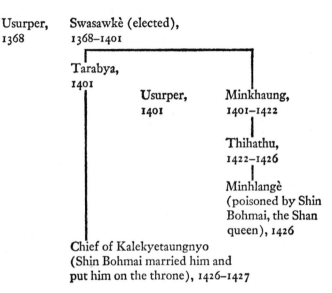

Usurper,   Swasawkè (elected),
1368   1368-1401

Tarabya,
1401

Usurper,   Minkhaung,
1401   1401-1422

Thihathu,
1422-1426

Minhlangè
(poisoned by Shin
Bohmai, the Shan
queen), 1426

Chief of Kalekyetaungnyo
(Shin Bohmai married him and
put him on the throne), 1426-1427

BURMESE DYNASTY

Mohnyinthado (married Shin Bohmai as a junior queen), 1427-1440
   (sons by the chief queen)

Minyèkyawswa,   Narapati, 1443-1469
1440-1443

Thihathura, 1469-1481

Minkhaung, 1481-1502

Shwenankyawtshin, 1502-1527
(assassinated by Shan chief Thohanbwa)

Shan chiefs' rule, 1527-1555

Kings of Hanthawaddy (Pegu), 1287–1539

Wareru, 1287–1306
Hkun Law (brother of above), 1306–1310
Saw O (nephew of above), 1310–1324
Saw Zein (brother of above), 1324–1331
Usurper, 1331
Saw E (nephew of Saw Zein), 1331
Binnya E Law, son of Hkun Law, 1331– ?
(Various claimants to the throne)
Binnya E Law's son, Binnya U, in 1353 emerges as the king of the Mons

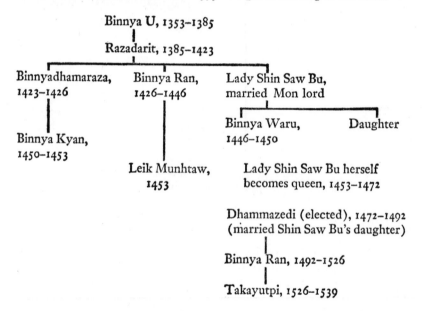

Binnya U, 1353–1385

Razadarit, 1385–1423

Binnyadhamaraza, 1423–1426

Binnya Ran, 1426–1446

Lady Shin Saw Bu, married Mon lord

Binnya Kyan, 1450–1453

Binnya Waru, 1446–1450   Daughter

Leik Munhtaw, 1453

Lady Shin Saw Bu herself becomes queen, 1453–1472

Dhammazedi (elected), 1472–1492 (married Shin Saw Bu's daughter)

Binnya Ran, 1492–1526

Takayutpi, 1526–1539

Burmese rule, 1539–1550
Smim Sawhtut rebels against Burmese rule, 1550–1551
Smim Htaw, brother of the last king Takayutpi, declares himself king
and is defeated by Bayinnaung, 1551
Burmese rule, 1551–1740
Smim Htaw Buddhaketi (Lord of the Striped Elephant), 1740–1747
Binnya Dala, 1747–1757

Toungoo Dynasty, 1486–1752

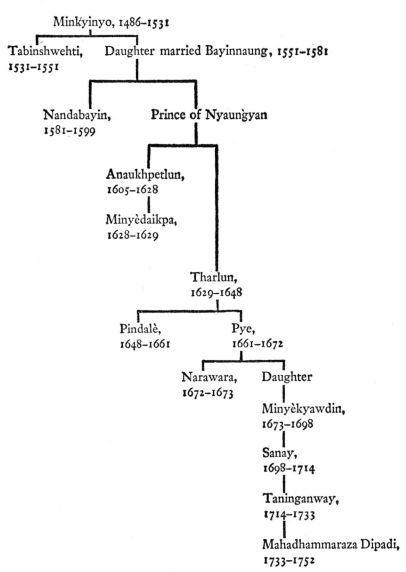

Minkyinyo, 1486–1531

Tabinshwehti,
1531–1551

Daughter married Bayinnaung, 1551–1581

Nandabayin,
1581–1599

Prince of Nyaungyan

Anaukhpetlun,
1605–1628

Minyèdaikpa,
1628–1629

Tharlun,
1629–1648

Pindalè,
1648–1661

Pye,
1661–1672

Narawara,
1672–1673

Daughter

Minyèkyawdin,
1673–1698

Sanay,
1698–1714

Taninganway,
1714–1733

Mahadhammaraza Dipadi,
1733–1752

Alaungpaya Dynasty, 1752–1885

Capitals: Shwebo, 1752–1763; Ava, 1763–1783; Amarapura, 1783–1859 (the court moved to Ava as a war measure in 1823 and returned to Amarapura in 1837); Mandalay, 1859–1885.

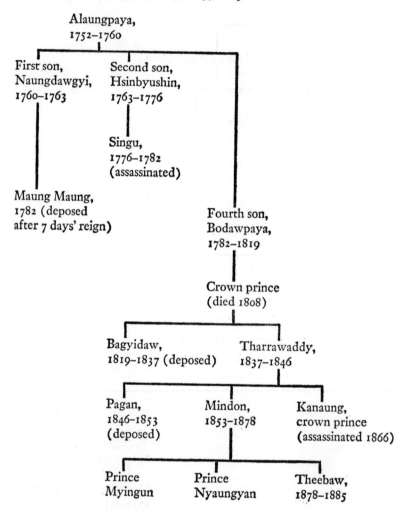

Alaungpaya,
1752–1760

First son,
Naungdawgyi,
1760–1763

Second son,
Hsinbyushin,
1763–1776

Singu,
1776–1782
(assassinated)

Maung Maung,
1782 (deposed
after 7 days' reign)

Fourth son,
Bodawpaya,
1782–1819

Crown prince
(died 1808)

Bagyidaw,
1819–1837 (deposed)

Tharrawaddy,
1837–1846

Pagan,
1846–1853
(deposed)

Mindon,
1853–1878

Kanaung,
crown prince
(assassinated 1866)

Prince
Myingun

Prince
Nyaungyan

Theebaw,
1878–1885

Appendix III   Bibliographical Notes

General Remarks

This is the first work, written in English, which attempts to trace the history of Burma in its entirety. Indeed, there have been only four histories of Burma written in English. The first, Sir Arthur Phayre, *History of Burma* (London: Truber, 1883), naturally dealt only with the pre-British period. The second, G. E. Harvey, *History of Burma* (London: Longmans, 1925), stopped at the point when the British frigates, ready for the kill, entered Rangoon harbor in 1824. The sequel, *British Rule in Burma, 1824–1942* (London: Longmans, 1946), was a study in government and not a history. The third, D. G. E. Hall, *Burma* (London: Hutchinson, 1952), focused attention only on the British period, being merely a handbook of British rule in Burma. The fourth, John F. Cady, *Modern Burma* (Ithaca, N.Y.: Cornell University Press, 1958), concerned itself with the British period and after, although as a prologue it gave an account of the period 1784–1824. Both Hall, *A History of South-East Asia* (London: Macmillan, 1955, 1964), and Cady, *Southeast Asia: Its Historical Development* (New York: McGraw-Hill, 1964), however, gave brief accounts of the history of Burma in the various periods of southeast Asian history.

Most of the facts that I present in this history of Burma are already known to scholars and students of Burmese history. However, in presenting those facts, I endeavor to interpret and explain them in such a way as to show that there is a definite pattern behind them. Although I attempt to be as objective and as detached as possible, I am but a

Burmese, and my view of the history of my country is of course the Burmese view. The reader doubtless finds that my interpretations are entirely different from those of Hall and Cady. Hall, a member of the Imperial Education Service while at the University of Rangoon, naturally looks at Burmese history from the official British point of view, and Cady, a member of the American Baptist Mission while at Judson College, a part of the University of Rangoon, understandably holds different opinions. I was a student at the University when Hall was a professor of history there, and I was contemporary with Cady as a lecturer before World War II. After the war, as Rector, I had the honor of having them on my staff as visiting professors. Like the Six Men of Hindustan, who described the different parts of the elephant, perhaps all three of us are equally right in our different views of the Burmese history, and also equally wrong. So that the interested reader can refer to their opinions, references to the relevant pages of their histories of southeast Asia are given in the bibliographical notes under each chapter heading.

Burmese Sources

My sources are mainly Burmese, and for the political events I use the following chronicles: *Hmannan Yazawindawgyi* (The Glass Palace Chronicle), Mandalay: Mandalay Press, 1908; *Konbaungzet Mahayazawin* (The Chronicle of the Alaungpaya Dynasty), Rangoon: Thudhammawaddi Press, 1922; *Thuthawdita Mahayazawin* (The Revised Chronicle), Rangoon: Thudhammawaddi Press, 1933.

Hmannan ends with the events of the year 1869. *Konbaungzet* incorporates those chapters from the *Hmannan* dealing with the Alaungpaya period with new chapters on the reigns of Mindon and Theebaw. *Thuthawdita* incorporates *Hmannan* with *Konbaungzet*, rewriting some passages. However, *Hmannan* remains the standard Burmese chronicle (it was even Phayre's main source). Most of my information is from *Hmannan*, but I have not given the page references as footnotes, for to the reader who does not know Burmese such references will be of no practical value, and to the reader who knows Burmese they will be redundant, as the printed versions of these chronicles have very detailed tables of contents, almost as complete as a general index of events. When the source of a particular item of information is not *Hmannan*, I have indicated the source either in the text itself or in the bibliographical notes under each chapter heading. I have used also the lesser known

343 Bibliographical Notes

"Arakanese and Mon Chronicles" (not yet printed), the manuscripts for which are in the Burma National Library, Rangoon. U Ba Than, *Myama Yazawin* (A History of Burma), revised edition, Mandalay: Pidakataw Pyanpwayay Press, 1951, gives a summary of *Hmannan* with critical comments and some additional information.

For ecclesiastical history, I have relied on the following: Maha Dhamma Thingyan, *Sasanalankara* (A History of Buddhism), Rangoon: Hanthawaddy Press, 1956; *Sasana-bahusutapakasani* (Notes on the History of Buddhism), Rangoon: Hanthawaddy Press, 1953. Again for reasons given above with regard to *Hmannan*, I have not given the page references to these works. Using *Sasanalankara* as his main source, one of King Mindon's great monks wrote in Pali *Sasanavamsa* (A History of Buddhism in Burma), which has been translated by B. C. Law (*Sacred Books of the East*, Vol. XVII, London: Luzac, 1952).

For the history of Burmese literature, I used the following standard works: U Pe Maung Tin, *Myama Sarpay Thamaing* (A History of Burmese Literature), Rangoon: Thudhammawaddy Press, 1940; U E Maung, *Anusarpay Kaukhnote-chetmya* (Readings from Burmese Literature), Rangoon: Pyinnya Gonyaung Press, 1958; Major Ba Thoung, *Myama Sarsodawgyimyar Ahtokpatti* (Biographies of Burmese Authors), Rangoon: Ava House, 1962.

Burmese Chronicles

With European scholars *Hmannan* has an unfavorable reputation, yet most of the facts given in Harvey, Hall, and Cady for at least the period after 1044 have their source in *Hmannan*. Even before it was written *Hmannan* had become the victim of malicious propaganda on the part of the British envoy, Crawfurd, who visited the Court of Ava in 1826. In more recent times the chronicle was criticized for its acceptance of certain legends and folk-tales as history. But this criticism could be valid only with regard to the first few chapters dealing with the period before 1044. Moreover, some of the so-called fairytale accounts relating to events before 1044 have been shown by archaeological evidence to be founded on historical facts. For example, Harvey insisted in 1924 that the kingdom of Prome could not have existed before A.D. 800. Since then, however, archaeological finds have made it clear that the kingdom was in full bloom by at least the second century A.D. Critics made much of the fact that dates given in the chronicles did not agree with the dates given in the inscriptions at Pagan. But they forgot that they could understand the full purport of the inscriptions only by using the chronicle accounts as a check list, as it were. Moreover, they ignored also the fact that the committee of scholars who composed the *Hmannan* had access to the inscriptions. The same critics attempted to prove the chronicles wrong with regard to certain events, and distorting and misreading the inscriptions they put forward the most fantastic theories.

Unfortunately for historical scholarship, the only portions of *Hmannan* which have been translated into English happen to be the portions dealing with the period before the fall of Pagan in 1287: G. H. Luce and Pe Maung Tin, *The Glass Palace Chronicle of the Kings of Burma* (Rangoon: Burma Research Society, 1923). In their translation of the text, Luce and Pe Maung Tin were on the whole accurate, but unfortunately they used an involved, archaic, and semi-poetical style of English, reminiscent of the "forged" medieval poems of Thomas Chatterton. This style, beautiful in many ways, gave a note of unreality and romance to the translated version of the chronicle and tended to make the reader think of the ancient kingdoms of Prome and Pagan as a Keatsian fairyland, forlorn. For the periods after Pagan, *Hmannan* gave a well-balanced, accurate, and continuous account of Burmese history, and *Konbaungzet* carried the story down to 1885. It is true that both chronicles continued to record the signs and portents that preceded a king's death, but then, even in twentieth-century America, there are those who are believed to have the gift of prophecy and interpret signs and omens. The accuracy of the chronicle could be checked with contemporary writings of various times. For a violent criticism of *Hmannan* (for the "old Burma" period only), see Luce, "A Century of Progress in Burmese History and Archaeology," *Journal of the Burma Research Society (J.B.R.S.)*, Vol. XXXII (1948), Part I. For the defense, see U Tet Htoot, *The Nature of Burmese Chronicles*, in Hall (ed.), *Historians of South-East Asia* (London: Oxford University Press, 1961), and Maung Htin Aung, "A Defense of the Burmese Chronicles," a paper read before the XXXVII International Congress of Orientalists, Ann Arbor, Michigan, August, 1967 (*in press*, N. V. Martinus Nijhoff's Boekhandelen Uitgerversmaatschappij, The Hague).

Chapter I

E. H. G. Dobby, *Southeast Asia* (London: University of London Press, 1950), gives a good idea of the geographical unity of the region. Brian Harrison, *South-East Asia: A Short History* (London: Macmillan, 1954), sketching the history of the region on a smaller canvas, shows the general pattern of the history of the region.

Chapter II

All writers on southeast Asian history rely on G. Coedes, *Les Etats Hindouises d'Indochine et d'Indonesie* (Paris: Boccard, 1948), for the history of the region in the early centuries. But perhaps he over-emphasizes Hindu "colonization" of the region. His *Les Peuples de la Peninsula Indochinoise* (Paris: Dunod, 1962), translated into English by H. M. Wright as *The Making of South East Asia* (Berkeley, University of California Press, 1966), attempts to show the close cultural relationship between the old southeast Asia that existed before the thirteenth century and the new southeast Asia of the twentieth. For a summary of the Thai view that Suvarnabhumi (Sanskrit) or Suvannabhumi (Pali) was in Thailand, see *In Commemoration of 2500 Years of Buddhism*, published in Bangkok in 1956 by the Royal Commission for Celebrating the 2,500th Anniversary.

Luce, "Early Chinese Texts about Burma," *J.B.R.S.*, Vol. XIV (1924); Luce's translation of *Man Shu* (Ithaca, N.Y.: Cornell University Press, 1961); and E. H. Parker, *Précis of Chinese Imperial and Provincial Annals relating to Burma* (Rangoon: British Burma Press, 1893), give the reader details of the various Chinese historical texts, containing references to Burma.

Luce, "The Ancient Pyu," *J.B.R.S.*, Vol. XXVII (1932), contains a detailed and appreciative account of Pyu culture, but summarily rejecting *Hmannan* accounts, Luce accepts the vague and hearsay accounts given in *Man Shu* as authentic. U Po Lat, *Myamar Yarzawin Hnint Yinkyayhmu Thutaythana* (Researches in Burmese History and Culture), Rangoon: Pyinnya Nanda Press, 1962, refutes Luce and shows that archaeological evidence supports the chronicles. The Sinhalese chronicle *Mahavamsa* (translated into English by W. Geiger and published by the Government Press of Colombo, 1912) testifies to the importance of Ceylon to southeast Asia in the early centuries. For a summary of these references, see Sirima Wickrama Singhe, "Ceylon's Relations with South-East Asia, with special reference to Burma," *The Ceylon Journal of Historical and Social Studies* (Colombo), III (1960), 1.

Hall, *A History of South-East Asia* (1964 ed.), pp. 133–37; Cady, *Southeast Asia*, pp. 112, 113.

Chapters III and IV

U E Maung, *Kyauksar Kaukhnotechetmyar* (Selections from the Inscriptions), Rangoon: Pyinnya Nanda Press, 1959), is a valuable source.

Luce, in his "Mons of the Pagan Dynasty," *J.B.R.S.*, Vol. XXXIV (1950) and "Old Kyaukse and the Coming of the Burmans," *J.B.R.S.*, Vol. LXIII (1959), contends that the Burmese entered Burma from the Shan plateau only in the later half of the ninth century A.D., basing his conclusions on his interpretations of the Burmese inscriptions and *Man Shu*. Leading authorities on Burmese inscriptions, namely U Po Lat, formerly Director of Archaeology, Professor U E Maung, Daw Mya Mu, and *Thuriya* U Thein Maung do not accept his findings. Luce also contends in *Mons of the Pagan Dynasty* that the name of the king of Thaton who was defeated by Anawrahta was Makuta instead of Manuha, and that Kyansittha's daughter married Makuta's grandson. He asserts that Kyaukse district was originally inhabited by the Mons. He also casts doubts on the correctness of *Hmannan* accounts regarding Buddhism at Pagan. For refutation of all the above theories advanced by Luce, see U Po Lat, *Myamar Yarzawin*, and Maung Htin Aung, "A Defense of the Burmese Chronicles."

Dr. Than Tun, in various articles published in 1958 in a Rangoon weekly and in 1959 in *J.B.R.S.*, accepted and expanded the theories advanced by Luce. These articles reached the European scholars, as they were written in English, but the essays and articles refuting them, written in Burmese, are not known outside Burma. Unfortunately, my own article giving a summary of the main arguments put forward by the Burmese scholars was not accepted for publication by the editorial board of *J.B.R.S.* in 1960. In any case, the position of those articles by Than Tun is now unclear, because in an essay published in *The Work-*

ing Peoples' Daily, Rangoon, February 12, 1965, he rejects all the theories of Luce. For a refutation of the suggestion made by Luce and Than Tun that Ceylon raiders killed Alaungsithu, see Singhe, "Ceylon's Relations with South-East Asia."

For an account of the pre-Buddhist religion of the Burmese, see Maung Htin Aung: *Folk Elements in Burmese Buddhism* (London: Oxford University Press, 1962).

For Anawrahta's influence on Siam, see W. A. R. Wood, *A History of Siam* (London: Unwin, 1929), and *The Chronicle of the Emerald Buddha* (English translation; Bangkok: Bangkok Press, 1929).

For the fall of Pagan, see Edouard Huber, "La Fin de la Dynastie de Pagan," *Bulletin de L'Ecole Française d'Extrême Orient*, Vol. IX (1909), and Marco Polo, *The Book of Ser Marco Polo* (translated by Sir Henry Yule; London: Murray, 1871).

Hall, *A History of South-East Asia*, pp. 137–47; Cady, *Southeast Asia*, pp. 114–28.

Chapter V

For Chinese accounts of their relations with Burma during this period (and also for later periods) see Parker, *Burma with Special Reference to Her Relations with China* (Rangoon: British Burma Press, 1893). *Razadarit Ayaydawbon* (The Royal Crisis of Razadarit), written soon after his death, gives a detailed account of his campaigns (not yet printed; manuscripts in National Library, Rangoon).

Hall, *A History of South-East Asia*, pp. 147–57; Cady, *Southeast Asia*, pp. 128–30, 145–53.

Chapters VI and VII

My Siamese sources are Wood, *A History of Siam;* Nai Thein, "Intercourse between Siam and Burma as recorded in the Royal Autograph Edition of the History of Siam," *J.B.R.S.*, Vols. XXV (1935) and XXVIII (1938); U Aung Thein, "A Translation of *Our Wars with Burma*, by Prince Damrong," *J.B.R.S.*, Vols. XXXVIII (1955) and XXXIX (1956).

For the Portuguese episodes, see F. C. Danvers, *The Portuguese in India; Being a History of the Rise and Decline of their Eastern Empire*

(London: India Office, 1894); Maurice Collis, *The Land of the Great Image* (London: Faber, 1943); and Maung Htin Aung, "Bayinnaung and the Sacred Tooth," *Sunday Times of Ceylon* (Colombo), February 18, 1962.

Hall, *A History of South-East Asia*, pp. 238–54, 353–80; Cady, *Southeast Asia*, pp. 190–95, 285–89.

Chapter VIII

Alaungpaya Ayaydawbon (The Royal Crisis of Alaungpaya), compiled soon after his death; not yet printed; manuscripts in National Library, Rangoon.

Siamese sources are those in the previous chapter.

Luce, "Chinese Invasions of Burma in the Eighteenth Century," *J.B.R.S.*, Vol. XV (1925), is a detailed and scholarly account, based on Chinese sources.

Raise a Ladder to the Sky, extract from a Burmese nursery rhyme, and *Quester after Silver*, extract from Maung Htin Aung, *Epistles Written on the Eve of the Anglo-Burmese War, 1824* (The Hague: Martinus Nijhoff, 1967).

Hall, *A History of South-East Asia*, pp. 381–92; Cady, *Southeast Asia*, pp. 289–92.

Chapters IX, X, and XI

For a fuller account of the bogus missions exchanged between Bodawpaya and the Chinese emperor, see U Kyaw Thet, "Some Aspects of the Sino-Burmese Diplomacy during the Reign of Bodawpaya," in *Burma*, a bulletin issued by the Ministry of Information, Rangoon, July 1951.

Dorothy Woodman, *The Making of Burma* (London: Cresset Press, 1962), discloses many official secrets regarding Britain's relations with Burma and presents revealing extracts from British official papers. The book makes it clear that the Burmese were by no means the aggressors in the Anglo-Burmese wars. Saul Rose, *Britain and South-East Asia* (Baltimore: Johns Hopkins Press, 1962), shows that the conquest of Burma was merely a part of Britain's expansion in southeast Asia. Maung Maung, *Burma in the Family of Nations* (Amsterdam: Djambatan,

1956), and Maung Htin Aung, *The Stricken Peacock: Anglo-Burmese Relations, 1752–1948* (The Hague: Martinus Nijhoff, 1965), give the history of diplomatic intercourse between Burma and Britain in greater detail than this present work. W. S. Desai, *History of the British Residency in Burma, 1826–1840* (Rangoon: University of Rangoon Press, 1939), illustrates the difficulties and problems of Anglo-Burmese relations after the first war.

For additional information regarding the various palace groups and rebellions, my sources are the unpublished notes and memoranda of Myothawundauk Kadaw (wife of Myotha Wundauk, junior minister for Foreign Affairs, deputy to Kinwun Mingyi, and a lady-in-waiting to Mindon's queen), who died in 1936); U An Tu (retired Deputy Commissioner and son of the Minister for Post and Telegraph under King Theebaw), who died in 1946; and U Pein (the author's father, Deputy Commissioner), who died in 1945.

For information regarding the bogus prince, my sources are the unpublished notes and memoranda of my father U Pein (see the footnotes in the relevant chapters in *The Stricken Peacock*).

Shwegaingtha, *Mandalay Ahnittayar* (Mandalay—One Hundred Years), Mandalay: Kyeepwaryay Press, 1959, contains valuable information regarding the reigns of Mindon and Theebaw. For additional details of the new literary forms, see Maung Htin Aung, *Burmese Drama* (London: Oxford University Press, 1937), and *Burmese Monk's Tales* (New York: Columbia University Press, 1966). The latter contains an introduction on the state of Burmese Buddhism on the eve of the British conquest.

Hall, *A History of South-East Asia*, pp. 554–607; Cady, *Southeast Asia*, pp. 293–302, 380–95.

Chapter XII

All European historians draw a veil over the British excesses in the so-called pacification of Burma. Even Maung Maung, *Burma in the Family of Nations*, fails to pierce the veil. Yet the contemporary press, both in India and England, featured and criticized the atrocities. See D. R. Singhal, *The Annexation of Upper Burma* (Singapore: Eastern University Press, 1960), and Rudyard Kipling, *Barrack Room Ballads: Ballad of Bo Dah Thone*. The poem is from Oolay, *Ballads of Burma* (Calcutta: Thacker, 1912). Oolay was the pen name of Major W. C.

Conway Poole, Imperial Police Service. For a British estimate of British rule in Burma, see Harvey, *British Rule in Burma, 1824–1942*, which gives only one side of the picture. Harvey had very strong prejudices against the Burmese, as his *History* would testify. A fairer estimate is made by Frank N. Trager, *Burma: From Empire to Republic* (New York: Praeger, 1966).

The only published work in English on the Japanese period is U Nu, *Burma under Japanese Rule* (translated by J. S. Furnivall; London: Longmans, 1954). There exist a number of pamphlets and memoirs of the Japanese rule by Burmese writers, which remain unused by historians.

I became a member of the Council of National Education while still an undergraduate and became its Honorary Secretary in 1933; I was a student at the University of Rangoon from 1924 to 1928 and was appointed lecturer in 1933. Therefore the accounts of the student movements and student aspirations are based on my own personal knowledge and experience. Maung Maung, *Burma's Constitution* (The Hague: Martinus Nijhoff, 1960), and *Aung San of Burma* (The Hague: Martinus Nijhoff, 1961), give valuable sidelights on the making of Burmese independence. Hugh Tinker, *The Union of Burma* (London: Oxford University Press 1957), is an unbiased and detailed account of the first ten years of independence. Trager, *Burma: From Empire to Republic*, makes a critical but sympathetic appraisal of the achievements of the Burmese political leaders, especially General Aung San, U Nu, and General Ne Win, in the face of many difficulties.

Hall, *A History of South-East Asia*, pp. 692–704, 735–40, 774–75, 779–80, 782, 792–99, 849–55; Cady, *Southeast Asia*, pp. 395–405, 506–27, 574–78, 598–99.

Index